A Dialogue of Voices

Karen Hohne and
Helen Wussow, editors

A Dialogue of Voices

Feminist Literary Theory and Bakhtin

University of Minnesota Press • Minneapolis • London

Published by the University of Minnesota Press
2037 University Avenue Southeast, Minneapolis, MN 55455-3092
Printed in the United States of America on acid-free paper

Library of Congress Cataloging-in-Publication Data

A Dialogue of voices : feminist literary theory and Bakhtin / edited by Karen Hohne and Helen Wussow.
p. cm.
Includes bibliographical references and index.
ISBN 0-8166-2295-7 (alk. paper). — ISBN 0-8166-2296-5 (pbk. : alk. paper)
1. Feminist literary criticism. 2. Bakhtin, M. M. (Mikhail Mikhaĭlovich), 1895-1975—Criticism and interpretation. I. Hohne, Karen Ann. II. Wussow, Helen.
PN98.W64D49 1994
801'.95—dc20 93-8711
CIP

To Sandra
With thanks for
all your help
& encouragement—
Denise
3-25-94

Contents

Introduction

Karen Hohne and Helen Wussow

> A verbal-ideological decentering will occur only when a national culture loses its sealed-off and self-sufficient character, when it becomes conscious of itself as only one among *other* cultures and languages . . . there will arise an acute feeling for language boundaries (social, national and semantic), and only then will language reveal its essential *human* character; from behind its words, forms, styles, nationally characteristic and socially typical faces begin to emerge, the images of speaking human beings. . . . Language (or more precisely, languages) will itself become an artistically complete image of a characteristic human way of sensing and seeing the world.[1]

In this hope we are as optimistic as Bakhtin. A period of interchange, of dialogue between many voices and many forms of criticism, is approaching or, some would argue, has already arrived. This development may be the predecessor to the period Bakhtin describes above, a state of "decentering" in which a number of voices, "social, national, semantic," and *gendered* (we would emphasize), will speak simultaneously. One of the ways this state of affairs is moving toward a reality is through the growing dialogue between Bakhtin's writings and the various points of view that fall under the rubric of "feminist."

Such a dialogue does, of course, have its problems. In any verbal interchange, one may speak with the other's words, but such an appropriation is fraught with dangers. Bakhtin himself was aware of the difficulties inherent in appropriating the voices (and thus views) of an/other and the additional problems of having one's own voice appropriated for an end one finds abhorrent.[2] Several feminist critics point to the dangers of taking on the voice or the theory of any male critic, including Bakhtin; they argue that in doing so feminist critics risk finding their own voices drowned out by patriarchal theories and languages developed by men to write about literature written by men. But as Bakhtin would argue, all languages are influenced by one another. There cannot be a 100 percent pure feminist criticism, just as there is no unalloyed Bakhtinian reading of literature. The importance is the simultaneous reaction, a lively dialogue between the heteroglossic languages of Bakhtin and feminist theory.

The argument that Bakhtin is not useful for (or perhaps should not be used for) solving problems raised by feminist analysis of cultural texts on account of (1) his being male and/or (2) the absence of a treatment of gender in his philosophy does not seem valid. To reject him on the basis of his gender not only is to act as if gender determines all that one is (other aspects of oneself are excluded or irrelevant) but also is to decide that experience is pure—purely masculine or purely feminine—and thus monologic, closed, dead, a question of static being instead of a process, a becoming, a movement Bakhtin himself would insist on. Rejecting him because he does not treat gender as a determining factor in language/ideology would be like rejecting any and all literature written by straight white men. There are indeed literatures written by that group that are well worthy of rejection, and these are characterized by their refusal to have truck with any other viewpoints or voices except as objects. But Bakhtin is accessible and valuable to feminism not only in terms of his philosophy, which is specifically directed at celebrating, highlighting, bringing to the fore the vitalizing force of dialogism—that is, the incorporation and interweaving of various voices to create a sum far greater and more generative than the parts—but even in terms of his form. Certainly Bakhtin has never been criticized for being too linear; in fact, many have bemoaned his lack of order. Even in his language his rule-breaking word inventions give voice to his essentially otherly philosophy. In short, although he nowhere openly discusses gendrified language, he certainly exemplifies it. The only real danger in using Bakhtin's philosophy is the one we encounter when using any philosophies (including those of feminism)—we can fall into dogmatism. The error of dogmatism is not, however, one we will learn from Bakhtin, but one we might bring to him, and this ought to remind us just how much control we the readers have over what the text ends up being/saying.

As both Josephine Donovan and Michael Holquist have argued, Bakhtin is more than just a simple pluralist.[3] Bakhtin argues that not all languages bear hearing; rather, all the languages, concepts, ways of being in an utterance must be sorted and identified. A dialogic is formed by the different meanings within and between utterances. Thus, the bringing together of different theories of feminist criticism and the various emphases on those parts of a whole called "Bakhtin" result in a type of dialogism. Perhaps a more pertinent question than whether Bakhtin is, as a male thinker, worth using is whether Bakhtin's philosophy has anything to contribute to feminism. Could his philosophy elucidate problems raised by/in feminism? More interesting than a flat rejection of Bakhtin because of his gender or because he did not speak on gender are the possibilities that his concepts, such as heteroglossia and dialogism, hold for feminist writers. The question of what feminine *écriture* is/should be and whether it is even necessary is one that Bakhtin serves well to address.

But what would be a "feminist dialogics"? Patricia Yaeger, Dale M. Bauer, and Susan Jaret McKinstry state that a feminist dialogics would emphasize gender,[4] a topic that many feminist critics of Bakhtin underscore that he has left unexplored. For both Bauer and Ann Herrmann, a feminist dialogics would disrupt patriarchal hierarchy.[5] Bauer claims that the "female voice" disrupts the "surveillant" male gaze.[6] Here, as in many feminist criticisms, the female voice is referred to but is not defined. Is the female voice simply the voice of a female author or character? And what is this emphasis on singularity, on unity, on *voice* rather than *voices*? If we agree with Bakhtin that, given the heteroglossia of dialogism, each voice, whatever its gender(s), will contain the voices of others, then the singularity of the female voice is at best an illusion, at worst a silencing of the many experiences and contexts about which and within which women have spoken through the ages.

An example of the heteroglossic nature of the feminine or "otherized" voice is discussed in Siobhan Craig's essay in this volume, "Monstrous Dialogues: Erotic Discourse and the Dialogic Constitution of the Subject in *Frankenstein*"; she points out that Frankenstein's creature speaks with the voice of patriarchal authority, although he is denied any power by his creator and by society and is forced to the margins of his world. The creature speaks against his oppressors but appropriates their speech. While Frankenstein sees him as the enemy, the creature perceives Frankenstein as his oppressor. If we regard the creature as representing the other, the feminized voice in the novel, is it empowering to define this feminized voice as a simple opposition to the voice of power and authority? If the "female voice" or female writing, feminine *écriture*, is defined as being the opposite of the masculinist products of a patriarchal culture, then we end up only validating masculinism.

There is the problem of the word to which feminine *écriture* is reacting or opposing itself—call it masculinist, authoritative, monologic, phallogocentric, whatever. We all know from our own practice of analyzing cultural products that there is no such thing as pure unalloyed speech. Even if a language manages to "cleanse" itself of all otherly words, so that, for instance, only one vocabulary level remains, what is *not* there still modifies the text (as does the context). It might seem that Bakhtin, whose conception of monologism and authoritative language has been so helpful to those interested in dissecting authoritarian ideologies, is being ignored here, but Bakhtin himself noted that there can be no such thing as pure monologism. Everything is reacting to everything that has been said previously or may be said in the future. Thus, it would be difficult to create a new feminine language in response to a language existing in its pure form only in the imaginations of conservatives.

But let's say that there is some alchemically rendered version of masculinist language, the two hundred proof stuff. If feminine writing is the opposite of that, we end up only validating masculinism. Writing a nonlinear language to counter or oppose masculinist linearity is just as impoverished as Satanism, which must accept the dogma and power of the Church in order to exist. This sort of *être* is static, a mirror image, reversing but not changing. To counter objectification with its inversion is to fall into the trap of binarism that Bakhtin rejected in Saussure and in the concept of dialogism itself (Bakhtin visualized speech interaction as tripartite, being composed of speech, response, and context). Indeed, the only place where Bakhtin falls prey to binarism is some of his thought associated with carnival and its tendency to invert—top/bottom, death/life, high/low. It is too bad that it is often exactly this aspect of his philosophy that has been taken up in cultural analysis.

Many feminist critics have created a woman versus community binary as a form of definition in their writings. But, we ask, to what extent is this a viable binary? We must consider, in our discussions of women's writing, how the author ventriloquizes society's voices—gendered, racial, class—in the novel and ask if there are ways of separating these voices or whether these methods are in themselves exclusionary. We must ask if an emphasis on female voices means that in listening to "voices" we are really listening only for a distinguishable female voice (note the tautology of this approach). We must, says Herrmann, rewrite Bakhtin by positing subject as gendered.[7] Yet emphasizing female over the previously valued male suggests a binary method in opposition to Bakhtin's theories of dialogism and simultaneity. We must be careful not to turn dialogism into mechanical dialogue, into a Manichaean conversation between self and other, female and male, I and you. Feminist dialogics is not to be a monologic discourse that emphasizes the emphatically female voice to the exclusion of other social utterances. We must watch for a monologic privileging of the (female) gendered other and her voice.

An example of this type of exclusionary essentialism, despite their arguments to the contrary, can be found in the writings of Hélène Cixous and Luce Irigaray. Several essays defend these authors from this criticism,[8] but we would argue that there is a determinism in both writers' methods. In this volume, Lisa Gasbarrone points out in " 'The Locus for the Other': Cixous, Bakhtin, and Women's Writing" that Cixous speaks to the exclusion of all other voices. Cixous's writing is not dialogized; although it attempts dialogue with the various mouths with which a woman speaks, the result is not a conversation between many voices but statements made by a privileged, single voice.

A similar criticism can be leveled at Irigaray's work. Although she states that the voice of woman is "two-lipped," the "I" of her discourse perpetually addresses a silent "you."[9] Thus yet another silenced other—the audience of the newly vocal female locutor—is created. The unfortunate thing is that in Irigaray's discourse, the silent "you" is female. Therefore, one woman speaks for another, a method that African-American feminist critics have denigrated as a practice in contemporary feminist literary theory.[10] We may, then, ask to what extent does Irigaray's Western, white voice speak for women in general?

If we are to talk about feminine *écriture* in Bakhtinian terms at all, difficulties are bound to arise. For instance, there is no such thing as a *woman's language*, or for that matter women's languages, in Bakhtin. There cannot be, and, we would argue, there should not be a language totally possessed by one class, one gender, one social body. Bakhtin dislikes all claims to oneness, and to speak of a single-sexed language is to move toward a monologism that is at once reprehensible and dogmatic. In Bakhtin's terms, women's languages need male languages, although to use these appellations we beg the question of whether these languages even exist.[11] Bakhtin argues that language is never unitary and that utterances are always spoken in response to another's word.[12] Thus, in order for a patriarchal language to exist, it must speak in conflict with the languages of the others it tries to marginalize and silence. The same, therefore, is true of what may be termed matriarchal language.

Feminist critics have complained that Bakhtin is not interested in the languages of gender, in the strata of women in society.[13] Bauer has suggested that "how the reader finds a space of resistance in interpretive communities is the question of feminist dialogics."[14] But the question remains of whether the reader or critic can be assured that this space, this strata, is essentially female. To what extent do others speak within this space? We are thinking of Hispanics, lesbians and gay men, African and

Native Americans, and other marginalized peoples whose voices have been and, unfortunately, continue to be devalued and silenced. Feminine language is usually defined as "marked by process and change, by absence and shifting, by multivoicedness."[15] Perhaps these attributes are not so much essentially feminine as they are the mark of any oppressed group of people who, having experienced the pain of silence, are determined not to impose it on others and thus allow different voices to be heard. Both Clive Thomson and Patricia Yaeger have argued that a feminist dialogics is that which explores the relation of three fundamental categories—gender, race, and class.[16] We would point out, however, that neither Bakhtin nor his feminist appropriators have managed to discuss these multiple issues simultaneously. Although feminists complain that Bakhtin focuses only on male authors, a similar complaint might be made that feminist critics tend to focus on one or two of these categories at the expense of the other.[17]

Another problem evident in appropriating Bakhtin to feminist causes is the untheorized manner in which critics have used Bakhtin's concept of carnival. Many have found in carnival a method of combating patriarchy's laws.[18] It is important to note that in these apologies for carnival, however, the emphasis is on formalist defamiliarization and quick fixes rather than a close conceptual study of how or if carnival should be appropriated for feminist causes. It must be stressed that in Bakhtin's definition, carnival continues to exist within authority's framework. Carnival is a controlled period of subversion and inversion, of heteroglossia that happens on limited occasions during the year with the approval of the society that it ostensibly subverts. Instead of smashing social frameworks, carnival reinscribes them by being contained within them. Clair Wills and Nancy Glazener point out that Bakhtin's carnival is a "fetishising of the repressed,"[19] that his "concept of the carnivalesque folk-body harks back to a golden age in which 'the people' were clearly separate from official culture and therefore capable of making their critique from a conceptionally pure 'outside.' "[20] Such a location in time and space (a chronotope, by Bakhtin's own terms) outside the dominant culture of authoritative society is impossible. Indeed, as Glazener has suggested, Bakhtin's attempts to rationalize Rabelais's misogyny "merely reinscribe the symbolic conceptual burden that 'woman' bears for the implicitly masculine subjectivity in the text."[21] In this collection, Denise Heikinen indicates in "Is Bakhtin a Feminist or Just Another Dead White Male? A Celebration of Possibilities in Manuel Puig's *Kiss of the Spider Woman*" the ways that the carnivalesque can be controlled within society's framework, as portrayed in the film version of Puig's book.

Perhaps instead of speaking of women's languages or feminine *écriture*, we should be talking about a feminine *être*. Such a process might well lead us to a feminist dialogics, for dialogism is exactly a way of being. Feminist dialogics is more than "a rhetorical criticism."[22] It is a way of assessing not only our voices as women but our whole way of acting in a world that is at once our own and someone else's. Feminist dialogics is more than just the study of the polyphonic, ever-changing voices that many insist go into making novels by women. It is a way of living, an ethics as well as an epistemology. As early as "Art and Answerability," his first published work, Bakhtin betrays the seriousness with which he always treats culture, suggesting that we must take responsibility for fashioning our lives and our art. He points to the intercourse between art and life as forming a way of being: "Art and life are not one, but they must become united in myself—in the unity of my answerability."[23]

To find the paths toward feminine *êtres* will not be easy. Feminists tend to perceive dialogism as a release, but, as suggested in the above quote and throughout all of Bakhtin's work, it entails a struggle. This conflict is comprised not only of the various utterances within novels by women and men alike attempting to make themselves heard and our own attempts to hear their words; an effort must also be made to avoid falling into the trap of monologism (which privileges oneness) by replacing dialogism with pluralism. To say simply "many is good; single is bad" is to create a binary system that plays false to the concept of dialogism.[24]

A feminine *être* will concern itself with points of view, with the interlocative dialogic self investigating both its own positions and languages and those of others.[25] It will consist of "a struggle among socio-linguistic points of view."[26] Bakhtin defines the "languages of heteroglossia" as made up of "specific points of view on the world."[27] Feminine *êtres* will be the ongoing attempts in life and art to remain aware of, acknowledge, and analyze these different languages and contexts, positions in space and time, in which and from which they are spoken.

The concept of feminine *êtres* would include the idea of a female chronotope, although, strictly speaking, no chronotope can be designated specifically by gender, as any location in space and time would necessarily include the other gender. A female chronotope, however, would consist of positing the female subject in the context of space and time. Two bodies, the female self and the female other, or the female self and the male other, can observe one another in simultaneous but different positions.[28] In this volume Suzanne Rosenthal Shumway in "The Chronotope of the Asylum: *Jane Eyre*, Feminism, and Bakhtinian Theory" suggests a way of discussing the female subject within and without her position in a patriarchal society. Chronotopes exist simultaneously within and without the societal, national chronotope at large. Often, however, chronotopes are fashioned by the society in which they occur (such as the chronotope of the asylum within the complementary chronotope of the English country home). The Bakhtinian chronotope is more than just a contradiction between central self and marginalized other, for chronotopes, like dialogism, include multiples of space and time. What a discussion of the female chronotope needs to consider is both the gendered aspects of space and time and the whole place of the female subject within these spatial and temporal dimensions. Holquist has argued that the "I" is a chronotope through which language passes.[29] Now is the time to posit the female "I" as a particular chronotope that has yet to be explored. A female chronotope may well go beyond the Bakhtinian equations of space and time to include gender in these matrices and/or to discuss gender as a whole new dimension.

Holquist has suggested that "heteroglossia is a plurality of relations, not just a cacophony of different voices."[30] Feminine *êtres* would emphasize the relationships between race, class, gender, time, and space, rather than simply the multiplicity of voices and strategies for utterance through which women make themselves heard. There is a continent for us—not the continent of our bodies, as Cixous argued, but a cultural continent located in time: matriarchy. In some ways, matriarchy is determined by physiology (specifically, reproduction) and to that extent is biological, but more important is matriarchy's cultural aspect, as rich and varied as that of patriarchy. Matriarchal elements could be compared to the internally persuasive word, which Bakhtin defined as

> a word [that] awakens new and independent words, that . . . organizes masses of our words from within, and does not remain in an isolated and static condition. It is not so much interpreted by us as it is further, that is, freely, developed, applied to new material, new conditions; it enters into interanimating relationships with new contexts.[31]

Further, the internally persuasive work "is either a contemporary word, born in a zone of contact with unresolved contemporaneity, or else it is a word that has been *reclaimed for contemporaneity*" (our emphasis).[32] There is no reason that such reclamation cannot involve (a dialogic) recreation as well.

But where is matriarchy? Some still argue that it never existed in human culture. For all the attempts to wipe it out, however, matriarchy is as preserved in our cultures as is anything that has been marginalized. It is often remembered turned inside out in images like the witch, the spinster, or the crone (the last of which, by the way, Bakhtin connected to carnival and which is probably the only thing worth saving from that part of his philosophy). Like the Medusa, the hag whom Bakhtin described as simultaneously dying and giving birth is distinguished by her laughter.

If we would find a feminine *être*, we should set about looking for the matriarchal in human and nonhuman cultures—not to hallow it (dogmatism is guaranteed to cause death somewhere along the line, whether in autos-da-fé or in purges), but to use it as a jumping-off point, as a motor, not a pattern to copy. Both research and invention, which are dialogic processes, can produce for us a feminine *être*, that is, a feminist dialogics.

Just as peculiarly African-American cultural modes such as blues have often been the places where blacks could talk about blackness, so women's "writing" (putting quotations around the word in order not to privilege the written word over any other kind of word, verbal or not), feminine *être*, can be the place where women talk about what it is to be a woman in a masculinist world (and possibilities for woman in other worlds). And just as blues is not always sad, but often funny and hopeful, so women's writing need not dwell on the oppression of women, but on our laughing back, just as the crone laughs at death, which cannot end her any more than mankind can end woman.

The essays collected here in *A Dialogue of Voices: Feminist Literary Theory and Bakhtin* are not arranged chronologically, thematically, or generically. Rather, they are assembled in a manner that emphasizes that these essays engage in a dialogue with one another, that they act and react with their neighbors dialogically. Thus within this single volume a plurality of voices and languages may be heard: arguments both for and against the appropriation of Bakhtinian theories for feminist causes; the privileging of feminist and Bakhtinian concepts over one another; and the possibilities of Bakhtinian discussions of lyric poetry. Discussions of literary genres of different periods are represented, such as nature writing, nineteenth-century novels by British women, contemporary romances, Irish and French lyric poetry, and contemporary Latin American prose. The essays speak with one another; although the approaches and opinions may differ, the topics are often the same. Discussed is the viability of Bakhtin's concept of the carnivalesque for a feminist agenda; whether there is such a thing as a feminist dialogics, and, if so, how it is manifested in writings by women and men across the genres; and in what way the theory of the chronotope may aid in revealing the time/space continua in work by men and women of several countries. This collection succeeds in marshaling a dialogue of voices in which many speakers of both genders and of different eras are heard, but none takes precedence.

Lisa Gasbarrone's essay, perhaps the most theoretical in the collection, seeks connections between Hélène Cixous and Mikhail Bakhtin. At first these connections seem possible, given the importance that both attach to laughter and language, and to their mutual rejection of official, authoritarian, monologic discourse. Women's writing, feminine *écriture*, is presented by Cixous as a fracture, which identifies it with Bakhtin's evaluation of the novel as separate from an epic past ultimately as culturally deaf as patriarchal writing is for Cixous. Gasbarrone argues, however, that Cixous's desire to disconnect from the past means that no dialogue with it is possible; such a rejection of dialogue is distinctly anti-Bakhtinian. Gasbarrone finds that Bakhtin's definition of unitary, monologic language unfortunately fits Cixous's concept of feminine *écriture*, and that Cixous's privileging of essentialist women's writing renders it authoritarian. Although the other helps constitute the self for Bakhtin, it always remains strange and separate from the self; in fact, this very separation sparks our existence. In contrast, for Cixous the other is superfluous—she is more interested in the relationship between selves than between selves and others. Gasbarrone concludes that Cixous's feminine *écriture* is essentially monologic and therefore incompatible with Bakhtin.

Whereas Gasbarrone privileges Bakhtin over female literary theorists, Elizabeth Butler Cullingford warns of the dangers of appropriating Bakhtin for feminist purposes. Yet her reading of W. B. Yeats's Crazy Jane poems through the lens of the carnivalesque demonstrates both the advantages and limitations of Bakhtin's method. Her historical poetics reveal Crazy Jane not as the eccentric spokeswoman for Yeats's private desires but as the figure for an eroticized politics of female transgression. Yeats's contention that the removal of crown and miter in the Free State would allow the Irish to "lay our heads on Mother Earth" provides a metaphorical starting point for an investigation of the relation of Bakhtinian carnivalesque and Yeatsian female masquerade both to each other and to the discourse of contemporary feminism. Throughout the poems spoken by Crazy Jane, the symbolic identification between the pure woman and the Irish nation, a product of male fantasy, is ironized and finally ruptured.

Crazy Jane speaks as a sexual woman, but she also represents one of the disenfranchised subaltern groups largely ignored by the new state: the rural poor. Both class and gender issues are focused in the personae of the defiant old peasant woman and her lover, Jack the Journeyman. Cullingford argues that Yeats's construction of the peasantry parallels Bakhtin's vision of the early Renaissance folk: both are consciously ideological and serve contemporary political ends.

Virginia Purvis-Smith's imaginative essay uses Monique Wittig's compositional style, employing theory-centered notes to enter into dialogue with her autobiographical description of a church service. Like

Cullingford's characterization of the Irish bishops, Purvis-Smith compares the chapel's menacing decor—stiff, male figures looming over the congregation—to Bakhtin's critique of religious language as dead monologue. She ties traditional Christianity's emphasis on the written word to a masculinism that devalues the visual, a means of expression the church considers suitable only for enticing the illiterate folk into the place of worship. Purvis-Smith connects monologic language and masculinism more explicitly when she discusses some of the metaphors traditionally applied to sermonizing, such as "virile" and "muscular." She argues, however, that it is possible to break through the exclusivity of authoritative speech, "the father's word," by such seemingly small acts as changing the masculine pronouns in hymns. This activity coincides with the intention of the particular service in which she participates, where dancing women celebrate spirituality and replace traditional, monologizing male preachers who read off prescriptive sermons. The "reading" of the scripture for the day by a blind woman is linked to Bakhtin's emphasis on the importance of context to meaning making. Purvis-Smith concludes that a recontextualizing of the Bible would transform it from the (dead, authoritative, masculinist) Word to (fluid, alternativist) communication.

Patrick Murphy arrives at a similarly interesting, alternativist reading of "anotherness" (rather than otherness) by way of discussing nature writing. Beginning from Bakhtin's assertion that a genre represents a point of view, he uses the *Norton Anthology of Nature Writing* to illustrate how that genre is presented to us as closed and dead, and thus its possibilities are marginalized in a manner similar to the type of sermonizing Purvis-Smith discusses and revolutionizes. Genre-bound nature writing à la John Muir didactically offers the threadbare man-versus-nature dichotomy. Murphy, however, shows how ecofeminist writers, who are often denied inclusion in the genre on such insubstantial grounds as being too "feminine," represent alternative relationships with nature by means of formal breaks with the generic formula. For instance, ecofeminists have stretched nature writing to include dialogues, poetry, and novels (like Ursula Le Guin's *Always Coming Home*, which is a departure from the traditional novel form as well). They have allowed nature to become subject, even hero, and they question such accepted concepts as alienation as possible masculinist constructs, proposing instead the multiplicity of anotherness as a replacement for the dichotomous otherness of the man/nature binary.

Siobhan Craig expands upon Murphy's concept of anotherness by questioning the self/other dichotomy in Mary Shelley's novel. The relationship between Victor Frankenstein, his creature, and the missing female characters is at the center of Craig's essay. Victor is to the creature as self/subject is to other/object. The creature, as a being outside of nature whom Victor meets in places beyond society, is the incarnation of transgressive erotic desire. Craig points out the homosexual undertones of their relationship as well as of that between Robert Walton and Victor; confession here has an erotic charge, yet it is a sexual exchange based not on genitalia but words. Like Bakhtin, Shelley steps outside the limiting binary of self/other to a transgressive area beyond hierarchies where positive alternatives, such as anotherness, reside. The creature's demand for an equal mate reflects his desire to enter into the kind of dialogic relationship that Victor refuses him. Craig argues that this female creature, whom Victor destroys before completion, is clearly related to another female "character," Mrs. Saville, the reader to whom Robert's letters are addressed and who therefore enables the entire story. Craig concludes by proposing that Shelley left both Mrs. Saville and the female creature incomplete in order that we ourselves would construct them. In doing so we as readers enter into a dialogic relationship not with an other but with another.

Eleanor Ty picks up the *ars erotica* thread introduced by Craig in order to show that romance novels are not mere reiterations of official ideology about gender roles. In fact, she argues, category romances are our *ars erotica*. The reader's pleasure in romances is not only erotic but literary, however, an enjoyment propelled by the romance's hybridization of language groups (such as concatenations of official languages). Romances make use of different languages, like those appearing in *GQ* or advertisements, in order to both affirm official discourse and put forward a female victory over masculine modes. Ty connects this concept to the appearance in romance of carnivalesque devices such as disguise and mistaken identity. She argues that these expedients appeal to female readers because in life playacting is mandatory for us. Romance novels allow that playacting to become an option rather than a necessity. In romances, when men fall in love with women not because of their looks or position (their playacting) but because of who they are in themselves, playacting becomes what it should be—play, not work. Thus, category romances present not a reactionary officiality but a carnivalization of officialdom that ends only with the characters' marriage, an event that necessitates reading yet another romance in order to recover carnival's refreshing alternatives.

Denise Heikinen uses Puig's *Kiss of the Spider Woman* to show how authoritative discourse can make versions of itself appear to be alternatives while denying alterity. By rejecting the opportunity to take on omniscient narration and pulling back from any but direct speech, Puig allows greater latitude for the reader to enter the work. A healthy confusion reigns: confusion arises for the reader about who's talking.

There is a confusion of official and unofficial in the form of footnotes on scientific studies of homosexuality on the one hand and narratives borrowed from B movies on the other. Confusion exists between and within the two outsiders, Molina and Valentin, who, despite their intense marginalization, have internalized certain aspects of official ideology. Heikinen picks out their bewilderment as positive, because it forces the reader to reevaluate the official line on gender without guidance from any authorial voice. Just as Ty shows how romance novels appear to reinforce traditional gender roles only then to carnivalize them, Heikinen demonstrates how movies meant to underscore traditional values may be reformed by the viewer's recollection and description of them and by the audience's comprehension of the plot. Thus, the Communist Valentin's consciousness is unexpectedly raised by Molina's retelling of what was originally Nazi propaganda. Context proves to be as important as content; that which allows officiality to appear seamless conversely provides a place for bent readings of authoritarian stories.

Whereas Heikinen underscores the idealism of Puig's novel, Julie Shaffer notes the satire of marital and narrative conventions in *Sense and Sensibility* by Jane Austen. Shaffer points out that what has long proved disturbing about *Sense and Sensibility* is its ambivalence toward its moral lesson, the rejection of sensibility and the fantasies of romantic love that novels of sensibility provide. She argues that conventional readings of satire as a genre require privileging one term over another; in the case of Austen's novel, this has meant viewing the world in which the Dashwood sisters move as the privileged norm by which sensibility can be satirized. The limitations of this kind of reading are obvious, for it is undermined by the retained appeal of sensibility and its double-edged satire: it not only reveals the limitations in Marianne's approach to the world but also suggests that there are limitations to the world with which Marianne is left after giving up her illusions. It is true that in *Sense and Sensibility* the most obvious target of deauthorization has been Marianne's sensibility. But as Bakhtin's theory of the dialogic nature of novelistic discourse makes clear, every language within the discourse of a novel is confronted and challenged by all other languages there. The bidirectional satire not only reveals Marianne to be misguided but, by questioning the value of consensual reality, also destabilizes the grounds upon which the authority of that version of reality is based, suggesting that it is an ideological construct like any other. By bringing the sisters' differing versions of the world into dialogic contact in a way that foregrounds the limitations of both, the unstable and destabilizing satire enacts a battle between the conflicting ideological constructs or competing versions of social experience offered within the novel.

Shaffer notes that the novel develops the appeal of sensibility by suggesting that it imaginatively satisfies needs that the dominant ideology or "reality" does not meet. As the two sisters' marriage plots dialogically interanimate each other, they reveal that, although Marianne's may move unrealistically, Elinor's moves by an ideology that has limited value and that therefore deserves deauthorization. *Sense and Sensibility* might best be seen as using its dialogism to dramatize its view that women like Marianne are caught in a double-bind situation: they live in an adequate reality from which they are unable to escape except through fantasies that may make them incapable of taking advantage of the limited satisfaction that can be theirs in this patriarchal society.

Suzanne Rosenthal Shumway's essay on *Jane Eyre* is a natural development from and expansion on Shaffer's work on dialogic discourse in *Sense and Sensibility*. In addition to Bakhtin's work on language and the conflict between ideologies and their utterances is his theory of the chronotope, a powerful device with which to stage a reaccentuation of texts such as *Jane Eyre*. Shumway recommends that a new chronotopic model be forged—that of the asylum—to approach female insanity within the novel. It is within the specific space/time continuum of the asylum that female madness and its concomitant subversion is represented and refracted throughout the text.

Shumway points to Jane Eyre's insistence upon heteroglossia. Eyre strives to maintain her independence from the restrictions of internally persuasive and authoritative language. She must pit the strength of her desire for heteroglossia against the authoritarian, patriarchal, and centripetal languages of Edward Rochester and St. John River. St. John is the most serious threat to her linguistic independence, for he practices a kind of authoritarian ventriloquism, appropriating the authoritarian word of the Bible in order to make Jane follow his desires.

Jane is also threatened by linguistic chaos. Shumway equates this linguistic anarchy to Bakhtin's concept of centrifugal language. She sees this verbal disorder as existing beyond heteroglossia; it is explosive, incendiary, subversive, involuntary speech that threatens verbal and mental stability with turmoil and insanity. Between the restrictions of authoritative language and extreme verbal centrifugality Jane must find a middle way. By the end of the novel, we realize that Jane has achieved heteroglossia, for she can manipulate and control not one narrative voice but a host of them: the language of gothic, of autobiography, of writing-to-the-moment, of feminism.

However, in the chronotope of the asylum, centrifugal language gains the upper hand. This chronotope is refracted and diffused throughout the narration; examples of it can be seen in Jane's incarceration in the red room and her journey to Marsh End. In the chronotope of the asylum, communication is ineffectual; centrifugal language exists in its extremity and the "madwoman" is divorced from the community. One question raised by *Jane Eyre* is, How can lack of language, or the nonlanguage of centrifugality, be represented within a verbal text? The insanity of Bertha Mason Rochester is signified by verbal absence (she never speaks to the reader; we "hear" her only through Jane's voice). Bertha, the Other, exists only in empty space. Yet although Brontë actually creates gaps in her text and refuses to fill them in, it may be said that *Jane Eyre* itself is utterance from within or beyond the chronotope of the asylum. To whom is Jane Eyre writing? Does she write only for herself? Who is her imaginary reader? Does she hallucinate her/his presence? Is her text similar to her pleas in the red room? Are both directed to an unseen and seemingly unresponsive audience?

Like Shumway, Karen Simroth James expands upon one of the topics raised by Bakhtin, that of poetic language. The lyric, according to Bakhtin, revolves around monologue and excludes dialogue. James's reading of Pernette du Guillet's *Rymes* suggests that Bakhtin may have too narrowly defined his category of the dialogic by restricting it to novelistic discourse. She insists that poetry too is open to the challenge of divergent or opposing utterances. The seventy-eight poems of Du Guillet's work question the relationship between truth and language and explore the acquisition of selfhood through speech. The dialogic quality of Du Guillet's poetry allows her to circumvent and challenge the ideal of silence that Renaissance society and literary conventions imposed upon women. In Du Guillet's dialogic poetry the speaking and writing subject refuses to be relegated or in turn to relegate the other to the role of silent object. The *Rymes* clearly possess the essential dialogic quality that juxtaposes divergent and at times opposing voices. The speaker/poetic narrator can often be associated with the persona of the poet herself, the beloved of the addressee. This speaker often calls attention to the conflict within herself and within her lover between virtuous, spiritual love and physical desire.

Many of the poems discussed in James's essay provide examples of this diversity of voices and of the contexts in which they speak. Du Guillet's poetry embodies the notion of a dialectic subjectivity described by both Bakhtin and Benveniste. The duplicitous nature of language, divergent voices, and opposing points of view allow for a new poetic subjectivity, one that refuses the traditional dichotomy that opposes the speaking subject to the silent object. James argues that the *Rymes* reject any such static hierarchy, emphasizing instead the exchange of speech and the coexistence of multiple voices and speaking subjects, as well as the relative nature of truth itself.

The essays in this volume are in dialogue not only with each other, but with Bakhtin. A good example is in the concept of rupture, transgression, overturning, which Bakhtin often codified as carnivalesque. Gasbarrone picks up on this in her discussion of Cixous's feminine *écriture*, Cullingford in her conception of Crazy Jane, Purvis-Smith in the dancing alternatives to virile sermons, Murphy with ecofeminist writings that break the rules of the genre, Craig in the transgression of self/other, Ty in the romance novels that both affirm and overturn the ideologies contained within their languages, and Heikinen in the wonderful confusion she finds ordering Puig. All touch upon the carnivalesque in some way, but each puts a unique spin on the concept, one that enables it, so that nowhere does the carnivalizing force remain the somewhat deadening binary it is in the original. Other authors in the collection do the same with other Bakhtinian concepts, such as chronotope. All of the essays are united in a dialogue that proves once again how very vitalizing dialogue is. We feel certain that your particular reading of these essays will confirm this for you.

Notes

1. M. M. Bakhtin, "Discourse in the Novel," in *The Dialogic Imagination*, ed. Michael Holquist, trans. Caryl Emerson and Michael Holquist (Austin: University of Texas Press, 1981), 370.

2. Ibid., 293.

3. Josephine Donovan, "Style and Power," in *Feminism, Bakhtin, and the Dialogic*, ed. Dale M. Bauer and Susan Jaret McKinstry (Albany: State University of New York Press, 1991), 85; Michael Holquist, "Introduction: The Architectonics of Answerability," in M. M. Bakhtin, *Art and Answerability*, ed. Michael Holquist and Vadim Liapunov, trans. Vadim Liapunov (Austin: University of Texas Press, 1990), xxiii.

4. Patricia Yaeger, "Afterword," 240; Dale M. Bauer and Susan Jaret McKinstry, "Introduction," 3, both in *Feminism, Bakhtin, and the Dialogic.*

5. Dale M. Bauer, *Feminist Dialogics: A Theory of Failed Community* (Albany: State University of New York Press, 1988), 2; Anne Herrmann, *The Dialogic and Difference: "An/other Woman" in Virginia Woolf and Christa Wolf* (New York: Columbia University Press, 1989), 7.

6. Bauer, *Feminist Dialogics*, 2.

7. Herrmann, *The Dialogic and Difference*, 148.

8. See, for example, Barbara Freeman, "Plus corps donce plus ecriture: Hélène Cixous and the Mind-Body Problem," *Paragraph* 11 (1988): 58-70, and Carolyn Burke, "Irigaray through the Looking Glass," *Feminist Studies* 7 (1981): 288-306.

9. Luce Irigaray, *This Sex Which Is Not One*, trans. Catherine Porter (Ithaca, N.Y.: Cornell University Press, 1985), 206.

10. See bell hooks, *Ain't I a Woman: Black Women and Feminism* (Boston: South End Press, 1981), 52.

11. Bakhtin, "Discourse in the Novel," 276.

12. Ibid., 288.

13. Diane Price Herndl, "The Dilemmas of a Feminine Dialogic," in Bauer and McKinstry, *Feminism, Bakhtin, and the Dialogic*, 10; Yaeger, "Afterword," 240, 244.

14. Bauer, *Feminist Dialogics*, 159.

15. Herndl, "Dilemmas," 11.

16. Clive Thomson, "Mikhail Bakhtin and Contemporary Anglo-American Feminist Theory," *Critical Studies* 1, no. 2 (1989): 158; Yaeger, "Afterword," 240.

17. An exception to this statement is Mae Gwendolyn Henderson's "Speaking in Tongues: Dialogics, Dialectics, and the Black Women Writers' Literary Tradition," in *Reading Black, Reading Feminist: A Critical Anthology*, ed. Henry Louis Gates, Jr. (New York: Meridian, 1990), 116-42.

18. Peter Stallybrass and Allon White, *The Politics and Poetics of Transgression* (Ithaca, N.Y.: Cornell University Press, 1986), 4; Mary Russo, "Female Grotesques: Carnival and Theory," in *Feminist Studies/Critical Studies*, ed. Teresa de Lauretis (Bloomington: Indiana University Press, 1986), 213-29.

19. Clair Wills, "Upsetting the Public: Carnival, Hysteria, and Women's Texts," in *Bakhtin and Cultural Theory*, ed. Ken Hirschkop and David Shepherd (Manchester, England: University of Manchester Press, 1989), 137.

20. Nancy Glazener, "Dialogic Subversion: Bakhtin, the Novel, and Gertrude Stein," in Hirschkop and Shepherd, *Bakhtin and Cultural Theory*, 114.

21. Ibid., 127.

22. Bauer, *Feminist Dialogics* 167.

23. Bakhtin, *Art and Answerability, 2.*

24. See Holquist, "Introduction," xxiii.

25. Ibid., xxvi.

26. Bakhtin, "Discourse in the Novel," 273.

27. Ibid., 291.

28. See the following for problems in discussing female character and authors with reference to the self/other binary: Ann Jefferson, "Bodymatters: Self and Other in Bakhtin, Sartre, and Barthes," in Hirschkop and Shepherd, *Bakhtin and Cultural Theory*, 152-77.

29. Michael Holquist, *Dialogism: Bakhtin and His World* (London: Routledge, 1990), 27-28.

30. Ibid., 89.

31. Bakhtin, "Discourse in the Novel," 345-46.

32. Ibid.

"The Locus for the Other": Cixous, Bakhtin, and Women's Writing

Lisa Gasbarrone

> There is hidden and always ready in woman the source;
> the locus for the other . . .

As it happens, I was a college student in Paris in 1975, the year in which Mikhail Bakhtin died and Hélène Cixous first published "The Laugh of the Medusa." I had barely heard of either of them at the time. It wasn't until a few years later that I encountered first their names and then some of their writings in the course of my graduate studies at Princeton. I dutifully read the assignments in each, in the context of different seminars: Bakhtin's book on Rabelais for a class in Renaissance literature; and *La Venue à l'écriture*, as I recall, because it was suggested additional reading in another class. I didn't truly grasp the former, I remember being very moved by the latter, and certainly I perceived no connection between them. It is only with the distance of a few years, with the greater range of my own reading, and through the back door of other projects, that I found myself reading both authors again. This second time around I, like many others, noted the tantalizing resonance between the two.[1] It was immediately very exciting.

As I set about attempting to understand and adapt the resemblance I perceived for the purposes of my own project, that resemblance began to unravel. As I read more of Bakhtin, and more about both him and Cixous, I began to hear discord rather than a harmonious convergence of voices. The tantalizing resonance lingered in phrases like the following, from "The Laugh of the Medusa":

> Writing is . . . undoing the work of death—to admit this is to want the two, as well as both, the ensemble of the one and the other, not fixed in sequences of struggle and expulsion or some other form of death but infinitely dynamized by an incessant process of exchange from one subject to another.[2]

A distinctly Bakhtinian note is sounded in passages such as this. Yet, as I listened closer, I heard more dissonance than the productive dialogic exchange I had anticipated. What I hope to outline here, chiefly through my reading of "The Laugh of the Medusa," is the nature of the conflict I perceive.

The discernible similarities—the echoes, if you will—between Bakhtin's theories and Cixous's writings remain striking. As Cixous describes feminine *écriture*, "women's writing" or the feminine practice of writing seems to embody many of the characteristics of what Bakhtin called dialogic discourse. As the earlier quotation suggests, the resemblance is especially apparent in those moments in which Cixous and other theorist/practitioners of women's writing describe the new relationship between self and other that they seek to establish through literary expression. Cixous writes in "The Laugh of the Medusa" that "there is hidden and always ready in woman the source; the locus for the other" (245). Playing on the metaphor of womb and text, she invites women to engage in a type of writing—a feminine *écriture*—that would cultivate this "locus," that would defy the monologue of patriarchy and express, through language, a relationship between self and other that might be called dialogic. For those who have sought or simply perceived a convergence of Bakhtinian theory and the feminist project of feminine *écriture*, such a "locus for the other" seems promising. Yet this promise remains, in Cixous's "Laugh of the Medusa," largely unfulfilled. As I hope to demonstrate, too much in Cixous's text is antithetical to Bakhtin. If there is indeed a "feminist dialogics," as many have suggested, I will argue that it is not to be found here.[3]

My purpose, then, is not to propose a Bakhtinian reading of Cixous's text, but rather to offer what might be called a Bakhtinian critique. I propose to read "The Laugh of the Medusa" principally for Cixous's model of the relationship between self and other, which reveals, through her expression of it, a promise of dialogue that feminine *écriture* does not in this instance fulfill. By setting Bakhtin's model here in opposition, I hope to suggest not only the important contribution, but also what I would call the necessary corrective, his thinking has to offer to theorists of women's writing.

To write and thus forge for herself the antilogos
weapon . . .

Hélène Cixous's "Laugh of the Medusa" has been considered variously a manifesto, an exemplar, and an expression of utopian longing. In many respects, it is all three. From the very first lines of her essay, in which Cixous calls for the creation of a new literary movement, a revolution in writing, "The Laugh of the Medusa" is rousing, irreverent, joyous, disturbing, and willfully inconsistent. Cixous issues a call to women, to bring them to writing; she seeks to demonstrate by her text both what women's writing *is* and "*what it will do*." This call to letters has been celebrated for its effort to break from official (and, by definition, masculine) control of writing, to break with what Cixous calls "an arid millennial ground" (245). The thousand-year literary tradition against which Cixous is writing, a tradition ironically rich in manifestos such as hers, must be abandoned, she claims, if women are to speak finally in their own voice: "Anticipation," she writes, "is imperative" (245). In place of the repressive past, women will, through their writing, "foresee the unforseeable" (245), uncover the *féminin futur*, for which "The Laugh of the Medusa" serves as both a model and an invocation.[4]

Cixous's call to writing is framed figuratively as a call to arms. There can be no mistaking her assertion that the break with the past must be immediate, violent, and complete. Women's writing must not reinforce the mistakes of history "by repeating them" (245). Her look to the future, to a time when feminine *écriture* in all its promise may be fully realized, is all the more significant in that she believes no dialogue with the past is possible. The "(feminine) new" must be brought forth from the "(masculine) old" ("la nouvelle de l'ancien"), definitively and absolutely: "there are no grounds for establishing a discourse" between the two (245). The relationship between women's writing and the masculine order of both history and literature is thus more than confrontational; it is openly combative. The language Cixous uses to describe the "struggle" of women's writing is suffused with violence: "We must kill the false woman who is preventing the live one from breathing. Inscribe the breath of the whole woman" (250). The whole woman emerges only with the violent death of her false counterpart, and women's writing with the toppling of the male literary order. Woman must make "her shattering entry into history, which has always been based *on her suppression*. To write and thus forge for herself the antilogos weapon" (250; emphasis in the original).

"The Laugh of the Medusa" is presumably a prototype of this weapon, and its effect is meant to be sweeping, cataclysmic. Indeed the only affinity Cixous acknowledges between woman and the old order is located in brief moments of (poetic) catastrophe: "At times it is in the fissure caused by an earthquake, through that radical mutation of things brought on by material upheaval when every structure is thrown off balance and an ephemeral wildness sweeps order away, that the poet slips something by, for a brief span, of woman" (249). Earthquake, upheaval, fissure, death—only in the imagery of such moments of separation, each of an extreme and violent nature, can femininity be inscribed: "Now, I-woman am going to blow up the Law; an explosion henceforth possible and ineluctable; let it be done, right now, *in* language" (257; emphasis in the original). This linguistic razing is what Cixous pronounces necessary if the masculine hegemony or "phallogocentrism" is to be overturned.

It is precisely in sentiment, if not in language, such as this, that readers have perceived an initial affinity between the feminist project of feminine *écriture* and the literary theory of Mikhail Bakhtin. The observation is not farfetched. Bakhtin locates the beginnings of the novel, the privileged form of dialogic exchange, in a definitive break with the patriarchal world of myth and epic. In his essay "Epic and Novel," Bakhtin writes that the novel was "powerfully affected by a very specific rupture in the history of Western civilization." He traces this rupture, and the novel's subsequent emergence, "from a socially isolated and culturally deaf semi-patriarchal society."[5] In "The Laugh of the Medusa," Cixous also writes of a cultural (and here gender-specific) deafness: "the deaf male ear, which hears in language only that which speaks in the masculine" (251). Cixous's phallogocentric order, the "millennial arid ground" she seeks to break, has much in common with Bakhtin's world of the epic. Both are types of what Bakhtin would call monologic discourse, grounded in patriarchal myth, deaf to other voices and discourses, and subvertible only through transgression of the linguistic and literary laws that govern them.

Feminist critics have duly noted the resemblance. Novelistic discourse for Bakhtin, like feminine *écriture* for Cixous, attempts to subvert the monologic world of patriarchy through various forms of transgression. Clair Wills, for example, perceives "an analogy between Bakhtinian carnival, hysteria and women's texts in terms of their capacity to disrupt and remake official public norms."[6] Cixous's repeated attempts at subverting masculine myths (the Medusa is one such myth; the Freudian account of female sexuality would be another) are consistent with Bakhtin's prescription for dialogic discourse. Myth and epic exert what Bakhtin calls a "homogenizing power . . . over language" ("From the Prehistory of Novelistic Discourse," 60). They transform events, the dynamic world of exchange and experience, into an absolute fixed past, "attaching them to the world of fathers, of beginnings and peak times—canonizing these events, as it were, while they are still current" ("Epic and Novel," 14-15). Like Cixous, Bakhtin celebrates the unraveling of this "world of fathers." The desired end in each case, whether dialogic discourse or women's writing, is expressed in remarkably similar terms. The means of achieving this end vary greatly, however. Despite Cixous's explosive language, it is not at all clear that "The Laugh of the Medusa" announces a type of discourse that Bakhtin might have called dialogic, or even transgressive.

Dialogic discourse overturns the world of the fathers not through violence, but through laughter.[7] In its emphasis on the present, on concrete human history and becoming, Bakhtin's dialogue looks neither to a hidden origin or source, nor to a utopian future of language and literary expression.[8] Dialogic discourse is radically *present*, a "living mix of varied and opposing voices," a process of "interanimation" in which self and other create one another continually ("Prehistory," 49, 47). Bakhtin welcomes rupture, transgression, and subversion of the language of authority. He sees in the novel, or rather in novelistic discourse, a demystification not only of epic and myth but also of an idea of language as unitary and timeless, exclusive and transcendent. Language and literature so conceived are ultimately incompatible with feminine *écriture* as Cixous describes and practices it. Women's writing in "The Laugh of the Medusa" is presented as both a return to origins—now a world of mothers, not fathers—and a hope for future deliverance.[9] Either chronology, the mythical past or the utopian future, recasts language in an idealized monologue, set apart from the Bakhtinian world of "concrete human historical discourse" ("Discourse in the Novel," 279).

According to Bakhtin, any type of discourse that proclaims itself "special," a language apart, risks becoming "a unitary and singular Ptolemaic world outside of which nothing else exists and nothing else is needed" ("Discourse," 286). The very idea of such a language is, Bakhtin writes further, "a typical utopian philosopheme of poetic discourse" ("Discourse," 288). Cixous's longing for women's writing and "*what it will do*" is clearly an expression of such a utopian desire. It is small comfort that Cixous anticipates precisely the point I am raising: "Once more you'll say that all this smacks of 'idealism,' or what's worse you'll splutter that I'm a 'mystic' " (262). There is no question that her description of feminine *écriture* idealizes and mystifies the practice of writing, albeit in an idiom distinct from those against which she is struggling. For Bakhtin, however, it is not enough to demystify the monologic language of authority, if one merely sets another type of myth or monologue in its place.

In "The Laugh of the Medusa" Cixous writes that "it is impossible to *define* a feminine practice of writing, and this is an impossibility that will remain, for this practice can never be theorized, enclosed, coded" (253). Despite this declaration of openness, Cixous assigns a number of rather exclusive qualities to women's writing: it is fluid, vibrant, dynamic. It overflows in floods and streams and waves. It enjoys a "privileged relationship with the voice" (251), and not merely the voice, but the "equivoice" (252). Unlike the phallocentric system it overturns, feminine *écri-*

ture writes the (female) body: "the rhythm that laughs you; the intimate recipient who makes all metaphors possible" (252). Alongside these seemingly indeterminate qualities, Cixous offers a very appealing, and in many respects very Bakhtinian, account of the promise such writing holds:

> Writing is precisely working (in) the in-between, inspecting the process of the same and of the other without which nothing can live, undoing the work of death— . . . infinitely dynamized by an incessant process of exchange from one subject to another. (252)

The feminine practice of writing will reveal writing's true nature: it is gendered, but nonetheless radically inclusive. Where difference is freely admitted rather than erased, feminine and masculine coexist in writing. Feminine *écriture* is thus, ideally, bisexual. By this Cixous means not the traditional bisexuality, in which masculine and feminine are diluted to become neuter, but rather what she calls "the *other bisexuality*," in which difference is preserved. Woman is privileged to imagine this new relationship to the other—for the first time not based on opposition, hierarchy, and ultimately domination—because she has always lived it. Beneath her apparent acquiescence to the masculine order, woman has always lived by an alternate and subversive law: "To love, to watch-think-seek the other in the other, to despecularize, to unhoard . . . a love that rejoices in the exchange that multiplies" (264). Such phrases are very much in the spirit of dialogic discourse, with its "living mix of varied and opposing voices"; but despite these claims, Cixous's privileging of feminine *écriture* confers upon it an exclusive "official" status inconsistent with the open and transgressive nature she declares it to have.

Unlike Bakhtin, who sees literary transgression as possible primarily through novelistic discourse, Cixous explicitly privileges the poetic. For Bakhtin, poetic discourse (which is, as for Cixous, by no means limited to poetry) inevitably restricts language by elevating it to a special status, assigning it rules, and granting it a fixed and transcendent value: "the language of poetic genres, when they approach their stylistic limit, often becomes authoritarian, dogmatic and conservative" ("Discourse," 288). I am not the first to suggest that a certain kind of dogmatism emerges inevitably from what is called women's writing; for in describing its achievements and effects, theoreticians of feminine *écriture* cannot avoid becoming prescriptive. Women's writing will have a certain *style*, which some writers, male or female, will exhibit to a greater or lesser degree than others. Those who conform to this style are judged to be within the feminine practice of writing (Cixous's own list in "The Laugh of the Medusa" includes Colette, Duras, and Genet); those who do not, by inference, must remain outside. So women's writing establishes a new and inclusive relationship to the other, but only, it seems, to a certain kind of other.[10]

In a particularly lively essay entitled *Femmes écrites*, Laurence Enjolras has noted the irony of a feminine *écriture* that becomes exclusive, even repressive in its turn.[11] In its claim to authenticity, to an unmediated feminine truth, women's writing repeats a gesture uncomfortably similar to the tradition with which it seeks definitively to break. For Bakhtin, such an absolute departure, whether patriarchal or feminist, is bound to fail. There can be no clean slate like the one Cixous imagines. "Only the mythical Adam . . . could really have escaped from start to finish this dialogic inter-orientation with the alien word that occurs in the object," Bakhtin writes. "Concrete historical human discourse does not have this privilege: it can deviate from such inter-orientation only on a conditional basis and only to a certain degree" ("Discourse," 279). As Cixous approaches the object and its alien word, she imagines that it is already feminine. In place of a mythical Adam, "The Laugh of the Medusa" proposes a mythical Eve.

Beyond the "singular Ptolemaic world" she creates for women's writing, Cixous's preference for the poetic reveals an even greater distance between her thinking and Bakhtin's.[12] Only poets, Cixous writes, have been able thus far to break free of the dominant male discourse:

> But only the poets—not the novelists, allies of representationalism. Because poetry involves gaining strength from the unconscious and because the unconscious, that other limitless country, is the place where the repressed manage to survive: women, or as Hoffman would say, fairies. (250)

Poets and practitioners of feminine *écriture*, like their compatriots—witches, fairies, hysterics—speak from the unconscious, a place that is secret, hidden, and repressed.[13] It is this "limitless country" that Cixous calls forth in women's writing. By contrast, the Bakhtinian model is never that of the private inner voice, but rather of the public conversation. An individual's "inner speech" enters into dialogue with the outside world, but it does so at the level of consciousness, in the reality of "concrete historical human" exchange.[14] Knowledge, expression, even being, for Bakhtin, stem from conscious interaction with the other, the alien word, that which is outside the self. The relationship is symbiotic, to be sure. The other is constitutive of the self, and vice versa; in this sense, there is always something of the other within each of us. But this other, without whom there can be no self, remains, nonetheless, necessarily separate; or in Bakhtin's idiom, "alien." Dialogic exchange occurs only among individuals (or texts) that possess an identifiable degree of autonomy. Otherwise there can be no difference, and no need for exchange. The self/other relationship is conceived then not as a convergence of difference emerging from within, but rather, as Michael Holquist has phrased it, "as *different degrees each possesses of the other's otherness.*"[15] Though Cixous expresses the desire for a dialogic relationship between self and other, the method she prescribes for its realization produces a very one-sided conversation. As I shall argue, Cixous's location of otherness totally within the parameters of the self results in its negation. In short, she cancels otherness out.

Her libido is cosmic, just as her unconscious is
worldwide.

In the new relationship between self and other that Cixous describes in "The Laugh of the Medusa," the other's otherness, or "difference," is ideally that which should be preserved. "In the beginning," Cixous writes, "are our differences" (263); and this is the premise on which the new history, which women (and eventually men) will write, is to be founded. Each of us, male and female, is invited to consider the presence of the other within. Cixous describes this dynamic in terms of the "other bisexuality" mentioned briefly earlier:

> Bisexuality: that is, each one's location in self (*repérage en soi*) of the presence—variously manifest and insistent according to each person, male or female—of both sexes, non-exclusion either of the difference or of one sex, and, from this "self-permission," multiplication of the effects of the inscription of desire, over all parts of my body and the other body. (254)

This attempt to locate the other within carries with it a certain risk: in the effort to avoid exclusion, the self may become all-encompassing. Though the desired relationship is one that admits and even welcomes difference, rather than erasing or "castrating" it, Cixous's ideal of nonexclusion recreates, albeit inadvertently, the very threat to otherness that it is designed to contain. The risk to the other is particularly great when expression originates with the unconscious, as Cixous claims it does. Inner speech, with its fluid and ever-expanding boundaries, may drown out the conscious world of social interchange. There is much by way of analogy, metaphor, and allusion to suggest that this is precisely what takes place in "The Laugh of the Medusa." Cixous's disclaimers notwithstanding, the primary relationship celebrated here is less that of self to other, Bakhtin's dialogue, than that of self to self. If the "false theater of phallocentric representationalism" has staged a drama of exclusion, the new wave of women's writing offers in its place a drama of limitless containment.

The elements of "The Laugh of the Medusa" that prove most troubling from a Bakhtinian perspective all reflect a look inward, an endless return to the self. This is neither surprising nor necessarily lamentable. The project of women's writing is a retrieval of feminine identity: it is, therefore, a project of *self*-knowledge, *self*-awareness, and *self*-expression. The need to establish feminine identity through women's writing accounts in part for Cixous's references to autoeroticism, narcissism, homosexuality, and—the predominant and most problematic of images—the womb. All of these imply relationships that are directed more toward self and sameness than toward the "alien word." All are related, as Cixous evokes them, to the private inner voice of desire. "Break out of the circles," she urges women; "don't remain within psychoanalytic closure" (263). Yet Cixous's incessant return to the libido, to the body and its relation to the unconscious, serves more to enclose her within official discourse than to free her from it.

In her deliberate effort to break with traditional male psychoanalysis, Cixous celebrates the richness of female sexuality.[16] It is multiple: "inexhaustible, like music, painting, writing: [the] stream of phantasms is incredible" (246). To illustrate this multiplicity, this sexual and aesthetic inexhaustibility, Cixous turns ironically to a world "all her own," one that is private, hidden, and self-reflective. She uses the image of masturbation, of erotic self-fulfillment, as emblematic of the knowledge and awareness women seek:

> I have been amazed more than once by a description a woman gave me of a world all her own which she had been secretly haunting since childhood. A world of searching, the elaboration of a knowledge, on the basis of a systematic experimentation with the bodily functions, a passionate and precise interrogation of her erotogeneity. This practice, extraordinarily rich and inventive, is prolonged or accompanied by a production of forms, a veritable aesthetic activity, each stage of rapture inscribing a resonant vision, a composition, something beautiful. (246)

Autoeroticism is thus an expression not only of sexuality but also of spirituality; it is a science, an epistemology, and an aesthetics, all rolled (significantly) into one. However worthy, rich, and inventive this practice may be, I feel certain that it is not dialogic. The autoerotic model, offered here as an alternative to the traditional, repressive hierarchy in which the feminine self is subordinated to the masculine other, is one in which the other has become superfluous.

Autoeroticism and homosexuality ("The Americans remind us, 'We are all Lesbians'; that is, don't denigrate woman, don't make of her what men have made of you" [252]) are necessary elements in the project of self-discovery and self-expression that is women's writing. Woman has, up until now, been "kept in the dark about herself, led into self-disdain by the great arm of parental-conjugal phallocentrism" (246). Men have created an "antinarcissism" (248) in which women have languished. For Cixous, the remedy lies apparently in another form of narcissism, one in which the self is elaborated not to exclude, but rather to *include* others: "[Woman's] libido is cosmic, just as her unconscious is worldwide" (259). Woman *becomes* the world, the world is woman: "Our glances, our smiles, are spent; laughs exude from our mouths; our blood flows and we extend ourselves without ever reaching an end" (248). Everywhere she looks, then, Cixous is looking in the mirror. Any encounter with the other is by definition an encounter with the self. Cixous's stated, and very Bakhtinian, goal is the preservation of otherness in relationship to the self, once the true feminine self has been articulated. Yet it is difficult to see how difference is *not* erased in her formulation, where there is most certainly a blurring of the distinction between self and other. Where nothing is alien, to use Bakhtin's terms, there can be no alien word. In Cixous's unreserved flow between self and other, the dyadic tension necessary to Bakhtin's dialogue is lost. The "cosmic libido" is all-encompassing, and therefore ultimately circular, solipsistic, monologic. In a parody of the scene on the analyst's couch, Cixous ends up (like Dora?) talking only to herself.

The womb serves as the organizing metaphor for the dynamic described. It is, precisely, the "locus for the other" that Cixous claims is hidden and always ready within every woman. But it is also, significantly, the locus within which the other is wholly contained. Even, or perhaps *especially*, in its spatial arrangement, the image of the womb conflicts with Bakhtin's concept of the dialogic self, in which "outsideness" (often rendered from the French as "exotopy") remains such an important category. No event, no person can be known or experienced completely from within, *not even* the self. As Michael Holquist explains, "It is only from a position outside something that it can be perceived in categories that complete it in time and fix it in space."[17] My existence depends in part on the ability of those outside myself to perceive me in the context of that which I myself am unable to see. The relationship is neither hierarchical, as Cixous interprets the traditional male version of it, nor coextensive, as in the image of the womb; it is based on reciprocity, rather than on domination or containment.

Bakhtin is surely among a very few male writers who have invoked and elaborated images of pregnancy and the womb. He does so most extensively in *Rabelais and His World*, where the womb is depicted, as Mary Russo has phrased it, as an element of Bakhtin's "semiotic model of the body politic."[18] I would take this image a step further and say that the womb represents something larger even than the body politic. For Bakhtin, it serves as a model for our very being. As such, it is both a liberating and disquieting figure. Fullness, swelling, childbirth, and procreative power have invariably positive associations in Bakhtin's repertoire of the body. But the image of the womb is a grotesque—which is to say, double-edged, both regenerative and frightening:

> All unearthly objects were transformed into earth, the mother which swallows up in order to give birth to something larger that has been improved. There can be nothing terrifying on earth, just as there can be nothing frightening in a mother's body, with the nipples that are made to suckle, with the genital organ and warm blood. The earthly element of terror is the womb, the bodily grave, but it flowers with delight and a new life.[19]

For Bakhtin, the ambivalence of the womb—its terror and delight—is precisely what defines it as a grotesque. Without this ambivalence, without the suggestion of both destructive and regenerative potential, the image cannot function, as Bakhtin writes of Don Quixote's death, to apply "the popular corrective of laughter" to a world in which the deadliest risk is the "narrow-minded seriousness" of "idealistic and spiritual pretense" (*Rabelais*, 22). Cixous, like other feminists, succumbs to this risk in her appeal to pregnancy and the womb as models for human relationships.

In her essay, "Female Grotesques: Carnival and Theory," Mary Russo discusses at some length Bakhtin's formulation of the womb and pregnancy as grotesque images. As Russo adapts Bakhtin's theories of carnival and the grotesque to feminist analysis, her discussion is appreciative, though occasionally disapproving. Although she acknowledges that "there are many reasons for questioning the use of the maternal in recent French criticism" (she cites specifically the tendency to portray motherhood as an "idealized category"), she remains suspicious of anything potentially negative in Bakhtin's appropriation of the imagery of childbearing. Bakhtin is useful to feminism insofar as his formulations conform to those of recent feminists: "In terms strikingly similar to Bakhtin's formulation of the grotesque body as continuous process, Hélène Cixous calls this body 'the body without beginning and without end' " (Russo, 221). Bakhtin is suspect, however, because, like most male theorists of his time, he "fails to acknowledge or incorporate the social relations of gender" in his analysis (Russo, 219).

Russo focuses her criticism of Bakhtin on his treatment of the figure of the "pregnant hag," the terracotta figurines that he discusses in his introduction to *Rabelais and His World*. As Bakhtin explains these figurines, he emphasizes again their ambivalent quality:

> In the famous Kerch terracotta collection we find figurines of senile pregnant hags. Moreover, the old hags are laughing. This is a typical and very strongly expressed grotesque. It is ambivalent. It is pregnant death, a death that gives birth. There is nothing completed, nothing calm and stable in the bodies of these old hags. They combine a senile, decaying and deformed flesh with the flesh of new life, conceived but as yet unformed. Life is shown in its two-fold contradictory process; it is the epitome of incompleteness. And such is precisely the grotesque concept of the body. (25-26)

The ambivalence of the figure centers, for Bakhtin, not on the female grotesque, but rather on the aging body. It is a mistake to assume, as I believe Russo does, an implicit fear or contempt in Bakhtin's interpretation of these objects. She explains that "for the feminist reader, the pregnant hag is more than ambivalent. It is loaded with the connotations of fear and loathing associated with the biological processes of reproduction and aging" (Russo, 219). My quarrel with Russo's reading is that I am not convinced Bakhtin experiences "fear and loathing" in the contemplation of these figures, or indeed of any biological processes, whether copulation, defecation, childbirth, or even death.

To characterize the hags as "old, senile, decaying and deformed" is to call them what they are, or at least what they are meant to appear to be: they are grotesques, after all.[20] We assume an absolutely negative connotation in our reading of these adjectives; but, although the assumption is more than understandable (and I don't wish to appear either disingenuous or hopelessly naive), I don't think we can transfer our own assumptions to Bakhtin. A balanced reading of the passage shows that the old hags are explicitly positive figures. They are "the epitome of incompleteness," as Bakhtin says. They celebrate life in its extreme intermediacy, in the fullness of its indetermination. Russo herself makes this very point, hesitantly, when she reminds us that "Bakhtin's description of these ancient crones is at least exuberant" (Russo, 219).

Russo's ultimate reproach to Bakhtin is the question she asserts "never occurred to [him] in front of the Kerch terracotta figurines—Why are these old hags laughing?" (Russo, 227). In my reading of the passage, the question has not only occurred to him, he has already answered it. Their laughter is the "popular corrective" that prevents us from taking them too seriously. Bakhtin's description of the terracotta figurines constitutes a defense of ugliness or deformity—the grotesque—against what he considers to be the lifeless quality, the absolute stasis, of the classical aesthetic. It is a mark, I think, of our implicit adherence to this aesthetic that we cannot even entertain the notion that Bakhtin's description of the hags is positive. I would suggest that age and ugliness become undesirable attributes through our eyes, more than through his. By extension, then, his depiction of the figurines seems to us imbued with the "fear and loathing" characteristic of misogyny. Like Cixous, whom she quotes, Russo conveys the idea that fear is the only response men have to pregnancy and the womb. In Bakhtin's case, I believe a more subtle reasoning applies.

The source of fear in Bakhtin's discussion of the womb is neither woman per se, nor the maternal, nor the supposed mysterious power of pregnancy. Carnival functions, according to Bakhtin, precisely to place the body, male and female, on demystifying display: there can be, as I quoted earlier, "nothing frightening" in it (*Rabelais*, 91). If the womb is "the earthly element of terror" in Bakhtin's account, it is not because, as Cixous writes, "it has always been suspected that, when pregnant, the woman . . . takes on intrinsic value as a woman in her own eyes and, undeniably, acquires body and sex" (261-62).[21] The source of terror in the image of the womb is spatial: the fear of being swallowed up, the loss of "outsideness" that is essential to selfhood as Bakhtin defines it. To equate this fear with an intrinsic fear of woman is to restrict the definition of femininity to the functioning of the womb, which is indeed a definition that many thinkers, feminist and antifeminist alike, endorse. Cixous, in certain passages of "The Laugh of the Medusa," seems to me to be among those who define the feminine in this way; Bakhtin, in my view, is not.

> Write your self. Your body must be heard. Only then will the immense resources of the unconscious spring forth.

Much as the womb defines the relationship between self and other that Cixous proposes, the body defines woman's relationship to language. "Her flesh speaks true," Cixous writes. "She lays herself bare. In fact, she physically materializes what she's thinking; she signifies it with her body" (251). Writing the body is a matter of calling forth the unconscious, that which has been kept hidden. The expansive (female) body is riddled with ever-multiplying desire; and when this immense source of libidinal, linguistic expression has been unleashed, its force (it comes as no surprise) is "explosive, *utterly* destructive, shattering" (256; emphasis in the original). In reclaiming the body through language, women's writing visits yet again the scene of a violent and shattering confrontation.

As Cixous sets out to write femininity, in open defiance of the way in which Freud and other fathers have written it, she insists on the transgressive nature of her undertaking. "The Dark Continent," she declares, "is neither dark nor unexplorable" (255). Yet this continent, once illuminated through feminine *écriture*, looks like a rather familiar place. In claiming a privileged relationship to it, Cixous does no more than confirm what male theorists have claimed for centuries.[22] Though Cixous writes that this is a "body without end, without appendage, without principal 'parts' " (259), nonetheless a great many parts are on display; and all of them—nipples, breasts, womb—are either uniquely feminine or have served traditionally to define femininity.[23] Attempting to subvert the "phallic mystification" of writing, Cixous produces, in a sense, its mirror image: writing is no longer seminal, she claims, it is lactic. Merely interchanging body parts or fluids does little, however, to upset the Freudian framework, the relationship between writing and the unconscious, which Cixous retains virtually intact.

In a chapter of *Sémiotikè* entitled "Le mot, le dialogue, et le roman," Julia Kristeva draws a distinction between truly subversive discourses and those that are merely parody.[24] Explicating and developing certain ideas drawn from her reading of Bakhtin, Kristeva defines dialogic discourse as "une *transgression se donnant une loi*"; that is, a transgression that creates or provides its own law (Kristeva, 152). Women's writing, as Cixous demonstrates repeatedly in "The Laugh of the Medusa," presents itself as such a discourse. In practice, however, feminine *écriture* seems more reminiscent of what Kristeva calls a "pseudo-transgression," or "la *loi prévoyant sa transgression*"; that is, a law that anticipates its own transgression (Kristeva, 152). Such a pseudo-transgression remains in the realm of the monologic, for it upholds the official discourse it claims to subvert.

If the source of writing is the unconscious, as Cixous claims, if true expression lies exclusively within or upon or across or through the body—even the cosmic "body without end"—then the "locus for the other" remains obscure. In valuing the unconscious, that which is hidden and unspoken, Cixous admits the existence of a dark continent, in her words the "limitless country," where the other is ultimately an unnecessary, if not unwelcome, intruder. Cixous's professed alternative to the dialectic, to the phallocentric values of opposition and hierarchizing exchange, is scarcely better. The limitless, all-inclusive, multiple, and multiply desiring self simply allows no place ' 'outside," precisely where difference must be located. The other's otherness could hardly be problematic according to this schema, which doesn't allow it to exist.

Cixous's desire for "the new love" that "dares for the other, wants the other" might be considered an admirable, if somewhat suffocating, ideal, were it not undercut by the climate of hostility that pervades "The Laugh of the Medusa." The repeated violent imagery to which Cixous has recourse sets a jarring context for "a love that rejoices in the exchange that multiplies" (264). The violence of her text is reserved, of course, for the others who have come before, those who are part of the patriarchal history with which she seeks to break. It is ironic, then, that she shares this climate of hostility with a variety of "fathers" against whose vision she is writing: Freud is certainly one; Jean-Paul Sartre is arguably another.

Paranoia has occasionally been called a twentieth-century disease. A glance at some of the century's most influential models of human interaction tends to reaffirm this. Whether the scenario is the family romance or the existentialist search for authenticity, the other is often viewed with wariness and distrust, if not outright hostility. That which is encountered outside the self, in the conscious world of human exchange, may prove to be the source of neurosis or bad faith. In either case, the other is viewed in some sense as an obstacle to self-fulfillment.[25] A brief consideration of the dynamics of the Oedipal complex for all concerned, including the excluded little girl, may lead one to concur readily with Sartre that Hell is indeed other people.[26] It is small wonder, then, that Cixous's solution to this very real dilemma is to expand the self to preclude any form of opposition, as the only opposition she can imagine is one in which the self is threatened. Bakhtin offers another and, in my view, more viable alternative to this hostile climate, one that may fulfill the promise of the Medusa's laughter better even than Cixous herself.

> You only have to look at the Medusa straight on to see her. And she's not deadly. She's beautiful and she's laughing.

"Laughter," Bakhtin writes, "demolishes fear and piety before an object" ("Epic and Novel," 23). What I have tried to argue here is that the Medusa is not truly laughing, not in the Bakhtinian sense, for the Medusa's laughter replaces whatever myth it subverts with another version of the same pious, perhaps even frightening, image. According to the myth, the monster is deadly. Merely to look upon her reduces the observer to silence, turns him to stone. Cixous encourages the look with inviting reassurance: "You only have to look at the Medusa straight on to see her. And she's not deadly. She's beautiful and she's laughing" (255). But Perseus, in Cixous's schema, meets the fate with which he was initially threatened. As the representative of official discourse, he remains precisely that which must be exploded, swept away, if the "new history" of feminine *écriture* is to be written. I am, of course, no more inclined than Cixous to preserve the old myth; but what troubles me in her text is the way in which the new myth resembles the old. In the official version, the sword-wielding Perseus silences the Medusa for fear of being silenced himself. In the subversive "unofficial" version, the Medusa's laughter, a product not of the masculine province of history but of the limitless feminine country of desire, includes (and thereby preempts) whatever Perseus may have to say. In either case, someone is silenced. In either version of the myth, no true dialogue can be maintained.

Bakhtin imagines a relationship between self and other in which silence is truly, reciprocally deadly. The moment the dialogue ends, whether violently or gently, both other and self have ceased to be. Bakhtin believes that official discourses can and should be subverted; the "culturally deaf semipatriarchal" world, like Cixous's deaf male ear, must, even for its own sake, be made to hear. But history cannot be rewritten in the way that Cixous proclaims. To attempt to do so is always to accept more of the language of authority than one rejects. Cixous's feminine *écriture* remains monologic because it seeks the unconscious, the other within, a presence internalized and therefore precluded, rather than the "living mix of varied and opposing voices," the conscious external conversation in which tension is not diffused and in which opposition is neither forestalled nor contained.

If we attempt, Tzvetan Todorov has written, "to grasp in a single glance the whole of Bakhtin's intellectual itinerary, we note that its unity is achieved in the conviction . . . according to which *the interhuman is constitutive of the human*."[27] The space between self and other, the "difference" that Cixous would seek through women's writing to preserve, is irreducible, absolute, and—this is key—productive. The distance between self and other is not a gap to be bridged or a void to be filled, either through domination or inclusion; for it is in this very space that "interanimation" occurs, that we as humans exist. To illustrate the originality of this position, Todorov compares Bakhtin to Jean-Jacques Rousseau, who "sees the other as necessary only in the process of coming to know a preexisting entity" (Todorov, 85); that is, the self. Cixous's feminine self is also a preexisting entity. Silenced up until now, she has always been there, beneath the surface. Once this silence is broken, the "whole woman" erupts in violence ("volcanic . . . an upheaval of the old property crust") and promptly submerges everything in her path in a wave of desire.

My preference for Bakhtin over Cixous, for his concept of dialogic discourse over her definition of feminine *écriture*, stems in part from my initial enthusiasm for her work. Her vision of "the one and the other, not fixed in sequences of struggle and expulsion . . . but infinitely dynamized by an incessant process of exchange" remains as compelling for me as the first time I read it. My purpose here has not been to question the redefinition of the relationship between self and other that Cixous proposes, but rather to suggest that Bakhtin offers a necessary corrective to her vision for women's writing. Indeed her "new" model, the one she claims women have always lived, finds its more benevolent expression in Bakhtin, whose rhetoric is considerably less violent and whose laughter is more welcoming than Cixous's. Her self-styled "self-seeking" text celebrates a union with the other for whom Cixous has no need and to whom, in the end, she has left no place. Reading "The Laugh of the Medusa," I must conclude with Todorov that Bakhtin's vision is "not only more generous than the other, it is more true" (Todorov, 85).

Notes

1. A number of publications have appeared in the past few years addressing the topic of Bakhtin and feminism. These include Mary Russo, "Female Grotesques: Carnival and Theory," in *Feminist Studies/Critical Studies*, ed. Teresa de Lauretis (Bloomington: Indiana University Press, 1986); Dale M. Bauer's *Feminist Dialogics: A Theory of Failed Community* (Albany: State University of New York Press, 1988); *Bakhtin and Cultural Theory*, ed. Ken Hirschkop and David Shepherd (Manchester, England: Manchester University Press, 1989); and David Lodge, *After Bakhtin: Essays on Fiction and Criticism* (London: Routledge, 1990).

2. Unless otherwise stated, Cixous's essay is quoted from "The Laugh of the Medusa," trans. Keith Cohen and Paula Cohen, in *New French Feminisms: An Anthology*, ed. Elaine Marks and Isabelle de Courtivron (New York: Schocken, 1981), 245-64.

3. My reference is to the title of Dale Bauer's book cited in note 1. In the introduction to a subsequent collection of essays, *Feminism, Bakhtin, and the Dialogic*, ed. Dale M. Bauer and Susan Jaret McKinstry (Albany: State University of New York Press, 1991), Bauer and McKinstry offer various (often negative) definitions of a feminist dialogics: "Dialogic consciousness or standpoint depends neither on essentialism nor truth, but on context and condition. A feminist dialogics is not just agonistic or oppositional; it also suggests an identity in dialectic response, always open and ongoing" (3). "For the object," they write further, "is not, ultimately, to produce a feminist monologic voice, a dominant voice that is a reversal of the patriarchal voice (even if such a project were conceivable)" (4). By such criteria, Cixous's endeavor fails.

4. See Verena Andermatt Conley, *Hélène Cixous: Writing the Feminine* (Lincoln: University of Nebraska Press, 1984), 77-78.

5. M. M. Bakhtin, "Epic and Novel," in *The Dialogic Imagination: Four Essays by M. M. Bakhtin*, ed. Michael Holquist, trans. Caryl Emerson and Michael Holquist (Austin: University of Texas Press, 1981), 11. Quotations from this essay and others in the volume are cited in the text by title and page number.

6. Clair Wills, "Upsetting the Public: Carnival, Hysteria, and Women's Texts" in Hirschkop and Shepherd, *Bakhtin and Cultural Theory*, 130-51. Feminist critics have adopted Bakhtin's theory of carnival more readily than his theory of the novel, though both function dialogically and may be equally subversive.

7. I shall return to this point later in my essay, as laughter is announced in her title and Cixous also prescribes a form of laughter, designed "to blow up the law, to break up the 'truth' " (258).

8. As Gary Saul Morson and Caryl Emerson have pointed out in *Mikhail Bakhtin: Creation of a Prosaics* (Stanford, Calif.: Stanford University Press, 1991), there is a utopian

strain to laughter as Bakhtin describes it, particularly in *Rabelais and His World*. The idea of a utopia—a place out of time, out of history—is ultimately foreign, however, to Bakhtin's world of becoming. As Morson and Emerson phrase it, laughter and carnival are "the utopia of an anti-utopian thinker" (94).

9. Consistent with her call for an "other bisexuality," Cixous urges that we get past the opposition mother/father: "Let us dematerpaternalize rather than deny woman. . . . Let us defetishize. Let's get away from the dialectic which has it that the only good father is a dead father" (261). Earlier in the essay, however, she proclaims the primacy of the mother: "A woman is never far from 'mother' (I mean outside her role functions: the 'mother' as nonname and as source of goods). There is always within her at least a little of that good mother's milk. She writes in white ink" (251).

10. Indeed, feminist readers often relegate Bakhtin to the outside for not having been (I am distilling the argument) a feminist. Such judgments are decidedly "agonistic and oppositional"; they serve "to produce a feminist monologic voice, a dominant voice that is the reversal of the patriarchal voice"—a project, it turns out, that is readily conceivable. (I am quoting here from Bauer and McKinstry, *Feminism, Bakhtin, and the Dialogic*, 4.)

11. Laurence Enjolras, *Femmes écrites: Bilan de deux décennies*, in Stanford French and Italian Studies (Saratoga, Calif.: ANMA Libri, 1990). Enjolras adopts what she calls an impudent, polemical tone to describe her frustration with apologists of feminine *écriture*, who remain somehow oblivious to the paradox of their own writing. Texts like "The Laugh of the Medusa," she writes, "convey nonetheless, even as they claim to denounce, undo, annihilate them—and it's perhaps the enormity of the paradox that is so infuriating—the same repressive elements, intrinsic to the system and established by men, which have allowed the latter, since time began, to keep women in a subordinate position" (4; my translation).

12. In Bakhtin's cosmos, the ideal is the outward-looking Copernican model, as opposed to the "singular Ptolemaic world" in which everything is seen to revolve around the self. Cixous's is rather, as she phrases it, "a cosmos tirelessly traversed by Eros, an immense astral space not organized around any one sun that's any more of a star than the others" (259). But it is a cosmos in which everything returns ultimately to the "body without end." No one star is dominant, but all are contained within the "immense astral space" of the (woman's) body.

13. Clair Wills sees these different female types on a continuum. All of them represent a feminine energy (what Cixous sometimes calls "libido") that has been traditionally beyond male control, outside of the public order. This is, of course, an idea that men have held for years.

14. For a discussion of the relationship between inner and outer speech, see Michael Holquist, *Dialogism: Bakhtin and His World* (London: Routledge, 1990), 51-55, in particular. For a discussion of Bakhtin's critique of the Freudian idea of the unconscious and the individual psyche, see Katerina Clark and Michael Holquist, *Mikhail Bakhtin* (Cambridge, Mass.: Harvard University Press, 1984), 171-85. Bakhtin's quarrel with Freud rests in part on his perception of the unconscious as an ahistorical category, and of Freud's idea of language as a predominantly "natural" rather than social activity. In *Freudianism: A Critical Sketch*, Voloshinov detected in Freud a "*sui generis* fear of history, an ambition to locate a world beyond the social and the historical, a search for this world precisely in the depths of the organic" (cited in Clark and Holquist, *Mikhail Bakhtin*, 176). Whatever Bakhtin's role in this book, the sentiment is surely one he endorsed. Cixous's adoption of the unconscious opens itself to criticism on similar grounds.

15. Holquist, *Dialogism*, 51; emphasis in the original.

16. And she does so, ironically, as Laurence Enjolras has pointed out, at Lacan's bidding. See Enjolras, *Femmes écrites*, 30-31.

17. Holquist, *Dialogism*, 31.

18. The phrase is from Russo's essay "Female Grotesques," 219. Subsequent quotations from this essay are cited by author and page number in the text.

19. M. M. Bakhtin, *Rabelais and His World*, trans. Hélène Iswolsky (Bloomington: Indiana University Press, 1984), 91. Subsequent quotations from this essay are cited by title and page number in the text.

20. Although a good case can no doubt be made for the misogyny of the originals, I think that is another question altogether.

21. Cixous suggests here that what has always been "suspected" about women is true: they do take on an "intrinsic value" when pregnant, even, and perhaps especially, in their own eyes. I find this assertion deeply troubling. The notion that a woman "acquires body and sex" if not solely, then somehow more rapidly and truly, through the experience of pregnancy serves to link feminine identity yet again to a reproductive function that has so often served as a justification for the subordination of women. The strain of "women's writing" that celebrates, even figuratively, the experience of pregnancy as a source of feminine power excludes by inference, and rather cruelly, women who have not borne children. What is the source of femininity or power for women who cannot become pregnant or who are unable to carry a child to term? The issues, according to Cixous's own terms, become even murkier when abortion enters the picture. If the womb is—again, even figuratively—the "locus for the other," a model for nonthreatening human relationships, how should we then characterize the act of voluntarily terminating an otherwise healthy pregnancy?

22. Enjolras, in *Femmes écrites*, 30-31, cites Lacan: "Women's power is infinitely beyond all of these male categories, of power, of knowledge, which are mere nonsense, nonsense which doesn't concern them. . . . Must women attempt to integrate male categories, they who are more at ease in the realm [lit: place] of the unconscious?" (my translation).

23. Again, Laurence Enjolras points out that all the female parts are present and celebrated, except the one that is traditionally absent: the head. See her chapter "Pour un corps décapité" ("For a beheaded body") in *Femmes écrites*. In light of this observation, the Medusa is an interesting choice of figure. Cixous wishes to rewrite the myth; but in her new version of it, the head still goes missing.

24. Julia Kristeva, *Sémiotikè, Recherches pour une sémanalyse* (Paris: Seuil, 1969), 143-73. Subsequent quotations from this work are cited by author and page number in the text.

25. This idea could have no meaning for Bakhtin, for whom the other, even in disagreement, serves as the vehicle for self-fulfillment.

26. From the famous last lines of *Huis clos*: "L'enfer, c'est les Autres."

27. Tzvetan Todorov, *Literature and Its Theorists: A Personal View of Twentieth-Century Criticism*, trans. Catherine Porter (Ithaca, N.Y.: Cornell University Press, 1987), 81; emphasis in the original.

The Historical Poetics of Excrement: Yeats's Crazy Jane and the Irish Bishops

Elizabeth Butler Cullingford

In 1930 Yeats suggested a paradoxical similarity between the Bolshevik cultivation of mass emotion and his own imaginative return to the oral popular culture of the Irish peasantry:

> "Is not the Bolshevist's passion for the machine, his creation in the theatre and the schools of mass emotion, a parody of what we feel? We are casting off crown and mitre that we may lay our heads on Mother Earth."[1]

Yeats's metaphor of "discrowning" also permeates *Rabelais and His World*, on which Bakhtin worked from 1934 to 1940 during the expropriation of the Russian peasant farmers and the Stalinist terror.[2] Although the historical analogies between Bakhtin's Marxist espousal of the folk and Yeats's aristocratic "Dream of the noble and the beggarman"[3] cannot be pressed too far, their juxtaposition is suggestive. Yeats, who had a lifelong interest in Sir James Frazer's *Golden Bough* and in popular folklore, was thoroughly familiar with the concept of carnival.[4] The "discrowning" populism he shares with Bakhtin defines itself in opposition to the social and political repression that followed the Irish and Bolshevik revolutions. When the Russian peasants were resisting forced collectivization, Bakhtin celebrated the spontaneous collectivity of folk festival and humor. According to Terry Eagleton, "Bakhtin pits against that 'official, formalistic and logical authoritarianism' whose unspoken name is Stalinism the explosive politics of the body, the erotic, the licentious and semiotic."[5] In posttreaty Ireland, the conservative and petit bourgeois politicians of the new Free State allied themselves with the clergy to construct a monologic and humorless version of Irish postcolonial identity as Gaelic, Catholic, and sexually pure. In the late 1920s and early 1930s Yeats, who had supported the nationalist rejection of the imperial crown, now opposed the Irish miter, the power of what he called the "ecclesiastical mind, Protestant and Catholic."[6] An erotic and licentious female figure, the old madwoman Crazy Jane, disputes through her ballad poetics and carnivalesque insistence on the grotesque body the chaste national identity constructed by a celibate clergy.

Robert Young has cautioned that "just about anyone can, and probably will, appropriate Bakhtin for just about anything." He argues that, while the Rabelais study is the most attractive of Bakhtin's works for Marxists, "carnival offers a liberal rather than a Marxist politics."[7] Tony Bennett, however, claims that "Bakhtin's study of Rabelais would seem fully to exemplify what a Marxist—that is, a historical and materialist—approach to the study of literary texts should look like."[8] But what if one is looking for a *feminist*, historical, and materialist approach to literary texts? Can Bakhtin, master of disguise, alias, and multiple voices, but, as Wayne Booth puts it, practically tone-deaf to female intonations, be recuperated for feminist criticism?[9] And if he can be so easily appropriated, is he worth appropriating?

Reading Yeats through the lens of carnivalesque dialogism demonstrates both the advantages and limitations of Bakhtin's method. A historical poetics reveals Crazy Jane not as the eccentric spokeswoman for Yeats's private desires, but as the figure for an eroticized politics of female transgression. Yeats's contention that the removal of crown and miter allows us to "lay our heads on Mother Earth" provides a metaphorical starting point for an investigation of the relation of Bakhtinian carnivalesque and Yeatsian female masquerade both to each other and to feminism.

The rhetorical invocation of "Mother Earth" is problematic. Is it the familiar symbolic containment of women within the stereotype of maternality and materiality or a challenge to male transcendence through the generative power of female immanence? Bakhtin's work is permeated by an uncritical equation of woman with womb, grave, and excrement. In celebrating the regenerative capabilities of the grotesque carnival body, he continually tropes that body as female, without interrogating the gender implications of his metaphors. In a rare intervention on the subject of gender, Bakhtin admits that Rabelais did not take a progressive position in the sixteenth-century *Querelle des Femmes*: "Rabelais . . . did not take the women's side. How can his position be explained?"[10] Bakhtin naively supposes that "the women's side" is adequately represented by the Platonizing male poets descended from the courtly tradition; the opposition is represented by clerics hostile to the female body as the incarnation of sin. Bakhtin distances Rabelais from the tradition of medieval religious misogyny and presents him as adhering to the comic, folk view of woman:

> The popular tradition is in no way hostile to woman and does not approach her negatively. In this tradition woman is essentially related to the material bodily lower stratum; she is the incarnation of this stratum that degrades and regenerates simultaneously. She is ambivalent. She debases, brings down to earth, lends a bodily substance to things, and destroys; but, first of all, she is the principle that gives birth. She is the womb. Such is woman's image in the popular comic tradition. (*Rabelais*, 240)

Bakhtin is so firmly wedded to the virtues of degradation that he cannot imagine a woman objecting to his characterizing her as the mindless representative of the lower body: the endlessly reproducing womb.

Stallybrass and White correct Bakhtin's joyfully positive celebration of carnival by reminding us that "the politics of carnival cannot be resolved outside of a close historical examination of particular conjunctures: there is no a priori revolutionary vector to carnival and transgression." The same is true of the sexual politics of festivity. The female role in Renaissance carnival was indeed ambivalent: in the process described by Stallybrass and White as "displaced abjection," carnival's violent energies might be turned not against the official hierarchy but against powerless marginal groups like Jews or women.[11] The woman's *symbolic* role in carnival practices, however, was central. Men dressed as dominant, unruly viragos, and "in hierarchical and conflictful societies that loved to reflect on the world-turned-upside-down, the *topos* of the woman on top was one of the most enjoyed."[12] Virginia Woolf suggests that such symbolic use of the female serves only to reinforce her social marginality: "Imaginatively she is of the highest importance; practically she is completely insignificant."[13] Her objection speaks to Bakhtin's idealization of carnival; as a licensed transgression and inversion it is no more than a "permissible rupture of hegemony, a contained popular blow-off."[14] Simple inversion of categories reinforces hierarchy. As Shakespeare acknowledges, "There is no slander in an allow'd fool" and, Woolf would add, no threat in the representation of a woman ruling a man.[15]

Yet Davis provides an optimistic reading of the trope of the unruly woman that may be applied to Yeats's Crazy Jane. She argues that the representation of the disobedient, transgressive, verbally abusive female may offer a politically useful model for domestic and public behavior. The model operates positively only in specific historical contexts, where

> sexual symbolism has a close connection with questions of order and subordination . . . [and] the stimulus to inversion play is a double one—

traditional hierarchical structures *and* disputed changes in the distribution of power in family and political life.[16]

Both of these conditions applied to posttreaty Ireland, where woman had traditionally been represented as virgin or mother, an image deployed to generate sacrificial idealism in patriotic males but seldom to incite women to independent action; and the pressures to modernize social and sexual life were resisted by government and clergy as emanating from the political enemy, England.

Yeats's early project had been the formation of Irish patriots through a poetics of desire for the free nation, imagined as a woman. As heir to the long generic confusion between the Virgin and the Beloved that originated in troubadour love poetry, however, Yeats envisaged such desire as ungratified except in death. His Cathleen ni Houlihan, "purer than a tall candle before the Holy Rood" (82), has had many admirers but "never set out the bed for any."[17] This idealization of the unattainable female and sublimation of sexual into political desire persisted in Irish cultural consciousness long after the need for it had disappeared with the establishment of the Irish Free State. It was maintained by a devotion to the Virgin Mary with which it had always been intertwined.

The establishment of the nation turned Cathleen ni Houlihan into a pious housewife. Yeats saw the Irish hierarchy and the politicians conspiring to impose censorship in order to deny and cover up the "life of the belly and the reproductive organs" (*Rabelais*, 21). He was inspired to poetic and political resistance by the bishops' Lenten pastorals of 1924; the agitations of the Irish Vigilance Association and the Catholic Truth Society; the train holdups by "holy gunmen" in search of filthy English newspapers;[18] the Christian Brothers' public burning of the old folk ballad about the pregnant Virgin, "The Cherry Tree Carol";[19] the setting up of the Committee of Enquiry into Evil Literature in 1926; and the Censorship of Publications Bill in 1929.

Mary Douglas argues that fetishization of purity is characteristic of threatened minorities, whose concern with political boundaries is displaced into an obsession with bodily orifices.[20] Ireland's boundaries were compromised from without by continued British presence in the treaty ports and from within by partition and the bitter legacy of civil war. The revolution was unfinished. Although the Catholics were not a minority within the Free State, insecurity about boundaries combined with the desire of the newly empowered to assert control at home. Attention was diverted from rural and urban poverty by a public obsession with sexuality, defined as "dirt." In their 1924 Lenten Pastorals, which Yeats described as "rancid, course [*sic*] and vague,"[21] the bishops lambasted "women's immodest fashions in dress, indecent dances, unwholesome theatrical performances and cinema exhibitions, evil literature and drink." Their leading obsession was "foreign corrupting dances," which were not "the clean, healthy, National Irish dances . . . [but] importations from the vilest dens of London, Paris and New York—direct and unmistakable incitements to evil thoughts, evil desires, and grossest acts of impurity."[22] *The Catholic Bulletin* described "Leda and the Swan" as "the filthy Swan Song of Senator Yeats."[23] In "The Three Monuments" Yeats responded by mocking the idea "That purity built up the State / And after kept it from decay," (227) but the establishment was bent on eradicating filth, censoring and silencing heteroglossic voices.

State regulation of sexuality through the refusal of divorce and contraception and the promotion of motherhood as a full-time occupation weighed heavily on Irish women.[24] In their 1927 pastoral the bishops reiterated that "in woman, especially, purity is the crowning glory."[25] In the Senate Yeats defended divorce, supported women's right to work outside the home, and opposed a censorship that, devised in part to ban periodicals that advertised contraceptives, would also exclude from Ireland "all great love poetry."[26] In an erotophobic culture that tried to define indecency as "calculated to arouse sexual passion,"[27] he deployed the love lyric as a strategy of poetic resistance; in a bourgeois culture he marshaled the popular resonances of the ballad. Throughout the Crazy Jane poems, the symbiosis between the pure woman and the nation, a product of male fantasy, is ironized and ruptured.

Crazy Jane speaks as a sexual woman, but also as one of the disenfranchised subaltern groups ignored by the new state: the rural poor. Class and gender issues meet in the personae of the defiant old peasant woman and her lover Jack the Journeyman. The cultural values of the new state after 1922 not only were Catholic, they were rural petit bourgeois. After the famine of 1848 small farmers increasingly adhered to the social system known as familism, which ensured the continuity of inheritance and prevented the splitting up of farms. The male heir married at a later age than before the famine; unwed daughters could enter the convent, domestic service, or emigrate; noninheriting sons could become priests or move to town. Sexual independence was discouraged as likely to lead to economic disaster. Arensburg and Kimball note that the small farmers of Clare in the 1930s identified violations of the familistic pattern with "the debased conduct of the lower ranks of the landless and disreputable of the countryside."[28] Yeats posited an image of the class below the farmers, the landless peasantry and migrant laborers or journeymen (a group that rapidly declined after the famine), as preoccupied with desire and sexuality. The journeyman, a craftsman who hires himself out for a day's wages, is a man of no property, free of the conservatism that springs from land ownership. Yeats intuits that, because the landless had nothing to inherit or bequeath, sexual caution was not economically mandated. Introducing Merriman's grotesque and bawdy Gaelic poem "The Midnight Court," in which an assembly of women demands that men satisfy them physically and that the celibate clergy marry, Yeats links the frank expression of female desire with carnival, with "the free speech and buffoonery of some traditional country festival."[29] Yeats's aristocratic populism constructs the landless peasantry as desiring subjects, and the new Free State as a political body open to desire.

Yeats's conception of the peasantry parallels Bakhtin's vision of the early Renaissance folk in that both serve contemporary political ends. Although in his youth he had accompanied Lady Gregory from cottage to cottage collecting folklore and fairy tales, the middle-class poet had never undertaken serious anthropological research. His attempt to combine the oral folk tradition with sophisticated poetic techniques resulted in a generic hybrid. There is no reason, however, to deplore this procedure. Jameson endorses "the reconstruction of so-called popular cultures . . . from the fragments of essentially peasant cultures: folk songs, fairy tales, popular festivals, occult or oppositional systems of belief such as magic and witchcraft."[30] As opposed to Nazi *Völkisch* propaganda or what Holquist describes as the "Stalinization of Russian folklore," both of which subsume a sanitized idea of the people within the totality of the state, Yeats and Bakhtin emphasized the messy, libidinous, and subversive powers of folk culture.[31] Yeats opens his sequence with "Crazy Jane and the Bishop," a sustained female curse against patriarchal ecclesiastical authority that begins with verbal abuse:

Bring me to the blasted oak
That I, midnight upon the stroke,
(*All find safety in the tomb.*)
May call down curses on his head
Because of my dear Jack that's dead.
Coxcomb was the least he said:
The solid man and the coxcomb.
(255-56)

Cursing, however, is not sufficient to express Jane's contempt for official culture. Her final Bakhtinian gesture is to spit at the bishop.

Arguing that Bakhtin's work is "open to feminist inflection," Robert Stam suggests that his categories "display an intrinsic identification with difference and alterity, a built-in affinity for the oppressed and the marginal."[32] Clair Wills asks if women may have an especially productive relationship to carnival as "they are both placed together in the zone of the anomalous." More cautious than Stam, however, Wills fears that if " 'public' women become associated in male fantasy with the witch and the prostitute," their outspokenness will reinforce negative stereotypes and reinscribe them as spectacles within the visual economy of the male gaze.[33] For women the politics of marginality can easily become the politics of inversion (Margaret Thatcher as parody male) or isolation (the fetishized "difference" of separatism). Bakhtin emphasized that only to the extent that it enters into antagonistic dialogue with "official" discourse, hybridizing it, can the energies of carnival become politically transformative. Stallybrass and White discard his occasionally simplistic opposition between the carnival grotesque and the classicism of the official canon for his more complex appreciation of the way in which "the grotesque is formed through a process of hybridization or inmixing of binary opposites, particularly of high and low."[34] This hybridization or mixing of messages corresponds both with the dialogism of Yeats's Blakean occult philosophy, in which "a contrary is not a negation,"[35] and with a "deconstructed" feminism, which undoes the binary oppositions of "masculine" and "feminine" in order to unsettle patriarchal prescriptions for gender identity.

A female voice created by a man, Crazy Jane is inescapably hybrid. Yeats sought poetic impersonality by speaking as a woman, but as the poems are signed this impersonality is shadowed by Yeats's masculine sexual identity. The voices of these poems are double: the poet as male is textually absent but contextually present. Crazy Jane was both Yeats's attempt to speak the Other and a strategy for evading his own internal censor. His wife's mediumship gave him an occult model for the writing of poetry: Crazy Jane became one of his "controls." The control was a way in which female mediums could express forbidden materials;[36] Crazy Jane offered Yeats a similar license. As a result he, to whom composition had been a torture, "never wrote with greater ease."[37] When he grew tired of Crazy Jane, he was unable simply to discard her: he needed to "exorcise"[38] or "shake [her] off."[39]

Crazy Jane counters Yeats's self-representation in "Among School Children" as a "sixty-year-old smiling public man" (216). "Senator Yeats," with his Nobel Prize, his silk hat, and his armed guards, was an establishment persona with whom Yeats was never completely at ease. Crazy Jane is both his opposite and his grotesque alter ego: unlike him she is female and mad; like him she is old and still a desiring subject. Anticipating his later declaration that "lust and rage" were as appropriate for the pensioner as for the man in his prime (312), Yeats sought to destroy the conventional image of the old as the peaceful repositories of wisdom and good counsel. Bakhtin has identified old age as a component of the oppositional grotesque (*Rabelais*, 25), and Yeats, in what David Lloyd has aptly termed a "poetics of old age," marshals all the power that anomaly, ambiguity, and hybridization can provide.[40] The central trope in this poetics is that of superfluous female desire: an old woman's lust has no place in the cycles of generation. Past childbearing, Jane lacks a Catholic justification for her sexuality. In the Irish countryside the "old person who has already had his or her day of childgetting and childbearing, and yet still persists in manifesting sexual aspirations, is a stock figure of fun."[41] Postmenopausal desire is also rare in love poetry; it violates generic expectations.

Crazy Jane is, therefore, occult, *unheimlich*, and anomalous. Her ambiguous position in society is a source of both power and danger. An aged female who calls down midnight curses at the blasted oak is figuratively a witch. Mary Douglas suggests that

> the existence of an angry person in an interstitial position . . . is dangerous . . . witchcraft . . . would be the anti-social psychic power with which persons in relatively unstructured areas of society are credited.[42]

The clergy were the traditional persecutors of witches; not surprisingly, Jane's primary antagonist is the bishop, who represents the forces of organized society and male culture arrayed against the marginal female figure.

In her deployment of the transgressive power of anomaly, Jane embodies the carnival folk grotesque. Her obsession with copulation, defecation, and degradation contaminates the purity of monologic Catholic doctrine. As Rabelais mocks the clergy, Jane, with her "flat and fallen" breasts, her public, open body "like a road / That men pass over," her preoccupation with "the place of excrement," and her continual obscene punning on "whole/hole," taunts the bishop. She is the unruly woman, "proud and stiff," a shrew and a termagent (259-60). "I can scoff and lour / And scold for an hour" she warns her lover, who responds resignedly, "*That's certainly the case*"(257). Her craziness is crucial,

> because madness makes men look at the world with different eyes, not dimmed by "normal," that is by commonplace ideas and judgments. In folk grotesque, madness is a gay parody of official reason, of the narrow seriousness of official "truth." (*Rabelais*, 39)

Jane appears more "gay" in Yeats's letters than she does in the poems.

Her parody of "official reason" targets a petit bourgeois shopkeeper's wife:

> Crazy Jane is more or less founded upon an old woman who lives in a little cottage near Gort. She . . . [has] an amazing power of audacious speech. One of her great performances is a description of how the meanness of a Gort shopkeeper's wife over the price of a glass of porter made her so despair of the human race that she got drunk. The incidents of that drunkenness are of an epic magnificence. She is the local satirist and a really terrible one.[43]

Jane is committed to the culture of orality. She uses her "amazing power of audacious speech" to tell satirical stories "of an epic magnificence," described by Yeats as "performances." The original of Crazy Jane belongs to the ballad world in which women were the primary transmitters of the oral tradition;[44] for example, Yeats described how "Barbara Allen" had "come down from mother to daughter."[45] Yeats conducts his resistance to censorship through a poetics of desire in which sexuality is celebrated in the metrics, stanzas, and refrains of the popular ballad form.

For Yeats the ballad was the oral expression of Irish folk culture, and Walter Ong's description of the "massive residual orality" of the Irish countryside suggests that he was right.[46] Unlike purist devotees of Child, however, Yeats did not despise the hybrid form of the urban street or broadside ballad, a genre particularly rich in Irish patriotic material. English broadsides, which had a long tradition of anti-Puritanism, were often used to disseminate verses too bawdy for genteel publication. Mixing the urban and the rural, the English and Irish traditions, Crazy Jane disputes with the bishop in "common measure," drawing her energy from the simple rhythm Yeats called "an old 'sing-song' that has yet a mathematical logic."[47] Yeats crosses the ballad meter with the folk lyric to create a hybrid: the poem of emotion framed in a form associated with anonymity and collectivity.

Although Bakhtin contrasted the unity of poetic style and form with the novel's heteroglossic carnival of voices,[48] the ballad Yeats inherits and uses is dialogic in both history and form. Ballads depend on a process of communal re-creation that disperses the monologic voice of the poet among the singers who modify and transmit his creation. The ballad also foregrounds speech, often in the form of questions and answers. In "Crazy Jane on the Day of Judgment" Jane's voice alternates with the laconic responses of her lover; in "Crazy Jane Talks with the Bishop" she satirically quotes the words of her clerical opponent. Most significant for a dialogic reading of the poems, however, is Yeats's use of the ballad refrain, a voice without a subjectivity that complicates and challenges the univocality of the poetic text. In "Crazy Jane Reproved" the refrain, "*Fol de rol, fol de rol*," flippantly derides the injunction "never hang your heart upon / A roaring, ranting journeyman" (256-57). In "Crazy Jane on God" the words one might expect from the bishop are in fact contained in the refrain, which is strikingly juxtaposed with Jane's account of her sexual openness:

> I had wild Jack for a lover;
> Though like a road
> That men pass over
> My body makes no moan
> But sings on:
> *All things remain in God.*
> (259)

The previously anonymous religious refrain becomes in the last stanza the voice of Jane's body, a shift that complicates Bakhtin's oversimple equation of the desiring woman with the materiality of the flesh.

Jane is also in dialogue with the male canon. Because Bakhtin understands language as rooted in social context, and words as having meaning in relation to the words of others, he sees texts as the site of many historical voices. When Crazy Jane situates herself under the "blasted oak" in order to curse the bishop, our sense of her occult power prepares us for her later allusion to Macbeth's witches: "fair and foul are near of kin." The "coxcomb" of the refrain "*The solid man and the coxcomb*" suggests Lear's fool, exposed like Jane to the elements on the heath and anticipating the storm that rages in "Crazy Jane Reproved." Practicing Bakhtinian carnival inversions, Shakespeare's prophetic witches and wise fools represent the uncanny in duplicitous dialogue with official reason.

Crazy Jane's farmyard curses are Bakhtinian "billingsgate" (*Rabelais*, 16-17), a low discourse that mimics the official Catholic rite of excommunication once pronounced by the bishop against her lover:

> Nor was he Bishop when his ban
> Banished Jack the Journeyman.
> (256)

Her spontaneous orality contrasts with his dependence on print. His "ban," which comes from a text, subtly reminds Yeats's audience that their bishops were eager to "ban" books:

> Yet he, an old book in his fist,
> Cried that we lived like beast and beast.
> (256)

Jane links potency and orality as she associates the bishop with clothing, textuality, and male impotence:

> I am tired of cursing the Bishop,
> (Said Crazy Jane)
> Nine *books* or nine *hats*
> Would not *make him a man.*
> (586, my emphasis)

The bishop had charged that her physical relationship with Jack was the mating of "beast and beast." Using the abusive catalogue or popular blazon that according to Bakhtin is "related to animal traits, bodily defects" (*Rabelais*, 430), Jane inverts the religious condemnation of the animal body by associating the bishop with various birds: goose, heron, and (once the bishop is identified with the "coxcomb" of the slippery refrain) cock. The bishop's cock, however, is flaccid, while Jack's is "solid," tree-like:

> The Bishop has a skin, God knows,
> Wrinkled like the foot of a goose,
> (*All find safety in the tomb.*)
> Nor can he hide in holy black
> The heron's hunch upon his back,
> But a birch-tree stood my Jack:
> *The solid man and the coxcomb.*
> (256)

The bishop's ban ended Jack and Jane's love before it had time to exhaust itself through fulfillment. Yeats wrote, "Sexual desire dies because every touch consumes the Myth, and yet a Myth that cannot be so consumed becomes a spectre."[49] Jane and Jack are bound to each other by unsatisfied longing, so Jack has become a "spectre" who "wanders out into the night" (256). The "Crazy Jane" of English folklore was traditionally represented as deserted by her lover,[50] but Jack's name, repeated in every stanza, may suggest the banished Jacobite prince of the popular Gaelic *aisling* tradition, in which colonized Ireland waits for an exiled Stuart to return.

In Jack's absence, however, Jane has entertained numerous lovers, some of whom have exploited her:

> That lover of a night
> Came when he would,
> Went in the morning light
> Whether I would or no.
> (258)

Bakhtin's celebration of woman as the open body leaves her vulnerable to male predators. If Jane resembles an unpaid prostitute, however, she affirms that although "men come, men go" still "*all things remain in God*" (258). Having chosen her way of life, she refuses to complain: "My body makes no moan" (259). In the Irish context Yeats's celebration of female sexual transgression has a double strength. It opens an imaginative space for women's desire and pleasure in a culture that occludes them, and it recuperates the desires and pleasures of women from Ireland's mythological past.

Jane's multiplicity of lovers and unquenchable sexual appetites associate her with the promiscuous Queen Maeve, who was "never without one man in the shadow of another."[51] The pre-Christian Irish tradition on which Yeats draws is notable for its queens, goddesses, and female warriors. Yeats uses the ancient figure of the woman-on-top to critique the contemporary dominance of the Virgin Mother. Crazy Jane is related to the Cailleach Beare, the magical old hag who, appearing in many guises in Irish folklore and literature, bestows rulership of the land upon her lovers. In an early Gaelic poem she laments her decrepitude, her fall into religion:

> I drank my fill of wine with kings,
> Their eyes fixed on my hair.
> Now among the stinking hags
> I chew the cud of prayer.[52]

Writing on women in Irish mythology, MacCana emphasizes "the importance of this idea of the land and its sovereignty conceived in the form of a woman."[53] Unable to find her proper mate, the goddess becomes old, ugly, and crazed, but she is miraculously restored to youth and beauty when she has sex with the rightful king. In Yeats and Lady Gregory's play *Cathleen ni Houlihan* (1902) the old crone becomes "a young girl . . .

[with] the walk of a queen" when she persuades a young man to die for her and for Ireland's freedom.[54]

The twenties were notable for literary revisions of the image of Ireland as a woman, the most scathing of which was Joyce's "old Gummy Granny."[55] The depiction of the ancient milk woman in the opening chapter of *Ulysses* also parodies the tradition:

> Old shrunken paps. . . . Old and secret she had entered from a morning world, maybe a messenger . . . a witch on her toadstool, her wrinkled fingers quick at the squirting dugs. . . . Silk of the kine and poor old woman, names given her in old times. A wandering crone, lowly form of an immortal serving her conqueror and her gay betrayer, their common cuckquean, a messenger from the secret morning.[56]

Yeats would have recognized his own Cathleen, who has turned back into the poor old woman; as Sean O'Casey put it, "the proud step gone that was once the walk of a queen; bent now like the old Hag of Beara."[57] Joyce's old woman is witch, crone, sexually promiscuous, but "maybe a messenger." Completing an intertextual transmission from Yeats to Joyce and back again, her "old shrunken paps" cue the bishop's taunt that "those breasts are flat and fallen now" (259). On the hint provided by Joyce's "common cuckquean" the virgin Cathleen ni Houlihan reverts to the randy Crazy Jane, whose decrepitude implies that, despite Ireland's political independence, the goddess of sovereignty is still unsatisfied. Blood sacrifice has failed to renew her youth, and in posttreaty Ireland no one is offering her any sex. Free of the English, Ireland has been reimprisoned by the church.

Yeats was, however, unwilling to concede the domain of the sacred to the bishops. Jane therefore argues in "Crazy Jane and Jack the Journeyman" that sexuality must express itself here and now to free the soul for its encounter with divinity. The famous lines "The more I leave the door unlatched / The sooner love is gone" are not lament but celebration, for:

> I—love's skein upon the ground,
> My body in the tomb—
> Shall leap into the light lost
> In my mother's womb.
>
> (258)

These poems deny not divinity, but the bishops' right to legislate how it may be attained. Jane does not invert the church's demand for purity with a monologic demand for carnality; she claims that soul and body must be joined. Women must challenge the priestly definition of their sexuality as the site of sin. Indeed, in a carnival inversion Yeats equates sinfulness with premature renunciation of the flesh:

> To seek God too soon is not less sinful than to seek God too late; we must love, man, woman, or child, we must exhaust ambition, intellect, desire, dedicating all things as they pass, or we come to God with empty hands.[58]

The bishop does not represent the male "high" against the female "low," for Jane claims both "bodily lowliness" and "the heart's pride" for the desiring phallic woman, "proud and stiff" in her pursuit of love. As she says in "Crazy Jane on the Day of Judgment,"

> "Love is all
> Unsatisfied
> That cannot take the whole
> Body and soul."
>
> (257)

The bishop tells Jane to observe the Platonic binary opposition between heaven and earth that informs patriarchal clerical contempt for female sexuality: "Live in a heavenly mansion, / Not in some foul sty." But she refuses to separate mansion from sty, grave from bed, lowliness from pride, or the whole from the ruptured: "Fair and foul are near of kin, / And fair needs foul"(259).

The obsession with sexual purity characteristic of Irish official discourse led to a displaced emphasis on bodily dirt, and the public debate over Irish sexual identity was couched in excremental terms. Yeats's reiterated defense of *Ulysses* caused his main press opponent, the *Catholic Bulletin*, to christen him and his friends "the Sewage School" and the "Cloacal Combine," consigning them to the "literary cesspool." "Leda and the Swan" was called the "putrid 'Swan poem' " and the "Stinking Sonnet."[59] The Dublin Catholic weekly, the *Standard*, recommended the censorship bill as "a sound measure of moral sanitation."[60] Yeats's response to these attacks was defiant: "What matter if the ditches are impure?"(235). Crazy Jane complicates the repeated insults of the Catholic press by connecting excrement with pride and love:

> "A woman can be proud and stiff
> When on love intent;
> But love has pitched his mansion in
> The place of excrement;

For nothing can be sole or whole
That has not been rent."

(259-60)

Yeats's strategy is a perilous one. The use of the drains as a displaced metaphor for sex, traditional in the negative discourse of the body from Saint Augustine to Bataille, springs from fear and contempt of female sexuality rather than from a joyful acceptance of the mingling of base and sacred during intercourse. Male depiction of female defecation in poetry is uniformly misogynistic. In "The Lady's Dressing Room" Swift's Strephon nauseatedly explores his nymph's chamberpot, which sends up "an excremental smell," and is overwhelmed with revulsion at the unsurprising truth that "Celia, Celia, Celia shits."[61] Rochester's jaunty rhyme cannot mask his horror at female bodily oozings:

It is a thing unfit
That men should fuck in time of flowers,
Or when the smock's beshit.[62]

Sharing the disgust of Swift and Pope, Eliot depicts Fresca at "needful stool" in the first draft of *The Waste Land*.[63]

Crazy Jane's assertion that "love has pitched his mansion in / The place of excrement" therefore risks siting itself in a misogynist Waste Land of bodily issues. Bataille argues that there are "unmistakable links between excreta, decay and sexuality": "the sexual channels are also the body's sewers; we think of them as shameful and connect the anal orifice with them. St. Augustine was at pains to insist on the obscenity of the organs and function of reproduction. 'Inter faeces et urinam nascimur.' "[64] The discourse of bodily shame and "obscenity" voiced by Irish supporters of censorship and intellectual pornographers like Bataille betrays a common revulsion from the female body as reproductive site.

Through symbolic substitution and contiguity, the connection between excreta and sexuality also models the connection between sexuality and death. In her essay on abjection, Kristeva argues that "these bodily fluids, this defilement, this shit are what life withstands, hardly and with difficulty, on the part of death."[65] Crazy Jane asserts that the inextricability of fair and foul is "a truth / Nor grave nor bed denied" (259). Her juxtaposition of grave and bed evokes what Yeats called "the old association of love and death,"[66] an association strikingly embodied in "Crazy Jane Grown Old Looks at the Dancers." The poem was inspired by his dream of a dancing couple:

> I knew that he did not know whether he would strike her dead or not, and both had their eyes fixed on each other, and both sang their love for one another. I suppose it was Blake's old thought "sexual love is founded upon spiritual hate."[67]

Bataille claims that "the female partner in eroticism was seen as the victim, the male as the sacrificer,"[68] but Yeats changes his dream to allow Jane to affirm a sexually egalitarian erotics of violence. He puts a knife in the woman's hand and leaves the outcome ambiguous:

> Did he die or did she die?
> Seemed to die or died they both?
> God be with the times that I
> Cared not a thraneen for what chanced
> So that I had the limbs to try
> Such a dance as there was danced—
> *Love is like the lion's tooth.*
>
> (260)

Like the analogous relation between sexuality and excrement, that between sexuality and death has been interrogated by feminists who regard it as constructed rather than essential. Benoite Groult claims that when desire is reduced to "the taste for that which is dirty, degrading, and destructive, which is to say, for death," it reflects male domination of and contempt for the female body.[69] Cixous implies that the association of women with death answers a male need:

> Men say that there are two unrepresentable things: death and the feminine sex. That's because they need femininity to be associated with death; it's the jitters that give them a hard-on! for themselves! They need to be afraid of us. . . . Let's get out of here.[70]

Jacqueline Rose, however, refuses to surrender the territory of the unconscious to social forces. Seeing sexuality as intractably violent, she accepts the validity of Freud's analysis of the death drive:

> As feminism turns to questions of censorship, violence and sado-masochism, psychoanalysis hands back to it a fundamental violence of the psychic realm—hands back to it, therefore, nothing less than the difficulty of sexuality itself.[71]

Rose does not deny that socialization, although incomplete and precarious, produces personality structures shaped by ideology, but she argues convincingly that ideology interacts unpredictably with a preideological stratum of the psyche.

In this problematic area of theory it is important to distinguish an acceptance of the death drive from its celebration in the form of de Sade's abuse of women, or Bataille's sexist philosophizing and pornographic practice. Here Bakhtin may help us to separate Yeats from the gynephobes and pornographers. He interprets emphasis on the interconnection of Eros and Thanatos as a positive oppositional strategy, a method of resistance and a commitment to regeneration:

> Degradation . . . means coming down to earth, the contact with earth as an element that swallows up and gives birth at the same time. To degrade is to bury, to sow, and to kill simultaneously, in order to bring forth something more and better. To degrade also means to concern oneself with the lower stratum of the body, the life of the belly and the reproductive organs; it therefore relates to acts of defecation and copulation, conception, pregnancy, and birth. Degradation digs a bodily grave for a new birth; it has not only a destructive, negative aspect, but also a regenerating one. (*Rabelais*, 21)

Bakhtin genders the birthing Earth as feminine, but Yeats's validation of female sexuality goes beyond Bakhtin's when Jane opposes the sterility of the celibate bishop without offering herself as an Earth Mother. Jane's sexuality is determined not by her reproductive function, but by her desire to keep repeating the intense moment when "looks meet" and she "tremble[s] to the bone." She affirms the pleasures of both deep passion (her love for Jack) and casual sex ("men come, men go") without the justification of maternity.

Bakhtin claims that the carnival use of excrement to mock all that is "high, spiritual, ideal, abstract" is positive: "in the images of urine and excrement is preserved the essential link with birth, fertility, renewal, welfare" (*Rabelais*, 19, 148). Crazy Jane, who praises Cuchulain's wife, Emer, because she is "great bladdered" (586), takes a similar view of the excremental. Her "foul sty" houses an animal that symbolizes uncleanness for both Jews and Christians, one that devours its own excrement and wallows in filth to protect its sensitive skin from the sun. Colonial discourse had long bestialized the Irish by association with their pigs. They were characterized as living in a "foul dunghill" in their "swinesteads."[72] The bishop mimics colonialist denigration of the Irish peasantry, but Crazy Jane affirms the vital energies of the "foul sty." She appropriates the stereotype to obtain transgressive power.

Like Bakhtin, Yeats sees the pig as ambivalent: merely material, as in "this pragmatical, preposterous pig of a world, its farrow that so solid seem" (238), or powerfully material. As chair of the Irish Coinage Committee he lamented changes imposed by the Ministry of Agriculture on the original design of the sow and her litter, because "with the round cheeks of the pig went the lifted head, the look of insolence and of wisdom."[73] When the *Catholic Bulletin* attacked these "grotesque designs from the farm and poultry yards of Yeats" as "un-Christian," it specifically targeted the sow and her brood, ridiculing what it called "the pig-litter coinage" and giving Yeats further reason to set the pig against the bishop.[74] The pig's "insolence and wisdom" befit that independent-minded inhabitant of the "foul sty," Crazy Jane. Yeats's friend Arthur Symons had written an antifeminist poem in which suffragettes are depicted as descending into the "mire" with men, fighting "for leave to ply / A friendly muckrake with him in his sty."[75] Yeats positively revalues the metaphor.

For Yeats, excrement is a route to the divine. Recalling Bloom defecating in the outhouse, he speaks of "James Joyce in his Ulysses lying 'upon his right and left side' like Ezekiel and eating 'dung' that he might raise 'other men to a perception of the infinite.' "[76] Coprophilia grants prophetic status: the low is not opposed to the high but provides access to it. Yeats had earlier observed that Donne's "pedantry and obscenity" were "the rock and loam of his Eden,"[77] obscenity and "loam" being paired. As Bloom makes his way to the outhouse, he too meditates on the properties of loam:

> Want to manure the whole place over, scabby soil. . . . All soil like that without dung. Household slops. Loam, what is this that is? The hens in the next garden: their droppings are very good top dressing. Best of all though are the cattle, especially when they are fed on those oilcakes. Mulch of dung. Best thing to clean ladies' kid gloves. Dirty cleans. Ashes too. Reclaim the whole place.[78]

"Dirty cleans" expresses Bakhtin's notion that degradation digs a grave for a new birth, that destruction and regeneration are linked. Only those obsessed with the Manichaean claim that the body is inherently sinful fail to apprehend that waste and death are not the binary opposites of purity and life, but their necessary complements. Because the 1934 Congress of Soviet Writers had declared *Ulysses* "a heap of dung teeming with worms," Bakhtin could not mention Joyce in *Rabelais and His World*.[79] Yeats, however, publicly compared *Ulysses* to Rabelais in 1924; and in the Senate in 1928 he argued that Rabelais "is looked upon as one of the greatest masters of the past, and what is to be said of James Joyce may be said of Rabelais." Yeats praised Rabelais for escaping from the Catholic sense of sin by virtue of his "vast energy."[80]

Douglas argues that rituals of exclusion depend on the belief that "to be holy is to be whole, to be one; holiness is unity, integrity."[81] Blood, urine, feces, and spittle are taboo because they traverse the body's boundary. Cultures that

> most explicitly credit corrupt matter with power are making the greatest effort to affirm the physical fullness of reality . . . cultures which frankly develop bodily symbolism may be seen to use it to confront experience with its inevitable pains and losses.[82]

Through Crazy Jane, Yeats challenged the cultural exclusions through which the Free State was attempting to assert its body/boundary/identity against the encroachments of modernism. If "nothing can be sole or whole / That has not been rent," Ireland must symbolically accept the orifices and excreta of the body as part of the body politic. Writing on divorce Yeats asserted that union with the North could be achieved only through dialogue and the acceptance of difference. The Ulster Protestants "cannot be won if you insist that the Catholic conscience alone must dominate the public life of Ireland."[83] Yeats prophetically argued that the nation could not be made "whole" until it tolerated the "rending" of its ideological purity by minority views and practices: contraception, divorce, foreign dances, and books like *Ulysses*. His argument was largely strategic, for Ulster Protestantism, although it permits divorce and contraception, is otherwise illiberal in sexual matters. Yet Yeats's claim that a whole nation must comprise heteroglossic voices (women, the rural poor, the Anglo-Irish, even the Ulster Protestants) disturbs the totalizing monoglot discourse of Irish Catholicism.

Despite his insensitivity to the nuances of gender in the analysis of voice, then, Bakhtin's historical poetics offer feminists an enabling methodology. His blindnesses are occasioned by his utopian generosity and optimism, qualities that a feminist writing about a male canonical writer sorely needs if her critique is not to exhaust her reading pleasure. As Bakhtin argues and Crazy Jane demonstrates, satirical laughter can puncture the smug self-importance of bishops and unsettle their authoritarian pretensions. Bakhtin also helps to close the gap between historico-political and formalist readings of literature, a gap that has been artificially widened by current polemics against Marxist and feminist critical methodologies. Bakhtin's understanding of the socially rooted nature of language exposes the impotence of a method that would separate words from material reality. Both a formal analysis of Yeats's ballad poetics and a historical contextualization of his celebration of the excremental but eternally desiring body are needed to appreciate the transgressive force of Crazy Jane.

Notes

1. W. B. Yeats, *Explorations*, selected by Mrs. W. B. Yeats (New York: Collier, 1962), 336.

2. Michael Holquist, "Introduction," in M. M. Bakhtin, *Rabelais and His World*, trans. Hélène Iswolsky (Bloomington: Indiana University Press, 1984), xvii-xix.

3. W. B. Yeats, *The Poems Revised*, ed. Richard J. Finneran (New York: Macmillan, 1989), 321. Subsequent quotations from this work are cited by page number in the text.

4. Warwick Gould, "Frazer, Yeats, and the Reconsecration of Folklore," in *Sir James Frazer and the Literary Imagination*, ed. Robert Fraser (London: Macmillan, 1990), 144-46.

5. Terry Eagleton, *Walter Benjamin or Towards a Revolutionary Criticism* (London: Verso, 1981), 144.

6. W. B. Yeats, *The Senate Speeches*, ed. Donald R. Pearse (London: Faber, 1961), 117.

7. Robert Young, "Back to Bakhtin," *Cultural Critique* 2 (1985): 74, 92.

8. Tony Bennett, *Formalism and Marxism* (London: Methuen, 1979), 95.

9 Wayne Booth, "Freedom of Interpretation: Bakhtin and the Challenge of Feminist Criticism," in *Bakhtin: Essays and Dialogues on His Work*, ed. Gary Saul Morson (Chicago: University of Chicago Press, 1986), 154.

10. Bakhtin, *Rabelais and his World*, 239. Subsequent quotations from this work will be cited by title and page number in the text.

11. Peter Stallybrass and Allon White, *The Politics and Poetics of Transgression* (London: Methuen, 1986), 16, 19.

12. Natalie Zemon Davis, *Society and Culture in Early Modern France* (Stanford, Calif.: Stanford University Press, 1965), 136-38, 129

13. Virginia Woolf, *A Room of One's Own* (Harmondsworth, England: Penguin, 1945), 45.

14. Eagleton, *Walter Benjamin*, 148.

15. William Shakespeare, *The Complete Works*, ed. David Bevington, 4th ed. (New York: HarperCollins, 1992), 334.

16. Davis, *Society and Culture*, 131, 150.

17. W. B. Yeats, *Collected Plays* (London: Macmillan, 1952), 84.

18. Yeats, *Senate Speeches*, 177.

19. For Yeats's reaction to this event see "The Irish Censorship," in *Senate Speeches*, 175-80, and "The Need for Audacity of Thought," in *Uncollected Prose*, ed. John P. Frayne and Colton Johnson, 2 vols. (New York: Columbia University Press, 1970), 2:461-65.

20. Mary Douglas, *Purity and Danger* (New York: Praeger, 1966), 124.

21. Yeats, *Uncollected Prose*, 2:438.

22. *Irish Catholic Register* (Dublin, 1925), 559, 562, 563.

23. *Catholic Bulletin* 15,1 (1925): 4.

24. Marjorie Howes, lecture on *The Winding Stair*, Yeats International Summer School, Sligo, Ireland, 1990.

25. *Catholic Bulletin* 17,11 (1927): 1200.

26. Yeats, *Senate Speeches*, 177.

27. For Yeats's objection to this definition see "The Censorship and St. Thomas Aquinas," in *Uncollected Prose*, 2:477.

28. Conrad M. Arensburg and Solon T. Kimball, *Family and Community in Ireland*, 2d ed. (Cambridge, Mass.: Harvard University Press, 1968), 204.

29. Yeats, *Explorations*, 284.

30. Frederic Jameson, *The Political Unconscious* (Ithaca: Cornell University Press, 1981), 85-86.

31. Holquist, "Introduction," xix.

32. Robert Stam, "Bakhtin and Left Cultural Critique," in *Postmodernism and Its Discontents*, ed. E. Ann Kaplan (London: Verso, 1988), 141, 140.

33. Clair Wills, "Upsetting the Public: Carnival, Hysteria, and Women's Texts," in *Bakhtin and Cultural Theory*, ed. Ken Hirschkop and David Shepherd (Manchester, England: Manchester University Press, 1989), 138, 140.

34. Stallybrass and White, *Poetics and Politics*, 44.

35. W. B. Yeats, *A Vision*, 2d ed. (London: Macmillan, 1962), 72.

36. Alex Owen, *The Darkened Room: Women, Power, and Spiritualism in Late Victorian England* (London: Virago, 1989), 11.

37. W. B. Yeats, *Letters*, ed. Allan Wade (London: Hart Davis, 1954), 759.

38. For this comment see unpublished letter to George Yeats quoted in A. N. Jeffares, *A New Commentary on the Poems of W. B. Yeats* (Stanford, Calif.: Stanford University Press, 1984), 290.

39. Yeats, *Letters*, 788.

40. David Lloyd, lecture on Yeats's *The Tower*, Yeats International Summer School, Sligo, Ireland, 1990.

41. Arensburg and Kimball, *Family and Community*, 212.

42. Douglas, *Purity and Danger*, 102.

43. Yeats, *Letters*, 785-86.

44. Alan Bold, *The Ballad* (London: Methuen, 1979), 39-43.

45. W. B. Yeats, ed., *Broadsides* (Dublin: Cuala Press, 1935), 1.

46. Walter Ong, *Orality and Literacy* (London: Methuen, 1982), 69.

47. Yeats, *Uncollected Prose*, 2:462.

48. M. M. Bakhtin, *The Dialogic Imagination: Four Essays by M. M. Bakhtin*, ed. Michael Holquist, trans. Caryl Emerson and Michael Holquist (Austin: University of Texas Press, 1981), 264.

49. *W. B. Yeats and T. Sturge Moore: Their Correspondence, 1901-1937*, ed. Ursula Bridge (London: Routledge, 1953), 154.

50. See Ole Munch-Pederson, "Crazy Jane: A Cycle of Popular Literature," *Eire-Ireland* 14 (1979): 56-73, for a full discussion of this tradition.

51. Proinsias MacCana, "Women in Irish Mythology," *Crane Bag* 4,1 (1980): 10.

52. Brendan Kennelly, ed., *The Penguin Book of Irish Verse* (Harmondsworth, England: Penguin, 1970), 63.

53. MacCana, "Women in Irish Mythology," 7.

54. Yeats, *Plays*, 88.

55. James Joyce, *Ulysses*, ed. Hans Walter Gabler (New York: Vintage, 1986), 490.

56. Ibid., 12.

57. Sean O'Casey, *Inishfallen Fare Thee Well* (London: Pan, 1972), 148.

58. W. B. Yeats, *Essays and Introductions* (London: Macmillan, 1961), 483.

59. *Catholic Bulletin* 15,1 (1925): 1; 14,12 (1924): 1020; 14,10 (1924): 837; 14,11 (1924): 934; 15,1 (1925): 5.

60. Quoted in Michael Adams, *Censorship: The Irish Experience* (University, Ala.: University of Alabama Press, 1968), 42.

61. Jonathan Swift, *The Complete Poems*, ed. Pat Rogers (New Haven, Conn.: Yale University Press, 1983), 451. In the other poem in which this line appears, "Cassinus and Peter," the male overwhelmed with nausea at the fact that "Celia shits" is viewed ironically (ibid., 466).

62. John Wilmot, Earl of Rochester, *Complete Poems*, ed. David M. Vieth (New Haven, Conn.: Yale University Press, 1968), 139.

63. T. S. Eliot, *The Waste Land*, ed. Valerie Eliot (London: Faber, 1971), 23.

64. Georges Bataille, *Death and Sensuality: A Study of Eroticism and the Taboo* (New York: Walker, 1962), 58, 57.

65. Julia Kristeva, *Powers of Horror*, trans. Leon S. Roudiez (New York: Columbia University Press, 1982), 3.

66. Yeats, *Letters*, 828.

67. Ibid., 758.

68. Bataille, *Death and Sensuality*, 18.

69. Benoite Groult, "Night Porters," in *New French Feminisms: An Anthology*, ed. Elaine Marks and Isabelle de Courtivron (New York: Schocken, 1981), 68-69.

70. Hélène Cixous, "The Laugh of the Medusa," in Marks and de Courtivron, *New French Feminisms*, 255.

71. Jacqueline Rose, *Sexuality in the Field of Vision* (London: Verso, 1986), 16.

72. Stallybrass and White, *Politics and Poetics*, 132.

73. Yeats, *Senate Speeches*, 166.

74. *Catholic Bulletin* 18,1 (1928): 19-21.

75. Arthur Symons, *Knave of Hearts: 1894-1908* (London: Heinemann, 1913), 50.

76. Yeats, *Uncollected Prose*, 2:464.

77. Yeats, *Letters*, 570.

78. Joyce, *Ulysses*, 55-56.

79. Terry Eagleton, *Marxism and Literary Criticism* (London: Methuen, 1976), 38. R. B. Kershner, who notes the political problem faced by Bakhtin, concludes, "There is an undeniable sense in which, if Bakhtin did not celebrate Joyce, he should have." *Joyce, Bakhtin, and Popular Literature* (Chapel Hill: University of North Carolina Press, 1989), 17.

80. See the *Irish Statesman*, 23 August 1924, 753;Yeats, *Senate Speeches*, 147; Yeats, *Letters*, 807.

81. Douglas, *Purity and Danger*, 54.

82. Ibid., 120.

83. Yeats, *Senate Speeches*, 157.

ideological becoming: mikhail bakhtin, feminine *écriture*, and julia kristeva

virginia l. purvis-smith

the event

i should have remembered. boston is always like this in early spring—cold and overcast. it could be dusk, but it's only nine in the morning. why did i come? and why did i persuade my friend to come? this atmosphere is menacing. the dark wood paneling and high ceilings in the chapel absorb what little light there is. what? are those life-size figures of the apostles carved at each juncture of the paneling? they stand over all of us, as we huddle here in the damp cold. a conference on women and preaching. how can we ever speak out about <Preaching Wholeness to Our Daughters and Sons> *in the brooding presence of these men?*[1] *they dominate the space and guard what will be said and done, representing the orthodoxy of the christian religious tradition.*[2] *what is left for us to say?*[3]

the ministers are processing down the aisle. i'm not familiar with this hymn, so i'll scan the words first, as i always do, to make the changes from <man> *to* <one> *and try to eliminate the masculine pronouns for god. this gets so tedious. but the language in this hymn seems to be inclusive. what a relief. i'm able to sing straight through, with the rhythm.*[4]

the opening prayer sounds unusual. i'll have to remember that phrase: <We gather to acknowledge God in our midst.> *usually the liturgist says,* <Let us go to God in prayer.> *at that, i always giggle. someday, a whole congregation is going to be paying attention to the words and will get up and leave. the question is, where will they go?*[5]

i've not heard the scripture lesson read in this way before. the cadence of her voice is not that of a person reading a text. she's telling us the story. fascinating. those are the words of the text but her intonation is giving it a conversational tone, compelling my attention. oh, she's blind and she has memorized it. the words do not sound stilted and archaic, as they often do when scripture is read. she speaks them as contemporary words.[6]

i wonder why those three women are standing along the left side of the chancel with cloaks on. oh, no. liturgical dance. it always embarrasses me. usually when people physically occupy the space of the chancel they are immobile. the only movement is with hands, arms, and mouths as they gesture and speak. the expansive movements of dance feel like a violation of sacred space. in two leaps the dancers cross in front of the communion table.[7]

with their cloaks off, i can see their costumes. often the costuming is in poor taste, with thin, polyester leotards that accentuate the curvature of the women's breasts. why is it that liturgical dance is so frequently done by women or young girls? as i recall, i have seen only one man dance in a liturgy. but these costumes are of a heavier knit and the colors are soft: dark purples, pinks, and dark rose. the long full skirts complement the fluid jumps and spins. they seem to know what they are doing. they fill the chancel space with color and movement. we don't even need the words of the old testament lesson read aloud to understand their enactment of the story of naomi and her daughters-in-law.[8]

the voices of the preachers counterbalance one another. yolanda's soft, spanish accent does not rob the power of her speech; rather, it intensifies the anger in her voice that the latin american mothers have to search the morgues to find the bodies of their murdered children.[9]

and i think of virginia as an older sister as i listen to her preach on the passage from the book of daniel. *she plays with the image from the text that describes god as wooly-headed. i look at her short, straight, gray hair and her broad shoulders, and i trust the imaginative journey her words take me along, just as i have trusted her words in her books: the divine as a mother bear, a bakerwoman, a female pelican. they are not new images; they are ancient, but, until now, unspoken from the mouths of preachers i know.*[10]

the last hymn. i have to remind myself to relax. i do not need to brace myself against the onslaught of verses like <Immortal, invisible, God only wise, in light inaccessible, hid from our eyes.> not here. i want to sing the words of the hymn which are in front of me but my sobbing prevents me from forming any other sound. after the service, i walk up to goudey and she embraces me.[11] *i say,*

<goudey, i was able to worship without holding back. i heard my language spoken for the first time.>[12]

she says,

<i know, i know.>

we walk outside and the rain blows horizontally across the courtyard. our umbrellas are useless.[13]

the response

1. my textual inscription of this experience adapts several of monique wittig's devices from her novel *across the acheron*, a novel that repatterns dante's *divine comedy*. one device is her representation of dialogue by the use of parentheses rather than quotation marks. the way i read her parentheses reflects more accurately my sense of appropriating the words of others than the way i interpret quotation marks, which set apart the speech and the quoted text of others more sharply. once i hear another's words, they become part of my thoughts and speech and are no longer the possession of others, a phenomenon approximated more suitably by the signal of parentheses. however, parentheses have a number of meanings when used in essays, so i am using the configuration <>, which resembles parentheses, to recreate the effect wittig achieved. when i do use parentheses, their conventional meanings are to be understood.

by not using quotation marks when quoting another's words, i also intend to emphasize mikhail bakhtin's conception of utterance. he postulates that language is realized in utterance, by which he means both oral and written expression. the words we utter appear as part of a responsive chain in which we incorporate other people's words and utterances into our own thought. when the utterance of another is incorporated, whether by direct quotation or indirectly, a sort of dialogue within a dialogue occurs in which <the *change of speech subjects* has been internalized> (bakhtin 1986, 92). once internalized, the boundaries between utterances are weakened and the incorporated utterance of the other is permeable to that of the speaker. to stress this chainlike, internalized dialogue, i also do not indent longer segments of quoted text.

another way in which i textually enact bakhtin's description of utterance is to appropriate the endnote form to create the impression of the narrative as the event to which you, the reader, and i are responding. the notes represent my responses to the event, some of which occurred during the service in the chapel, many of which have taken shape as a result of my dialogue with the prior utterances of other writers, such as wittig and bakhtin. i would prefer that the texts run parallel—an upper text that inscribes the event and a lower text of response that uses the footnote form, producing an effect similar to reading a musical score. printing constraints, however, require a chronological arrangement of text and endnotes: event in its entirety followed by response.

the dialogue the texts enact is also meant to recognize the diverse readership of this essay. some readers will be feminists, some will be literary critics, some will be theologians, and others will personally and professionally identify with any number of these and other disciplinary stances. by using the two texts i am expanding the essay form to allow room for your conscious participation in the creation of the dialogues between event and response and between writer and reader. the dialogue between texts and the use of <> are thus meant to highlight the blurring of the distinction between writer and reader that occurs in the act of reading.

more than one reader has asked me whether i have thought about writing notes to the notes. although it might be textually possible, the essay's readability might become more complex than most readers would tolerate. just the two texts make unusual demands on you. even though creating notes to the notes might be a logical step to take in order to reflect textually the complexity of the dialogism of the utterance, it would not be possible to separate the texts enough times to denote accurately the multiple levels of utterances they contain.

bakhtin's summary of the dialogic complexity of the utterance as it appears in novelistic prose expresses well the intricacy of incorporating others' words in oral and written expression: <the utterance appears to be furrowed with distant and barely audible echoes of changes of speech subjects and dialogic overtones, greatly weakened utterance boundaries that are completely permeable to the author's expression> (1986, 93).

2. in the several years since this moment in the chapel at boston university's school of theology, i have re-visioned it in terms of a number of bakhtin's theoretical constructs, in addition to that of the utterance. the stance of the carved apostles hanging on the walls over us felt hostile. it seemed to me that they insisted we repeat their words, their utterances, verbatim. we would not be allowed to adapt them or add any of our own thoughts or expressions of our experience, a situation that i not only resent but find painful. such repression encourages dependency and immaturity. therefore, in order to understand my experience of the service in the chapel, i have also used bakhtin's conception of the maturation of the speaking subject as a <process of selectively assimilating the words [utterances] of others>, a process that he calls <ideological becoming> (1981, 341).

bakhtin talks about this selective assimilation by contrasting two possible modes of appropriating and transmitting others' words, two modes that are usually sharply separated in one's experience. in one mode lies the <authoritative word (religious, political, moral; the word of a father, of adults and of teachers, and so on) that does not know internal persuasiveness,> and in the other lies the <internally persuasive word that is denied all privilege, backed up by no authority at all, and is frequently not even acknowledged in society (not by public opinion, nor by scholarly norms, nor by criticism), not even in the legal code> (1981, 342).

bakhtin's discussion of authoritative discourse carries within it my sense of my relationship at the time of the conference to the religious language of the church and my relationship with those whom i identified as bearers, and guardians, of religious tradition—ordained ministers, seminary professors, church officials. at that point in my life all but two or three of these authorities were men. to shield myself from what felt like the absolute demands of their words, i incorporated bakhtin's words in their entirety upon first reading them, as though arming myself with his analysis, word for word, would effectively temper the force of religious authoritative discourse.

<The degree to which a word may be conjoined with authority . . . determines its specific demarcation and individuation in discourse; it requires a *distance* vis-à-vis itself. . . . Authoritative discourse may organize around itself great masses of other types of discourses (which interpret it, praise it, apply it in various ways), but the authoritative discourse itself does not merge with these . . .; it remains sharply demarcated, compact and inert: it demands, so to speak, not only quotation marks but a demarcation even more magisterial, a special script, for instance> (1981, 343).

bakhtin includes in his discussion of authoritative discourse an aside in which he observes that the authoritative word such as the religious discourse in many cultures is often spoken in a foreign language. he and i continue: <It is not a free appropriation and assimilation of the word itself that authoritative discourse seeks to elicit from us; rather, it demands our unconditional allegiance. Therefore authoritative discourse permits no play with the context framing it, no play with its borders, no gradual and flexible transitions, no spontaneously creative stylizing variants on it. It enters our verbal consciousness as a compact and indivisible mass; one must either totally affirm it, or totally reject it. It is indissolubly fused with its authority—with political power, an institution, a person—and it stands and falls together with that authority> (1981, 343).

those wooden apostles hanging over us in the dim light of the chapel seemed to permit no play in the architectural or liturgical space that they guarded. the very structure of the chapel represented a cultural orientation to religious authority which put it above, inaccessible, and indisputable to whoever worshipped in the space below, particularly those of us gathered there explicitly as women to preach <the Word.> in response, the brooding apostles communicated a menacing tone. to tamper with religious discourse would be to topple them.

once i realized i had absorbed the discourse of my religious tradition as an inert mass demanding demarcation from all the other discourses in my life, i began to differentiate myself from it and could affirm my questions about its demands. until then, i had not dared to tamper with it beyond my attempt to use gender-inclusive pronouns in the liturgy. even this amount of tampering can be intolerable for many who worship within the context of western religious discourse. a friend recently recounted two ordination services she had attended for two acquaintances, both episcopal women. they had requested that gender-inclusive language be used in the prayers of the services, certainly more accurate language given their gender. the bishop, a man, had denied both requests.

my refusal of capitalization in this essay is a bolder sign of my willingness to experiment with <spontaneously creative stylizing variants> on the authoritarian discourse represented by the posture of those wooden apostles (1981, 343). their discourse has been shaped through the centuries in large measure by one class of men: educated, and often white. they have put in place a system of naming that too frequently excludes the perspectives of women, other classes, and other races. that naming pretends its perspective is the only one, especially typical of a phrase such as <*The* Christian Tradition.> my refusal of capitalization is meant to reduce the privilege of any one perspective over another. other reasons for refusing capitalization emerge as the essay develops.

3. i am suspicious of dichotomies that require discrete choices between their two terms, for example, public/private, feminine/masculine. however, i am sketching a scene that sets up just such a dichotomy with the male figures encircling the women gathered in the sanctuary below. the scene could symbolize the tension between other seemingly oppositional terms as well, such as past/present, tradition/contemporary need; however, in this essay i propose to develop primarily the apparent gender tension.

i use the term <gender> to evoke the complexities of the many discussions about the necessity to distinguish between <sex> and <gender.> at one level, these discussions use <sex> to identify biological difference and <gender> to imply the processes of socialization whereby we become <woman> and <man.> while the distinction has provided a corrective to biological determinism, to make such a distinction is to imply that an identification of <naturally> determined traits as opposed to <culturally> determined ones can be made, a distinction that sets up yet another dichotomy of nature/nurture. as judith butler observes, maybe <'sex' is as culturally constructed as gender; indeed, perhaps it was always already gender, with the consequence that the distinction between sex and gender turns out to be no distinction at all> (1990, 7)!

i, too, suspect <sex> is as culturally constructed as <gender.> this perspective leads me to resist facile generalizations about how <women> approach anything. however, as much as i resist sex-role stereotyping at a theoretical level, i have been raised to be an anglo-american, protestant, middle-class, heterosexual woman in a culture that functions on a basis of sex-role stereotypes. i have to deal with them daily. the issues of <sex> and <gender> supply constant challenge, constraint, and frustration, as well as satisfaction—sometimes.

as this essay progresses, my dilemma about the feminine/masculine dichotomy will become ever more apparent. the authoritative discourse of my religious tradition, which is presbyterian and has as one source the branch of the protestant reformation identified with john calvin, has been recorded and transmitted for millennia almost entirely by men. as an ordained presbyterian minister who is a <woman,> i find much of this discourse foreign to my experience, alienating, and impossible to integrate into my own speech. my struggle to find voice in the context of this discourse does take on gendered overtones.

as a result, the terms of the french feminists' debate about feminine *écriture* seem to reflect my struggle: is <women's> writing (and speaking) even possible? is it identifiable as such? some of the participants in the debate say i have only two choices, another dichotomy. either i remain silent or, if i want to exercise my professional role and write and speak (especially in the rhetorical genre of the sermon), i have to adopt the male-gendered discourse of my tradition.

the debate over feminine *écriture* is colored by a despair that claiming language to reflect <women's> experience is an impossible task. in <is there such a thing as women's writing?> xaviere gauthier struggles with this issue because, for her, male control of the language of public discourse seems absolute. is our only option to remain mute and, therefore, outside the historical process? or shall we speak out and write, which means entering public discourse on <men's> terms? the setting of the chapel suggests that silence or embracing religious discourse on the apostles' terms are the only options if we women want to maintain our presence in that arena.

if we choose the second path, which those of us who have attended universities and seminaries and were taught by <men> have done, we enter history alienated. <And so, having lost their minds, women believed they could be men, equal their masters in adopting their grammar syntax. Completely divorced from themselves without knowing it, women were transformed into this Crazy Sex which was named the 'Second Sex'> (gauthier 1981, 162).

as i read these words and picture myself preaching, i do not know how to evaluate the image. i stand before the congregation in my robe—does it matter that some <women> buy colorfully embroidered robes or wear other than white clerical collars to signal their <feminity>?—which symbolizes my academic achievement and my ordination. but whose language do i speak? how much more of me does <the robe>cloak? on the other hand, is not the language of my religious tradition and the academy a part of who i now am?

gauthier concludes her essay with a resounding condemnation of my questions. <feminine> writing occurs in the <blank pages, gaps, borders, spaces and silence, holes in discourse>; once i try to explain myself, i am <compromised, rationalized, masculinized> (1981, 164). a contradiction, indeed! <women's> space is obscure; speaking out is compromise, presumably a compromise gauthier has chosen, herself, to make. her explanation is, after all, inscribed in a book.

hélène cixous presses the point about <women's> writing in <the laugh of the medusa> (1981). unlike gauthier, cixous trumpets a call for <women> to say something, to write ourselves. we must not be confined by the past. her call is meant to bring us to our senses and to our meaning in history. we are not destined to silence or to losing our minds.

what does cixous propose for women's writing? what will woman write when she has her turn to speak? first, herself, that is, her body: her pleasures, her organs. second, we must seize the occasion to speak and write, from woman toward woman. although cixous insists that <it is impossible to *define* a feminine practice of writing,> she will not be caught in the contradiction that gauthier posits, which she calls being caught between the medusa and the abyss (1981, 253). instead, she urges all of us to <laugh> and to <fly.> her writing throbs with possibilities: possibilities that our flight and our inscription of our bodies will transform phallogocentric language and <female> silence.

i appreciate cixous's energy, even though it seems to convey a frantic quality at times. her powerful words inspire and she is capable of maintaining a tension in her essay that lifts <woman> and <man> together. however, i am skeptical because she represents all the energy for change coming from the <mediating woman.> i am also skeptical about the implications of pressing <woman> and <man> to the level of metaphor as she does. such a position replaces the medusa/abyss dichotomy with the feminine/masculine one. i do not want to destroy the wooden apostles hanging on the walls, only to remove them from their elevated position and engage them in dialogue.

in the terms of the french feminist debate of the past several decades, i am much more responsive to simone de beauvoir's perspective because it moves away from defining the issues of women's location in public discourse, of <feminine *écriture*,> in either/or categories. whereas cixous's flight feels like a flight of fancy, de beauvoir's observations are anchored in social and political concerns. her 1949 comments in *the second sex*—<One is not born a woman; one becomes a woman>—are echoed in a 1976 interview with alice schwarzer: <On the one hand it's a good thing that a woman is no longer ashamed of her body, of her pregnancy, of her menstruation. . . . But it would be an error to make of it a value and to think that the feminine body gives you a new vision of the world. . . . The eternal feminine is a lie, because nature plays an infinitesimal role in the development of a human being. We are social beings. Because I do not think that woman is naturally inferior to man, I do not think either that she is naturally superior to him> (Schwarzer 1981, 153). her comments open the discussion of women's speaking and writing to more levels of complexity than cixous's negative characterization of <man's> phallogocentrism opposed to <woman's> boundless generosity.

julia kristeva's perspective about the expressive possibilities for women in public discourse further redefines the terms of the debate. this perspective emerges with particular clarity in an interview between gauthier and kristeva (kristeva 1981). kristeva notes that the literary avant-garde has been introducing ruptures and blank spaces into language for at least a century—and these writers are, by and large, men. in kristeva's scheme, phallic language users are the ones who are masters of their speech, regardless of gender. avant-garde writing either denies or traverses this position. she chooses the word <traverse> intentionally for it implies a sexual difference, not as a <fixed opposition ('man'/'woman'), but as a process of differentiation> (165). in this way, she reframes the issue, away from the metaphoric grandeur of cixous's <woman> /<man> and gauthier's silence/compromise. kristeva observes that traversal is characteristic of <great> literature because it captures a quality of all speaking subjects, that is, a certain bisexuality.

kristeva does see an emerging ability of woman to play with language with some skill and to achieve the ruptures that other avant-garde writers have. potentially, the writing subject is left in a continual position of sexual differentiation and contradiction.

she believes, however, that for women who write, the process of writing their sexual differentiation is at its initial stages and still follows one of two extremes: either the woman opts for power and the phallic dominates, that is, mastery in <science, philosophy, professorships, etc.,> or she elects denial, that is, silence (166). it seems we cannot completely escape the threat of gendered dichotomies: phallic mastery/feminine silence.

perhaps a great deal remains to be said by women, but the discoveries of what that might be and how it might be accomplished are not, apparently, straightforward tasks in the terms established by the debates over feminine *écriture*. the options that are offered lead to no clear resolution of my uncertainty about either the possibility or the advisability of speaking out as women, huddled as we are in the silent, cold space of the sanctuary.

4. bakhtin says we are born into a sea of language, actually, a sea consisting of waves and eddies of many <languages,> of limitless ways of construing meaning, which he calls heteroglossia. but all is not free-flowing change, a dynamic bakhtin calls the operation of centrifugal forces. he notes that social systems also exert centripetal forces on language to stratify and codify it; the two forces constantly pull and push at language (1981).

my usual posture in a worship service is one of resistance against the centripetal force of the church's discourse, gendered primarily as masculine in its scriptures, its liturgy, and in the persons of those in leadership positions. as a result, i am rarely in step with the rhythm of the service at any point. in this service, however, i was not positioned at the margin. from the moment of the opening hymn, my characteristic stance was the stance of the majority. consequently, in doing what i usually did, i was now an active participant. the change in my subject position in relationship to the unfolding service was disquieting.

5. whereas my stylistic use of *across the acheron* includes my use of modified parentheses, which have the added benefit of reflecting bakhtin's concept of the utterance, my thematic use of *across the acheron* can be described by comparing these phrases: <Let us go to God> and <We gather to acknowledge God in our midst.> their comparison reflects the contrast of dante's imagined universe with wittig's repatterning of it.

the comparison invites discussion of yet another of bakhtin's constructs, that of the <chronotope (literally, "time space")> (1981, 84). as i move further into my narrative about the service in the boston chapel, i am accumulating data that i hope will equip me to reformulate the time/space configuration that was, initially, so repressive. if wittig can repattern the chronotope of dante's cosmos, can i repattern the rhetorical space of the sanctuary, represented as it is by its architecture?

<chronotope> is bakhtin's coined word for the <process of assimilating real historical time and space in literature> (84). in his discussion of dante's universe, bakhtin describes its chronotope as <an external and immobile place on the extra-temporal vertical axis> (84). dante has stretched the historical images and people of his epoch along the other-worldly, vertical axis of the circles of hell beneath the earth, those of purgatory above, and those of paradise at the top, reminiscent of the relative postures of the apostles high and lifted up and the women huddled below. <Below, a crude materiality of people and things; above, only the Light and the Voice,> and it all occurs within a single time: <sheer simultaneity> (157). the historical figures who people this universe continuously strain against this verticality, which creates the <extraordinary tension that pervades all of Dante's world> (158). similarly, the women in the chapel were corralled in the architecturally symbolic timeless space of worship.

the hell, purgatory, and paradise that dante constructs are repressive. their rigid structures and hierarchical arrangement must be traversed in order. every circle has its designated place and its inhabitants are there through some reprehensible act, or lack, of their own doing. once in their place, they will never be released. the rigidity and inaccessibility of paradise are well described by beatrice in canto XXIX. she tells dante she has seen paradise, <where every *where* and every *when* are centered. Not for the gain of good unto Himself, which cannot be, but that His splendor might, in resplendence say, *I am*; in His own eternity, outside of time, outside of every other limit . . .> (dante 1952, 150). absolute place and absolute time and absolute being. in order to worship such a being, one must leave one's time and place and <go to Him.>

what a contrast are wittig's hell, limbo, and paradise! whereas dante differentiates places and freezes time in eternity, wittig's places seem to be simultaneous matrices that take shape as her perspective alters. her place and her time are <here> and <now.> the inhabitants of wittig's hell are not being punished for something they have done. the lost souls are females who are captive to subservient and victimized roles. they and their victimizers are together in hell. the female souls have been socialized to accept their roles; they are unaware; they are powerless. their situations are desperate and escape is nearly impossible, but wittig's hell is not so rigid that escape is out of the question. in fact, she and manastabal, her guide, will assist any of the damned souls in their release if they think the rescue has a chance. and wittig describes her providence as one who does kind deeds, not a prime mover.

the arrangement of wittig's three realms is in no way hierarchical. wittig has leveled dante's topos. the desert, <the route which must be taken to arrive in Hell,> is flat (1987, 7). it is on the same plane as hell, limbo, and paradise. each simply appears to occupy a different dimension on the plane of the earth's surface.

<center> achieves its definition by the location of the person at any particular moment; the <father> does not define the center. there is no every *where* or every *when*, no resplendent *I am*. <The space [of the desert] is flat, flat enough to reveal the circularity of the planet on the horizon. So we seem to be walking at the exact center of the earth> (7).

the effect of the change from the liturgical injunction to <Go to God in prayer> to the descriptive words <We gather to acknowledge God in our midst> was to reorient my sense of time/space from a dante-like structure to one resembling wittig's. rather than having to leave our location and scale the heights to paradise, we had only to call attention to the divine matrix among us, a matrix that wittig would say is constructed through discourse.

the only <lower> dimension in the novel seems to be that of the abyss of forgetfulness, into which the river acheron empties. that would be a void, without words, without discourse. wittig implies that assuming silence as a characteristic posture is choosing non-being. perhaps the conundrum of speaking in liturgical space, and thus of being either compromised or remaining silent, as represented by the feminine *écriture* debates, must be transformed in at least two aspects: one that uses kristeva's attempt to traverse issues of sexuality and the other that draws on wittig's cosmic reconfiguration of time/space.

6. what was striking about the scripture reading was the woman's rejection of the pious, monotone-like speaking voice typical of people who are reading text sacred to them. her approach sounded similar to a dramatic reading, but she was so well prepared and adept that her presentation lacked that quality of self-conscious performance. she spoke the words in a compelling, but conversational, manner.

again, i find bakhtin's portrayal of the utterance helpful as i reflect on the effect of this <reading.> as a person molds an utterance, her plan for it emotionally colors the words that she co-opts, as does an author's intent for any creative utterance. bakhtin pictures the utterance as radiating its expressive purpose to its words. although the words selected for live speech communication already have an emotional valuation as words of others, once they become part of the speaker's utterance, they also carry the revaluation of the current speaker. as bakhtin examines literary authorship, he asks whether the authentically creative work contains any single-voiced words, that is, the equivalent of reciting verbatim what one has heard. perhaps the creative voice can be only the second voice, the one that takes the speech of another, even an imagined other, and recasts it with her or his own emotional valuation. the author <is a person who is able to work in a language while standing outside language, who has the gift of indirect speaking> (bakhtin 1986, 110).

in this sense, the woman reading the scripture was the author of the text she presented. she was not conveying authoritative words cloaked in magisterial script; she had recast the words by the power of her own voice, and she gave them to us as contemporary speech.

7. just as the <reader> recast the words of the scripture text by the power of her voice, the dancers redefined the meaning of the chancel space. in many churches, the chancel is defined by its elevation and its distance from the congregation. in most christian traditions, it is the site of the altar and/or communion table, as well as the pulpit. the pulpit is further set apart by its size and added elevation, by its hierarchical representation of power and authority.

in order to recreate the pulpit's austerity and the aura that can surround the chancel area, in contrast to the exuberance of the dance, i remind you of herman melville's pulpit in *moby dick* (1952, [1851], 29-30). it shares a design and function basic to that of many pulpits—its distinctness lies only in the exaggerated aspects of its architecture. melville's chaplain gains his <lofty height,> not by stairs, but by a rope ladder. once the height is gained, the chaplain pulls the ladder after him into the pulpit, <leaving him impregnable in his little Quebec.> the pulpit design is that of a ship's bow: <What could be more full of meaning?—for the pulpit is ever this earth's foremost part; all the rest comes in its rear; the pulpit leads the world. From thence it is that the storm of God's quick wrath is first descried, and the bow must bear the earliest brunt. From thence it is that the God of breezes fair or foul is first invoked for favourable winds. Yes, the world's a ship on its passage out, and not a voyage complete; and the pulpit is its prow.>

the design of the pulpit complements what will happen in that space. the preacher is to assail the listeners with *the* authoritative word of <God's quick wrath.> typical in the homiletic literature are images that convey a sense of the preacher up in the pulpit aiming remarks *at* a congregation.

one of the more graphic of these images was expressed by henry ward beecher in the first of yale university's lyman beecher lecture series on preaching in 1872, a series that continues as one of the most prestigious annual lecture series on preaching to this date. beecher describes good preaching as preaching that <takes aim> (1902, 10). he compares his first real sermon with his first kill. he had had great success in firing off his gun—a smoke, a report, but nothing fell. writing before freud, he is bold to say: <I fired off my gun as I see hundreds of men firing off their sermons.> one day his father helped him. henry kept cool and took aim. he fired at a squirrel. <That was the first thing I ever hit; and I felt an inch taller, as a boy that had killed a squirrel, and knew how to aim a gun.>

the fluid movements of the dancers were such a contrast in form and function to melville's pulpit, beecher's preacher, and the chancel space they define. my embarrassment should have been for them, not for the dancers who transformed the chancel. they, the woman <reading> the scripture text, and the call to worship that restructured the cosmos were so unaffected and graceful in their gender inclusiveness that i began to be convinced that we could, after all, gather as <women> and <Preach Wholeness to Our Sons and Daughters.>

however, the form and function of the chancel and its pulpit and the expectations of what will be done and said there, and how it will be delivered, have more explicitly gendered overtones than i have yet disclosed. in *the feminization of american culture* (1978), ann douglas includes a quotation from lyman beecher, henry's father, the popular nineteenth-century revivalist preacher after whom the yale lecture series was named. the quotation appears in the context of his description of what he thought caused the success of his first revival at east hampton, long island, in 1807: <'Finally I resolved that I would preach the doctrine of Election. I knew what that doctrine was and what it would do. . . . My object was to preach cut and thrust, hip and thigh, and not to ease off. I had been working a good part of a year with my heart burning, and they feeling nothing. Now I took hold without mittens'> (1902, 40).

cut and thrust, hip and thigh. taking aim. lest you think that this vivid, aggressive, phallic imagery was quietly left in the nineteenth century, let us revisit the series in its 1959 version. in that year it was delivered by joseph sittler, a lutheran theologian. when i picked up his published lectures, i suppose i had expected that they would provide a contrast to the explicitly phallic language the beechers used to talk about preaching. as i glanced at the jacket cover, i read the claim that the book is <a virile reassessment of the minister's role as preacher in contemporary society> (1961). virile. i wondered what that could mean.

it seems as though sittler is concerned about how preaching has become lackluster and disorderly. he urges <every man [preacher] to order his life> and offers specific suggestions about how that might be done (1961, 88). he is concerned that the language of business dominates american speech, and, from his perspective, especially characteristic of this language is its <paucity.> he says it is simply not adequate language to do justice to the kind of community the church knows <herself> to be, and he offers as a model paul's epistle to the roman church, chapter eight. he describes the language as compact and building in intensity. he continues by quoting yet another theologian that paul's <'words come as water jets in uneven spurts from a bottle held upside down'> (54). paul's is a language of <joy and release,> a <muscular and postive code,> contorted, tense, until the release of the thirty-fifth verse, which passes into that song of intolerable joy that ends the chapter (54).

virile, indeed. i suppose i can affirm part of sittler's agenda, which is to explore the potential of language. his impulse, though, is to pick up phallic imagery, imagery that was not his alone but already part of the tradition of commentaries about paul's language and latent in that language itself. although most members of american, protestant congregations do not have these particular images of the pulpit or of the preacher's task and language at the forefront of their awareness as they sit in the pews of a sanctuary, these images embrace the stereotypical tone and expectation of what will happen in the chancel rather well. the space is defined by hierarchy, and it is masculine territory.

before the conference, i, too, was not fully conscious of these expectations. i simply had a feeling of awkwardness and self-consciousness when the use of the chancel or pulpit expanded beyond the customary functions. after the initial discomfort, however, i would enjoy how some ministers would open that space in some way, for instance, by preaching from behind the communion table or in the middle of the chancel. their choice of preaching location had implied a disavowal of the removed, privileged space of the pulpit and a statement of their perception of preaching as an inclusive activity: everyone is symbolically gathered around the table or altar, including the preacher, who is not alone in a pulpit imparting <the Word> to the congregation.

but dance opened the space even more. initially, i was embarrassed by the exuberant, physical presence of the women. but their leap into that masculine-defined space was the jolt that made me conscious that those of us gathered in the sanctuary had claimed the whole space for our own—and i was no longer embarrassed.

8. embedded in bakhtin's conception of <text> lies a theoretical base to carry on a discussion of the <language> of dance. if <text> is <any coherent complex of signs,> works of art can be included in the study of texts (bakhtin 1986, 103). by extension, in this essay i am <reading> the entire service, the ritual itself, as <text,> instructed by bakhtin, the debates of the french feminists, and wittig's novel.

in order to explore more fully the power of the dance, i also enlist susanne langer's distinction between <discursive> and <presentational> symbols. in *philosophy in a new key*, langer admits that speech is <the readiest active termination of that basic process in the human brain which may be called *symbolic* transformation of experience> (1942, 44). but we do have other expressive means in our repertoire. we also use ritual, myth, and art as active terminations of symbolic transformations of experience. when dealing with objects and concepts that are charged with meaning for us, that is, that which is sacred to us, we have access to modes of symbolism such as ritual, as well as speech. langer defines ritual as an articulation of feeling, not a free expression of emotion, but a disciplined rehearsal of <right attitudes> (153).

langer places religion, which she defines as <a gradual envisagment of the essential pattern of human life,> in the arena of ritual (155). ritual is of a different symbolic order than is propositional thought. ritual is a presentational symbol; propositional thought lies in the domain of discursive symbolism. discursive symbolism limits our ability to express apprehensions of pattern and attitude for this reason: discursiveness is linear. that is, it requires ideas to be strung out, as in the statement <kay sees jane.> langer says such a statement appears as linear progression, but the action the statement represents is simultaneous. the ideas rest within one another. any idea that cannot lend itself to a linear form is discursively incommunicable, and langer reminds her readers of the logicians' claim that that which cannot be projected in discursive form is inaccessible to the human mind.

no, langer says. discursive use of language is not our only articulate product. for example, visual forms are capable of articulation. true, as langer notes, they present their parts simultaneously in one act of vision and are complex. they present too many relationships from the beginning of their apperception to the end and are too subtle for linguistic expression. the semantic of visual form is presentational symbolism, very different from the semantic of discursive symbolism, but a conveyor of meaning nonetheless. the elements of a presentational symbol such as a picture, or a dance, are not units of independent meaning, as are the words of discursive symbolism. they have no fixed meaning apart from context, nor can they be defined in terms of other presentational symbols. although discursive and presentational patterns show a formal difference, both conceptualize what they convey; they both carry meaning and function as elements of understanding.

an expansion of the discussion of presentational patterns to include margaret miles's (1985) work discloses even more significance in the liturgical dance in terms of religious discourse. miles offers that the discursive uses of language are a corrective to centrifugal forces, by which she means the adaptation of cultural forms by individuals to their own situations. she points out that culture uses language as a corrective, unifying force in instruction and education, which become increasingly sophisticated at the <advanced> levels in the training in the use of language.

but she notes that, in the first place, education is not equally available to everyone. second, at its more advanced levels, academic language aims at objectivity and analysis. this <language, through its universality and its discursive method, is uniquely suited to the analysis of experience, of 'what went wrong'> (140). this use of language can be constructive in that it contributes <to one of the constant and continuing tasks of every culture—its own self-healing by analysis and diagnosis> (141).

however, discursive language's preeminence falters when claims are made about its universality in the formation of the identity of peoples over time. <Language becomes coercive when it is used not therapeutically—to examine, interpret, and suggest—but as a standard, in alliance with social, political or ecclesiastical institutions that require universal assent to particular formulae> (145). miles observes that <the alternative to the critical use of language is to be used *by* language, to be forced to grasp feelings, objects, events, and ideas only in their sloganistic or stereotypical form, to fit one's experience to clichéd language> (135).

i hear most liturgical language in this way: trite and senseless. when i am listening to the radio, the tone and cadence of the speaker's voice indicate in the first word that i have tuned into a religious broadcast. and the words used are invariably stock phrases strung together to make a so-called sermon. after hearing one such sermon, you will have heard them all. in addition to being used by their language, these speakers demonstrate a lack of creativity, in bakhtin's terms. in their attempt to replicate authoritative discourse, they strive for what amounts to verbatim recital, a <literal, single-voiced word> that is <naive and unsuitable for authentic creativity> (bakhtin, 1986, 110).

in addition to the critical use of religious discourse, miles urges a growing awareness of the messages received from images, which communicate to larger groups of people. image contemplation played a more significant role in the formation of individuals prior to the catholic and protestant reformations, but with those movements <the therapeutic capacity of religious language was explored and extended as never before,> that is, its ability to analyze <what went wrong,> to the neglect of contemplation—and the neglect of much of the population (150). moreover, <the intellect, engaged by language, is religiously trained,

but [because contemplation has been neglected] the emotions are less effectively engaged> (150). the elevation of language use, in its discursive sense as miles offers it here, leaves emotion, our feelings, with fewer expressive avenues. miles thinks that presentational symbols offer an expressive capability underutilized in contemporary religious discourse.

miles asserts that the imprecision of presentational symbols such as visual image (i would add liturgical dance) is part of their strength. if the person receiving the image cannot apprehend it, part of the problem might be an untrained artistic intelligence, perhaps more of a problem for those who <think of themselves as essentally structured by a verbal nucleus> (127). the comparison miles makes is between the use of visual imagery to study history and the use of written texts. she points out that most of the literary texts of christianity before the modern period were <almost exclusively the product of culturally privileged, highly educated, male, and most frequently monastic authors> (9). the critics of visual imagery in the churches were a few theologians who equated the spiritual with the verbal. pictures, stained glass windows, and sculpture (and dance) were adequate for the common, simple folk, but the sacred things of god were to be celebrated in holy writings (and, with the protestant reformation, in expository preaching) (38).

langer and miles help me understand another part of my discomfort with liturgical dance. my education had predisposed me to devalue the use of presentational symbols in favor of discursive, more <spiritual> symbols. that training had left me defenseless against the flood of emotion which the dance evoked. my <higher> education had taught me to appreciate the intricacy of well-reasoned argument, of expository sermons, but i was unaccustomed to granting the capability of other forms of expression to speak as effectively to the depth of human experience as does expository mastery.

as we have already seen, this mastery is the mark of phallic domination, according to kristeva (1981). the christian religious tradition grants the exercise of its discursive forms, the more highly valued and more <spiritual> forms, to men. perhaps that is why men appear less frequently in liturgical dance.

9. by the time we got to the sermon, i must have been prepared for all my expectations of what could happen in a worship service to be overturned. i no longer felt self-conscious about female presence in the chancel; i was prepared to listen, i thought. again though, i was not expecting the emotional impact yolanda's voice and stories would have. rev. yolanda pupo-ortiz, one of the first puerto rican women to be ordained.

bakhtin's analysis of speech genres provides one avenue for thinking about her sermon's effect. because bakhtin postulates that language is realized in utterance, in oral and written expression, he examines utterance quite closely (1986). every sphere of human activity makes use of language; every sphere develops its own typical forms of utterances called speech genres. the variety of genres is boundless, but even in their multiplicity the genres are amenable to analysis.

speech genres are of two types: primary and secondary. the primary genres constitute the raw material of unmediated communication. direct, everyday conversation and personal letters are examples. the secondary genres signal complex and organized cultural communication, usually written—novels, drama, and i include sermons.

because the speaker fashions the utterance in response to any number of prior utterances and in anticipation of response, bakhtin uses the relationship of the speaker to the addressee as an organizing principle for the classification of speech genres. bakhtin acknowledges that sometimes the relationship between the speaker and addressee is simple; all the speaker need determine is the addressee's scope of knowledge about a particular subject. if the relationship of the speaker and addressee is familiar, the constraints of social convention are loosened. when the proximity of the speaker-addressee relationship narrows to intimacy, the framework of social convention dissolves. <Intimate genres and styles are based on a

maximum internal proximity of the speaker and addressee (in extreme instances, as if they had merged). Intimate speech is imbued with a deep confidence in the addressee, in his sympathy, in the sensitivity and goodwill of his responsive understanding> (1986, 97).

in contrast, as the distance between the speaker and the addressee grows, the speech genre exhibits a more standard and external structure. i conceive of the sermon as traditionally exhibiting such a formalized and official structure. however, the combination of yolanda's soft voice and the terrible, intimate content of her stories broke into the formal relationship traditionally established between the preacher and congregation. in turn, that combination transformed the formal structure of the speech genre <sermon.>

the sermon is a genre that has been almost exclusively identified with the male voice for centuries in many christian traditions. the change of voice, alone, refocused the listeners' attention, because it recast the genre of <sermon> outside the bounds of the accepted formal structure of the genre. but the content of her sermon—narratives about the anger of grieving mothers—further altered the sermon's formal structure. rather than the characteristically discursive sermon explicating the scripture passage, her intimate narratives implicated the listeners in the events she described and in the narrative of the passage. langer (1953) calls this narrative use of language <poesis,> by which the artist provides the listener a created world, a space both can inhabit.

10. dr. virginia mollenkott teaches in the english department at william paterson college and is a feminist theologian. from the way her sermon was structured and presented, i inferred that her approach was similar to the one i had been trained to use in seminary, although her religious tradition refuses to ordain women as preachers. the constraints on who is granted the authority to preach vary from tradition to tradition, but a summary of the process i went through and of the possible attitudes toward the authority of scripture will give a sense of the professional preparation for, and elements that lie behind, sermon preparation and delivery. the summary will also give a sense of why gauthier's condemnation of my choice to <master> this genre was so stinging—i am deeply ambivalent about the extent to which i have had to forgo speaking out of my own experience as part of the process of my professional training.

in my religious tradition, preaching is an exposition of scripture in the context of the life of a particular faith community, that is, a congregation. preaching is an interpretative task grounded in written texts—hebrew and greek scriptures—and the limitless commentaries on them.

in order to be granted the authority to preach as a minister from a pulpit, a candidate must be ordained as a minister of the word and sacrament. the governing body of the church, the session, can approve, in circumstances that warrant it, that lay preachers occupy the pulpit, and a minister can invite someone to preach who is not ordained, with the approval of the session. but to be ordained as a minister, the candidate must have a seminary education, or its equivalent, which includes courses in homiletics, new testament greek, and hebrew. in addition, a candidate must pass four nationally administered exams, including an exam in biblical exegesis. exegesis means drawing an interpretation out of a text by study of such aspects as its historical and theological context, which implies the use of secondary sources such as bible commentaries, its literary form, and its particular use of words and syntax, all in interaction with one's own intellectual and affective responses to the text.

during the four-hour exam in biblical exegesis, the student demonstrates an ability to use either hebrew or greek in her analysis of the given text; proposes an interpretation of the passage; and writes a brief sermon to demonstrate how that meaning of the passage might be applied to the concerns of a congregation. the student provides, as part of the exam, a profile of this imagined congregation. this is the pattern that we are trained to use in seminary, and it is the pattern yolanda and virginia's sermons seemed to follow, but also transform.

describing the variety of positions about the authority of scripture is more difficult. actually, i can only establish a spectrum of possibilities, and probably those who gathered to worship at the conference represented a number of positions on that spectrum. i have derived these positions from elizabeth schussler fiorenza's similar discussion in chapter 1 of *in memory of her: a feminist theological reconstruction of christian origins.*

first, the doctrinal perspective asserts that scriptural texts do not just communicate god's word; they *are* god's word. this approach decontextualizes scripture. the events and assertions are not part of a history of any particular people or place; the truth of the texts is timeless and uniform, its answers definitive—bakhtin's authoritative word in a capsule.

second, the dialogical-hermeneutical approach insists on trying to place each text in its historical setting. what events could have precipitated it? what issues was it attempting to address? not only was the text in dialogue with events and needs at the time of its writing, and, in many cases, again at the time of its multiple revisions (redactions), but we are in dialogue with the text. in addition, as our perspective changes, different aspects of the text emerge for us. the meaning is not fixed.

a third approach is to identify major theological themes of scripture and judge the merits of any one text on its faithfulness to that theme. for example, if one believes that all theology is engaged for or against the oppressed, intellectual neutrality in regard to scripture is not possible. some passages are faithful to liberation; some are not. the text is not uniformly <true.>

my own position moves between the second and third approaches. the meaning of the text is subject to constant review, and interpretation is not a benign activity. it does have social and political consequences. when i say the images virginia used of the divine as wooly-headed and as a mother hen had not passed the mouths of preachers i know, what was their source? those images had come from the hebrew and christian scriptures, but the authorship of those scriptures, their transmission, the arrangement of the lectionary (the three-year cycle of scripture readings that many denominations use in their weekly worship services), and the commentaries on those texts have been determined largely by men for millennia. feminine images for the divine emerge erratically in western protestant christian discourse and had not been communicated to me as carrying the same authoritative weight as did the masculine ones.

11. though i resist cixous's <woman> / <man> dichotomy and her exuberance about woman's speaking and writing <from woman toward woman,> my response to the women-led service was just such a response—one of gratitude, relief, and joy. my response was also wordless—i wept. perhaps that response is too typically gendered, one of retreating into the language of tears. only if crying is construed as retreat, as an ineffectual, <feminine> mode of expression. june goudey, the conference coordinator, did not construe it that way. she embraced me, and with her embrace she accepted my tears. i did not feel i had to choke them back or apologize for them. i did not have to hide or restrain my emotion, nor did i feel pressured to articulate in words what i was feeling. the tears were sufficient and i was not ashamed to weep.

earlier i used kristeva's comments about avant-garde writing, which implies denial of the phallic mastery of speech; traversal, as process of sexual differentiation; and wittig's time/space reconfiguration of dante's cosmos to surmount the dichotomies i find in the french feminist debate about feminine *écriture.* kristeva's concept of self-definition will make the possibility of traversal more clear. as one matures, the self-definition at which one <arrives> is not the solid, readily identifiable, individualized entity of which we, perhaps, conceive. she proposes that the speaking subject is, rather, the construal of <a network where drives, signifiers and meanings join together and split asunder in a dynamic and enigmatic process> (1987, 111). as a result, <a strange body comes into being, one that is neither man nor woman, young nor old.> our identities are <constantly remade and reborn>

(111). the service presented me with a particularly concentrated experience of language- and self-reconfiguration, not the first and undoubtedly not the last in my life. that repositioning could not be immediately translated into speech, and neither could the disquieting, but exhilarating, repositioning of my time/space perspective.

kristeva's concept of self-definition depicts the fluid sense i have of self, the self as matrix, the self as capable of such reorientations. this concept has reinforced my resolve to incorporate the textual device of not capitalizing in the dialogue that is this essay, especially not the personal pronoun <i,> except in quoted material. capitalization would imply a solid, objective entity that could be identified and permanently tagged. i only capitalize within quoted material, which is identified by the modified parentheses, and then only to display more graphically bakhtin's heteroglossia.

12. in her 1958 book *on shame and the search for identity*, the sociologist helen merrell lynd speaks about our lifelong search for significance. she observes that when we discover the possibilities of identifications with cultural contexts other than those already familiar to us, that is, when we discover the possibility of reconfigured networks of meaning, we perceive and are ashamed of our smaller, more limited selves. we can react in one of several ways. while the possibility of expanded identifications can be seen as offering the opportunity for an enlargement of self, as i experienced during the service, it can also be perceived as a threat to the familiarity and comfort of our smaller world—neighborhood, religious group, ethnic group, nation. enlarging our perspective and thereby transcending our shame means, lynd believes, adopting a comic frame of reference, a sense of proportion. the comic view <is the condemnation of the partial masquerading as the complete> (256). the disclosures during the service, that the space created by those wooden apostles was not inviolable and that theirs was not the only way to use religious discourse, were not likelihoods i had considered before the service—certainly not to the extent to which the space and language had been transformed. for that moment, their discourse, including its emphasis on discursive symbolism, had been condemned as partial.

i hope that the tendency of the debate about feminine *écriture* to offer either/or choices has become dated. in the 1970s, the debate had to take the ubiquity of male discourse seriously, but its either/or terms create a dilemma as women continue the struggle to find their voices. patricia yaeger talks about the seemingly contradictory implications of the arguments of the french feminists that insist that <women that must get out of male language> while they simultaneously use it (1988, 24). <What is at stake in devouring, erasing, exorcising the father's word is precisely 'the hope of the name,' the emancipatory, utopian desire that we will find some new name that cherishes us; that will give an 'outwardness' to our 'inwardness.'>

such hope is not to be taken lightly. such erasure, though infrequent, can take place.

13. as relieved as i was to discover the possibilities of wider identifications, i knew the moment represented by the service would pass, washed away as we almost were by the driving rain. such moments are not usual occurrences in christian worship; they take focused effort to create and are still highly dependent upon the combination of people present. the debate about feminine *écriture* that posits the seemingly inescapable contradiction of silence or compromise feels like the norm more often than not. bakhtin's constructs allow for some movement within language, but he is not naive about the power of centripetal forces, the power of those wooden apostles.

at the start of the service, i wondered what was left for us to say. i learned that a great deal was, but power configurations can more easily erase the matrix created by the service than we could erase the matrix of meanings established by <the father's word.> when the way we talk, which is as much an accepted part of our environment as the air we breathe, is called into question, changes that may be exhilarating to some are threatening to others.

in the case of the language for articulating religious experience, changes in it—in how we talk about the divine-human relationship, even whether there is one; the meaning of life; the moral and ethical nature of our communal life as human beings; our conception of who we are as persons—threaten, or affirm, the very ground of our worldview.

the wooden apostles still maintain their control over that space, unmoved. we had to leave, exposed to the torrents of rain. the matrices of meaning that we had constructed were dissolved.

works cited

bakhtin, mikhail. 1981 [1975]. *the dialogic imagination*, ed. michael holquist, trans. caryl emerson and michael holquist. austin: university of texas press.

______.1986 [1952-3]. *speech genres and other late essays*, ed. caryl emerson and michael holquist, trans. vern w. mcgee. austin: university of texas press.

beecher, henry ward. 1902 [1872]. *yale lectures on preaching: first, second and third series.* chicago: the pilgrim press.

butler, judith. 1990. *gender trouble: feminism and the subversion of identity.* new york: routledge.

cixous, hélène. 1981. the laugh of the medusa. in *new french feminisms*, ed. elaine marks and isabelle de courtivron. new york: schocken books.

dante alighieri. 1952 [*c.* 1307-21]. *the divine comedy*, trans. charles eliot norton. *great books of the western world* 21. chicago: encyclopaedia britannica, inc.

de beauvoir, simone. 1989 [1949]. *the second sex.* new york: random house.

douglas, ann. 1978. *the feminization of american culture.* new york: alfred a. knopf.

fiorenza, elizabeth schussler. 1988. *in memory of her: a feminist theological reconstruction of christian origins.* new york: crossroads.

gauthier, xaviere. 1981 [1974]. is there such a thing as women's writing? In *new french feminisms*, ed. elaine marks and isabelle de courtivron. new york: schocken books.

kristeva, julia. 1981 [1974]. oscillation between power and denial. In *new french feminisms*, ed. elaine marks and isabelle de courtivron. new york: schocken books.

______. 1987 [1977]. talking about polylogue. *french feminist thought*, ed. toril moi. new york: basil blackwell ltd.

langer, susanne. 1942. *philosophy in a new key: a study in the symbols of reason, rite and art.* cambridge: harvard university press.

______. 1953. *feeling and form: a theory of art.* new york: charles scribner's sons.

lynd, helen merrell. 1958. *on shame and the search for identity.* new york: harcourt, brace and company.

melville, herman. 1952 [1851]. *moby dick; or, the whale. great books of the western world* 48. chicago: encyclopaedia britannica, inc.

miles, margaret r. 1985. *image as insight: visual understanding in western christianity and secular culture.* boston: beacon press.

mollenkott, virginia r. 1988. *the divine feminine: the biblical imagery of god as female.* new york: crossroads.

schwarzer, alice. 1981 [1976]. simone de beauvoir. In *new french feminisms*, ed. elaine marks and isabelle de courtivron. new york: schocken books.

sittler, joseph. 1961. *the ecology of faith.* philadelphia: muhlenberg press.

wittig, monique. 1987. *across the acheron*, trans. david levay. london: peter owen.

yaeger, patricia. 1988. *honey-mad women: emancipatory strategies in women's writing.* new york: columbia university press.

Voicing Another Nature

Patrick D. Murphy

I

Nature writing has been for some two centuries one of those "marginalized" genres of modern writing.[1] Much of what has been labeled as such consists of prose essays or meditational volumes, which are neither novel nor poem, neither fiction nor science. It has been marginalized at least in part because nature writing fails to fit neatly any of the ongoing genre categories that organize criticism. It has also been marginalized because nature has been primarily an object of attention or a site for human endeavors since the Enlightenment rather than an entity in its own right, a speaking subject, a hero in the Bakhtinian sense, or a locus of sacred power. To the degree that a canon of nature writing is forming in the United States today, it remains generally limited to white males writing a particular type of prose, women who imitate them in that endeavor, and something called "romantic poetry," frequently heavily ego-bound and more often than not about the white male poet's sensitivities and intellectuality rather than its ostensible subject. In either case, alienation from the object of attention and alienation within the authorial subject appear requisite conditions.

A new text, *The Norton Book of Nature Writing*, which attempts to set the terms of the canonical debate for the genre/mode of nature writing, illustrates this orientation.[2] One may begin with the table of contents. Of ninety-four authors, only fourteen are women; only two of the authors—as far as I can determine—are nonwhite, and these both Native Americans. Twenty-one of the men have multiple entries, but only one of the women, so that the contribution of the women is reduced even further than their limited numbers might suggest. In the first paragraph the editors define "nature writing" as prose and primarily nonfiction: the "naturalist essay." The *father* of all this is Linnaeus; that is, nature writing is a product of the Enlightenment, of rationalism, categorization, and classification—patriarchal and hierarchical to the core. It is also fundamentally Judeo-Christian in its prolapsarian position on human origins and human essence. In the introduction to the *Norton*, editors Finch and Elder quote Gilbert White: "A constant theme of the nature essayists was the search for a lost pastoral haven, for a home in an inhospitable and threatening world."[3] A return to the garden and a definition of the present planet as a "howling wilderness," then, are the hallmarks of a mode of writing arising from colonialism, industrialization, and the growth of an urban leisure class, as the editors assert with approbation. Human alienation is the foundational ontotheology for the efforts to define and canonize this mode of writing.

Alienation provides the primary explanation for the near exclusion of Native American authors—"a certain kind of intense and self-conscious awareness of nature follows from a loss of integration between society and nature,"[4] and native peoples did not experience such a loss until it was forced upon them, nor have native authors tended to accept the permanency of such a condition.[5] It also provides a possible explanation for Annie Dillard's being the only woman to receive a double entry—the excerpt the editors have chosen from *Pilgrim at Tinker Creek* ends: "It is ironic that the one thing that all religions recognize as separating us from our creator—our very self-consciousness—is also the one thing that divides us from our fellow creatures" (she apparently uses a definition of religion exclusive of animistic and primal spritual beliefs).[6] And it explains Thoreau's receiving the most space in this collection. Thoreau, like Dillard, goes to nature to observe rather than to participate, forever aloof and transcendent, and to escape that part of nature known as human society. Alienation is disguised in both cases as autonomy, with Thoreau going to the extreme, as Barbara Johnson observes, of ignoring pregnancy entirely in *Walden*.[7]

As Max Horkheimer and Theodor Adorno argued nearly fifty years ago, "the Enlightenment has extinguished any trace of its own self-consciousness."[8] And the crucial element of the self-consciousness that has been extinguished is precisely the recognition that this "alienation," which has been enthroned as a necessary condition of rational existence and an absolute human state at least since the articulation of language, is generated and continuously reproduced by Enlightenment beliefs: "Myth turns into enlightenment, and nature into mere objectivity. Men pay for the increase of their power with alienation from that over which they exercise their power. Enlightenment behaves toward things as a dictator toward men. He knows them in so far as he can manipulate them. The man of science knows things in so far as he can make them."[9] In direct contrast to this Enlightenment acceptance of absolute alienation and the reduction of everything outside the human subject to objects upon which to cast the alienated, rationalistic gaze, Donna Haraway posits that "in a sociological account of science all sorts of things are actors, only some of which are human language-bearing actors, and that you have to include, as sociological actors, all kinds of heterogeneous entities. . . . this imperative helps to break down the notion that only the language-bearing actors have a kind of agency."[10]

At a time when feminist praxis and postmodernist critique have ruptured the assumptions of genre, canon, creativity, and inspiration, an effort is under way in this country to render nature writing a dead rather than living genre, so that only imitation can occur, rather than innovation. The applicability of what Bakhtin says about the novel at the opening of "Epic and Novel"—that it is "younger than writing and the book," "receptive to new forms of mute perception," and "has no canon of its own"—should be cause for celebration over the vitality of this marginalized form of written representation of human experience.[11] But Finch, Elder, and others seem to be regretting its liveliness and flexibility, perhaps precisely because nature writing has the potential to realize the "ability of the novel to criticize itself," which "is a remarkable feature of this ever-developing genre."[12] Instead, the proponents of canonical delimitation of nature writing as "the naturalist essay" prefer that we come to know nature writing, as Bakhtin notes, as "we know other genres, as genres, in their completed aspect, that is, as more or less fixed pre-existing forms into which one may then pour artistic experience."[13] The emphases on (1) nonfiction—fact rather than fancy in determining detail; (2) the essay—informational rather than artistic style; and (3) prose—referential rather than self-reflexive language: all point in this direction of deadening.

As such, then, nature writing will reproduce the absolutes of Enlightenment belief in the power of science over art, observation over imagination, and human systematization and ordering over any indeterminable structures of natural process.[14] In particular, such codification will guarantee the reproduction of existing hierarchies of value, because it will preclude nature writing's engagement with the present, depriving it of the novel's and the novelization of other genres' "zone of maximal contact with the present (with contemporary reality) in all its openendedness,"[15] which would necessarily include the possibility of the subversion and transformation of existing hierarchies, paradigms, and ideologies. Dillard's *Pilgrim* is an example of this movement toward "pre-existing forms." It imitates Thoreau's *Walden*, even to its structure of a year's visit to a body of water by an apparently autonomous single individual. Criticism of existing social institutions and human behaviors toward the environment will be wrapped in nostalgia and the fatalistic regret that accompanies permanent exile from the garden. The monological conceptualization of nonfictional prose furthers the precluding of subversion of contemporary institutions. The author is imaged as an individual speaking without anticipation of audience response, not conversing but only lecturing about individual perceptions, as John Muir so frequently does. It is a highly romantic, author/self-centered conception of the didactic text, with a concomitant definition of the audience as passive recipient, very much in the encoder-code-decoder mode of communication models, the very antithesis of a Bakhtinian utterance-based conception of participatory discourse.

This prescriptive, anthologizing, closing down of the genre is structured to exclude the insights and challenges of feminism to the ways in which knowledge and narratives are constructed. As Rachel Blau DuPlessis has noted, discussing Virginia Woolf's depiction of the fictitious Mary Carmichael, for a woman to write her own voice, her own consciousness, to present in effect her own perceptions of nature and human relationship within it, she must break the sentence: "To break the sentence rejects not grammar especially, but rhythm, pace, flow, expression: the structuring of the female voice by the male voice, female tone and manner by male expectations, female writing by male emphasis, female writing by existing conventions of gender—in short, any way in which dominant structures shape muted ones."[16] If such is the case, then a feminist nature writing will not be able to express the experiences and perceptions of women unless it breaks with the very genre structures, based initially on a certain period style, that Finch, Elder, and others are attempting to codify at this time.

That women are attempting just such expression can be seen across the entire range of genre categories, including nature essays. And they are doing so in far more dialogical ways than the dominant-nature writing tradition would allow, both as a result of self-conscious intent and out of the necessity of their subject positions within contemporary society, for "woman . . . negotiates differences and sameness, marginality and inclusion in a constant dialogue, which takes shape variously in the various authors, but with one end—a rewriting of gender in the dominant fiction"—that is, the dominant fiction of male universality in every genre of writing.[17] Women writers in the field of nature writing, then, are key figures in the degree of novelness to be found there, which is necessarily dialogical, because "novelness is a means for charting changes that have come about as a result of increasing sensitivity to the problem of nonidentity. Greater or lesser degrees of novelness can serve as an index of greater or lesser awareness of otherness."[18] Having posited human alienation from the rest of nature as the fundamental nonidentity in the form of a loss, the nature-writing codifiers appear bent on denying any other forms of otherness. They also deny the relation of such otherness to determining ways of negotiating the interanimating nonidentity of humanity/nature and the potential for *transgredience* that such interanimation provides, preferring lamentations of the loss of identity or paeans of moments of transcendence.[19]

DuPlessis's notion of dialogue, like that of Dale Bauer's in *Feminist Dialogics*, contradicts the male naturalist's imperious assertion of total human alienation from the rest of nature.[20] Many writers—women and Native Americans in particular—are countering with the question, Is alienation really the way of the world for human beings who have self-consciousness? Perhaps it is only an invention of those white males who are running around either trying to return to the mother and her womb, or trying to make the mother return and be once more obedient to them? What if instead of alienation we posit *relation* as the primary mode of human-human and human-nature interaction without conflating difference, particularity, and other specificities? What if we worked from a concept of relational difference and *anotherness* rather than Otherness?

Dialogics reinforces the ecofeminist recognitions of interdependence and the natural necessity of diversity;[21] that is, dialogue at the most basic levels of energy/information exchange, as in gene pools and cross-fertilization (*conversari*, the root for conversation, according to my desk dictionary meant "to live with," and was the medial form of *conversare*, "to turn around"). Such recognitions require a rethinking of "Other" and "Otherness," concepts that have been dominated recently by psychoanalytic rather than ecological models. "Anotherness" proceeds from a heterarchical—that is, a nonhierarchical—sense of difference. If the recognition of "Otherness" and the status of "Other" is applied only to women and/or the unconscious, for example, and the corollary notion of "anotherness," being another for others, is not recognized, then the ecological processes of interanimation—the ways in which humans and other entities develop, change, and learn through mutually influencing each other day to day, age by age—will go unacknowledged.[22] The degree to which patriarchy throughout its historical manifestations (including the Enlightenment in which the antiseptic and opaque veil of science was placed over its machinations and rationalizations) has placed both women and nature in the category of the absolute and alienated "Other" attests to the continuing refusal to recognize reciprocity as a ubiquitous natural/cultural process. Much of the ecofeminist critique in philosophy and the sciences has been devoted to exposing the bankruptcy of such categorization.[23] Bakhtin makes explicit the difference between relational and alienational otherness by the different Russian words he employs for "another" in "Toward a Reworking of the Dostoevsky Book" (appendix 2 of *Problems of Dostoevsky's Poetics*). There he points out that "in actuality a person exists in the forms *I* and *another*."[24] He also addresses, according to Gary Saul Morson and Caryl Emerson, the connections among " 'I for myself, the other for me,' and 'I for another' " in the untranslated "Toward a Philosophy of the Act."[25]

What all of the foregoing is meant to suggest is that in order to have a women's nature writing, there must be a breaking of genre conventions established by men, and accepted by women, working within patriarchal structures. Such efforts have always been imperiled by the dominant culture's variegated ideological strategems for silencing women's voices, or straining them through male normative discourses to conflate and deny difference. Today this imperiling is taking the form of codifying a patriarchal definition of nature writing. But unlike previous pivotal moments, women now have the benefit of an increasingly sophisticated conception of dialogic methods of discourse and critique and a voice from within the realm of nature philosophy itself, ecofeminism. A few examples will help to clarify how women writers have been and continue breaking the traditional bounds of nature writing, what we have to gain from such efforts, and the ways in which both feminism and dialogics inform our understanding of these texts as well as the texts themselves.

II

Let me begin my examples of women who break the traditional bounds of nature writing with an only recently rediscovered feminist environmental writer from the early twentieth century, Mary Austin. In 1903 she published *The Land of Little Rain*, which has been reprinted only in the past six years. In 1988 it appeared in paperback as part of the Penguin Nature Library series.[26] In one sense Austin's work needs to be analyzed as a turn-of-the-century text and placed in the context of its production. In another sense, though, because of its recent rediscovery and republication, it needs to be placed in the context of its current reception. Ed Hoagland's series introduction and Edward Abbey's book introduction, both of which precede Austin's text in the Penguin volume, attempt to contain the author and her writing within their ideological bounds, defining the genre and the book's contents for the reader rather than engaging Austin on her own ground. Listen to Hoagland: "Until quite recently indeed (as such things go), the whole world was a wilderness in which mankind lived as cannily as deer, overmastering with spears or snares even their woodmanship and that of other creatures, finding a path wherever wildlife could go. . . . Aristotle was a naturalist, and . . . Darwin and Thoreau. . . . Yet nature writing, despite its basis in science, usually rings with rhapsody as well—a belief that nature is an expression of God."[27] Wilderness seems to mean here a place in which people do not yet dominate their habitat. I say "not yet" because the rest of Hoagland's description is based on a competition rather than cohabitation model of human and other animal relationships. This competitive model is based on a myth of hunter-gatherer societies that ignores gathering as the stable, reliable, mainstay method of obtaining sustenance that it was and falsely establishes a patriarchal hierarchy of gender relationships in primal societies. Hunter-gatherer here is one of the patriarchal dichotomies of man/woman, hunter/gatherer, culture/nature, and heroic/menial. Note, too, the curious word choice so that even the deer are treated as having craft ("woodmanship") and a will to power ("*over*mastering" rather than mastering; they too must be seeking mastery of nature?). There is also the lineage of male thinkers who determine the genre, as well as the exclusionary definition of theism that posits a transcendent God outside of and separate from nature, in contradistinction to animism, Native American beliefs, and contemporary ecofeminist spirituality, represented by such people as Starhawk and Alice Walker, as embodied in her novel, *The Temple of My Familiar*.[28]

I assume that Hoagland commissioned Abbey to write the introduction, which begins with Abbey's dismissing Austin's thirty other books out of hand without having read them—a common response to works by women, especially feminist ones: I know they must be second-rate, so I haven't bothered with them. After pointing out that Austin "crusaded for the rights of American Indians and Mexican-Americans" and "was an active feminist at a time when that particular cause entailed risk and trouble"—as if it entails neither today and is merely one cause among many—Abbey then trashes Austin's style, which is "too fussy, even prissy." So what makes this a "living book"? "The accuracy of her observational power . . . The subject matter looms above and burns through the lacy veil of words, as a worthy subject will, and soon takes precedence over the author's efforts to show herself an author."[29] In other words, the value of this book has nothing to do with the woman who wrote it but results only from the degree to which she aligns herself with normative male thinking and writing on a traditionally male subject. Everything that marks Austin off from her male peers, everything that might suggest another sensibility and another worldview from the dominant one, is denigrated by Abbey and reduced to the problem of an effeminate style practiced by all nature writers at the turn of the century. In effect, Abbey has established in his own mind a contemporary equivalent of an "epic discourse" against which Austin and all others will be measured and found wanting. Abbey's contention is not really over authorial style four score and twenty-odd years ago, but over the dictating of an official style for nature writing today, with, as Bakhtin would say, "its reliance on impersonal and sacrosanct tradition, on a commonly held evaluation and point of view—which excludes any possibility of another approach—and therefore displays a profound piety toward the subject described and toward the language used to describe it."[30]

Both editor and introducer conveniently omit that feminist researchers, recovering the neglected works of women writers, first revived public interest in Austin's work, not naturalists and not male editors. The structure of this book, then, reveals itself as a heated dialogue between masculinist and feminist viewpoints about the nature of writing, the nature of nature, and the tradition and future of nature writing, with two (at the time) living men ganging up on one dead woman.

The gendered character of this polemic is heightened by the reprinting of another version of Austin's work the year before the Penguin edition was published. In 1987 the Rutgers American Women Writers series published *Stories from the Country of Lost Borders*, which contains the stories from *The Land of Little Rain*, the 1909 *Lost Borders*, and a lengthy introduction by Marjorie Pryse.[31] What a different introduction we find here. Austin, who had had a desire to tell stories since the age of four, suffered a nervous collapse while in college, and her male doctor suspected that it "might have something to do with the natural incapacity of the female mind for intellectual achievement."[32] No doubt he supposed this to be an "accurate" observation of nature. Further, Pryse reveals the importance of the relationships among women writers both for Austin's own development and for her assistance to others, as well as placing Austin in a literary tradition that Abbey utterly ignores, that of the "late nineteenth-century women writers who worked in the genre of literary regionalism."[33] Further, Abbey omits mention of her involvement in the suffrage and women's labor movements. Perhaps this is because both Hoagland and Abbey are more concerned with universalizing their perceptions of proper experience than recognizing its particularities, including the experiencer's gender. But as Michael Holquist notes in *Dialogism: Bakhtin and His World*: "Existence, like language, is a shared event. It is always a border incident on the gradient both joining and separating the immediate reality of my own living particularity (a uniqueness that presents itself as only for me) with the reality of the system that precedes me in existence (that is always-already-there) and which is intertwined with everyone and everything else."[34] For Austin the land is the shaping precedent; and, in the desert of which she writes, if individuals do not adjust their particularities of behavior and belief to that shape, their existence will quickly cease.

In the opening and title story of *The Land of Little Rain*, Austin begins by defining the territory through its ancient Indian name, "the Country of Lost Borders," not the name imposed by recent white invaders, because it "is the better word." The power of naming is invoked here, and that power remains with the inhabitants who live along its frontiers, "Ute, Paiute, Mojave, and Shoshone," while white men are defined as visitors. White society and its states, rules, and structures are not allowed prominence but placed in perspective: "Not the law, but the land sets the limit." And although people may not live in the desert heart of this country, "void of life it never is."[35] Austin recognizes that the land may have an ecosystem that neither requires nor facilitates human participation. "This is the nature of that country," to be a thing-in-itself and for-itself, rather than a thing-for-us, a crucial ecological recognition. As Pryse notes, "In Mary Austin's work, the land solely determines the nature of the region"; in addition, it enters the story, as Austin herself claims, "as another character, as the instigator of plot."[36] Thus it becomes a hero in the Bakhtinian sense, with Austin unfolding its narrative both in terms of its presenting "a particular point of view on the world" and through continuously depicting the land's own ecosystem behavior as a viewpoint "on oneself."[37] Although not a speaking subject, the land does function as a signifying agent, with its significations interpreted and represented by Austin.

Throughout this story in which the desert is the hero and the white man the antagonist, Austin repeatedly gives primacy to nature as a dynamic interactive system in which people can participate if they follow the lead of the land: "Most species have well-defined areas of growth, the best index the voiceless land can give the traveler of his whereabouts."[38] This line may be read as both informational and polemical, returning to the issue of who is the inhabitant and who the invader, suggesting that the white settlers of California coming into conflict with the native inhabitants already identified might learn to limit their "areas of growth."[39] Interestingly enough, Austin's publishers wanted her books to be coffee-table editions of exotic stories for urban easterners, but Austin saw herself as writing for the locals who were in contact and confrontation with the land, attempting to educate them about the world they could not see because they were monologically focused on "overmastering" it. That my doubled reading of "The Land of Little Rain" is motivated rather than capricious can be seen from the final lines in which Austin directly addresses her audience, placing its members in specific relationship to the rest of nature: "It is hard to escape the sense of mastery as the stars move in the wide clear heavens to risings and settings unobscured. They look large and near and palpitant; as if they moved on some stately service not needful to declare. Wheeling to their stations in the sky, they make the poor world-fret of no account. Of no account you who lie out there watching, nor the lean coyote that stands off in the scrub from you and howls and howls."[40] The relationship here of one species of animal to another, and of both to the larger natural systems, seems quite clear.

Much of Austin's work has been neglected or buried and only in recent years have her contributions to an American women's literary tradition, to nature writing, and to critical analysis of Native American literature been reexamined and reprinted. Yet this recovery clearly has not been a simply informational project. Women's writing and feminist perspectives on ecology and human history remain heavily contested terrain. Critical synthesis of ecology, feminism, and dialogics is needed to recognize and appreciate not only what Austin writes about, but also how she writes, and why she does so. And Austin's case indicates that recovering women's nature writing and its breaking with male normative traditions and discourses remains a significant and polemical task.

III

In many ways, conditions have not improved much for writers since Mary Austin who attempt to unite women's issues and nature writing in individual works. Susan Griffin's *Woman and Nature: The Roaring inside Her* (1978) proves a case in point.[41] For many feminists and virtually all ecofeminists this has been a touchstone text. Yet it is almost never taught in a nature-writing course or defined as nature writing by male teachers or critics. It does not "fit" the genre because its dialogical novelness explodes the monological, restrictive conceptions being imposed as a prescriptive definition. Griffin employs a postmodernist metanarrative structure, polemically critiques what she observes, posits a utopian conclusion, and includes humans as part of the nature they study—all of which cannot be appreciated from a monological worldview but can and will be celebrated from a dialogical feminist worldview. Dialogics enables the critic to articulate not only *Woman and Nature*'s organization but also the variety of double-voicing throughout that gives it so much power and that accounts for the significant tonal shifts as the debate of the text gradually resolves toward the voice of a community of women in nature. A discussion of Griffin's text can illuminate some of the many ways in which feminist thought can novelize the nature-writing genre to maintain and develop it as a tool of cultural critique.

In the 1982 anthology *Made from This Earth*, Griffin provides an introduction for the extracts from *Woman and Nature* reprinted there that includes a few remarks about its structure: "It moves by the force of echoes and choruses, counterpoints and harmonies. In one way, the book is an extended dialogue between two voices (each set in different type face), one the chorus of women and nature, an emotional, animal, embodied voice, and the other a solo part, cool, professorial, pretending to objectivity, carrying the weight of cultural authority" (note that she does not say a "male voice," a biologically essential one, but rather an ideologically constructed one, which historically has been predominantly mouthed by men).[42] It also consists of a metadialogue over the ways in which nature has been and can continue to be perceived and in which the degree of listening, learning, and self-revaluation on the part of the gendered participants is both depicted and evaluated. The relationship of ideology to the constraints on dialogue about nature is revealed because for Griffin "a speculation about dialogue is also a speculation about ideology."[43] And further, in "The Way of All Ideology," Griffin suggests an explanation for the emphasis on nonfictional prose in the codification of nature writing:

> Audre Lorde has made an illuminating connection between this civilization's fear of the associative and musical language of poetry (a language which comes from the depths of reason beneath rational consciousness, from dark, unknown regions of the mind) and the same civilization's fear of black skin, of the female, of darkness, the dark other, Africa, signifying an older, secret knowledge.
>
> For, of course, it is not simply inventiveness which is feared. The new machine, the new gadget is worshipped. What is really feared is an open door into a consciousness which leads us back to the old, ancient, infant and mother knowledge of the body, in whose depths lies another form of culture not opposed to nature but instead expressing the full power of nature and of our natures.[44]

Griffin seems to be utilizing a conception of the unconscious similar to that employed by Jacques Lacan in positing that "the unconscious is the discourse of the Other," but with a crucial difference.[45] For Lacan this Other is absolutely alienated, a lack never fulfilled until death, but for Griffin this Other is *Another*, another part of ourselves just as we are another part of nature.

In the preface to *Woman and Nature*, Griffin observes that the recognition of false dichotomies does not make them disappear. The two sides must rather be brought into dialogue and relation in the process of dissolving the polarization. Griffin will use parodic double-voicing as one technique for exposing the illusion of objectivity and separation that philosophical and scientific discourses have attempted to perpetuate: "Since patriarchal thought does, however, represent itself as emotionless (objective, detached, and bodiless), the dicta of Western civilization and science on the subjects of woman and nature in this book are written in a parody of a voice with such presumptions."[46]

The prologue of *Woman and Nature* sets out through voice and countervoice the text's point-counterpoint thesis: the patriarchal structures of Western civilization alienate man from both woman and nature, which are seen as related, and in that relation both are established as proper subjects for domination; and, women and nature are interrelated, and in that interrelation is to be discovered women's strengths and a way past patriarchy's destructive limitations. Book 1, then, is a study of the development of Western civilization's definitions of "Matter," particularly as they arise from the prevalent mind/body dualism of Western philosophy and religion. The voicing here consists almost entirely of the ideas of "great" Western male thinkers rendered as anonymous indirect discourse. The value of this form of narration lies in the ability of indirect discourse to strip away the emotive, affective, and stylistic subterfuges that the original quotations so often display. This is a result, as V. N. Voloshinov argues, of "the analytical tendency of indirect discourse," which "is manifested by the fact that all the emotive-affective features of speech, in so far as they are expressed not in the content but in the form of a message, do not pass intact into indirect discourse. They are translated from form into content, and only in that shape do they enter into the construction of indirect discourse."[47] Thus Griffin is able to enter into critical dialogue with these historical thinkers through narrative structure, and to place her readers in a more critical posture than they would occupy if reading the originals. This results both from their anonymity and from the situatedness of the utterance: "Indirect discourse 'hears' a message differently; it actively receives and brings to bear in transmission different factors, different aspects of the message than do the other patterns. . . . Analysis is the heart and soul of indirect discourse."[48]

Not until six pages into the first chapter of book 1 is the feminist counterchorus allowed voice, and then it only emphasizes the lesson already well established primarily by the "Church Fathers" that sin is a product of the earth and that women are closer to the earth and that woman sinned first: "*And we are reminded*," announces the counterchorus, "*that we have brought death into the world.*"[49] Crucially, Griffin renders this as active-voice direct discourse and does not have the counterchorus speak again until after presenting a chronology of the four centuries of European witchcraft trials and executions and the attendant development of Renaissance philosophy. Griffin faithfully represents the near-total exclusion of women from theology, philosophy, and science except as objects by devoting almost forty pages to patriarchal thought. When the feminist counterchorus does appear, it records the interpellation of women as inferior beings ignorant and fearful of their own nature.

In the next seven chapters of book 1 the reader begins to hear a little more frequently from the counterchorus as the dialogue relies more and more heavily on the patriarchal ideas and practices of the past few centuries. The final chapter is perhaps the most devastating for readers to engage. After the chapter titled "Cows," Griffin juxtaposes "Her Body," which emphasizes the ways in which men have attempted to deny women scientific knowledge of their own bodies as well as to make them over physically in some ideal image. To indicate the extent to which both of these behaviors are based in the misogyny endemic to patriarchal thought, Griffin begins each subsection of "Her Body" with an epigraph on the tortures imposed on "witches," beginning with Henri Boguet's venomous cry: "I wish they all had but one body, so that we could burn them all at once, in one fire!"[50] Not surprisingly, Griffin ends with a parenthetical entry describing the surgical procedures for a hysterectomy.

Book 2, "Separation," continues with the same kind of discourse structures as the first book, covering such topics as "His Power," "His Control," "His Certainty," and ending with "Terror." Then book 3, "Passage," with only two chapters, initiates the modern feminist response to the two preceding books. The first chapter, "The Labyrinth," uses a narrative voice that mimics the dominant discourse, reporting a kind of experience that cannot be understood from within the parameters of patriarchal paradigms. The other chapter, "The Cave," is written entirely in the counterchorus voice except when directly quoting specific women. And both the labyrinth and the cave are refigured by Griffin in a dialogical inversion that lays bare the patriarchal ideology behind their classical mythological structuration and the matrifocal prehistory it was meant to suppress. This matrifocal prehistory is then restored by inverting the original inversion to recognize the labyrinth and the cave as vaginal, uterine symbols of power and understanding, not distorted by dreams of domination and the divorce of rationalistic logic from the other emotive and affective processes of the mind.

Book 4, "Vision," is divided into two long sections with subchapters—"The Separate Rejoined" and "Matter Revisited"—in which all that has been torn asunder and all that has been separated, calculated, classified, and ossified is brought back into relation, connection, and correction (in the sense of healing, not intellectualizing). Even here Griffin maintains the dialogical structure of narration, but now the polemical indirect discourse has been dropped. Instead, the dialogue is between "Herstory" and women's understanding, with some sections composed entirely of the latter, as the counterchorus becomes a chorus bursting into lyricism and dithyramb. The final chapter of the book is titled "Matter: How We Know." Even here in the most utopian moment of Griffin's analysis, the dialogue continues, as her visionary remarks on possibility are counterposed to her own mother's actual experiences. And Griffin calls for continuing dialogue in her final, but not finalizing, words:

> Because I know I am made from this earth, as my mother's hands were made from this earth, as her dreams came from this earth and all that I know, I know in this earth, the body of the bird, this pen, this paper, these hands, this tongue speaking, all that I know speaks to me through this earth and I long to tell you, you who are earth too, and listen *as we speak to each other of what we know: the light is in us.*[51]

Like Mary Austin, Susan Griffin ends not only with direct rather than indirect discourse but also with direct address, challenging her audience to participate in the dialogue the text establishes.

Griffin's work demonstrates the ability of nature writers to engage postmodernity, specifically through the blurring of genres and metanarrative reflexivity. More importantly, her work demonstrates the ability of ecofeminists to write polemically *and* dialogically, which simultaneously exposes the monological character of masculinist normative discourses in science, philosophy, and naturalist nonfiction. Further, if Austin is recognizable as a nature writer, although with a gendered difference, Griffin clearly is not in *Woman and Nature*. Yet Griffin's text is a type of environmental writing and can serve as a limit text to critique existing genre definitions.

IV

In this final section I mention briefly several other kinds of works worthy of the attention given the preceding two that further demonstrate the need to rewrite the definition of nature writing and thwart the attempts to establish a nature-writing canon. Like Susan Griffin, Donna Haraway could be defined as a postmodernist nature writer. Her most recent text, *Simians, Cyborgs, and Women* (1991) is subtitled *The Reinvention of Na-*

ture. Haraway explains this collection as being "a book about the invention and reinvention of nature—perhaps the most central arena of hope, oppression, and contestation for inhabitants of the planet earth in our times," which "treats constructions of nature as a crucial cultural process for people who need and hope to live in a world less riddled by the dominations of race, colonialism, class, gender, and sexuality."[52]

In other words, Haraway's historical analyses of the ideologies that have structured scientific discourse and the paradigms that have guided scientific research give the lie to Abbey's naturalizing depiction of "observation" as being merely a question of an "accuracy" that can be measured against some unmediated reality. They also reveal the naïveté underlying such a claim as Thomas J. Lyon's in *This Incomperable Lande*: "I have limited this book to essays on natural history and experiences in nature, believing that in fiction and poetry, though there are often beautiful descriptions of nature, other themes and intentions tend to predominate."[53] Apparently, Lyon believes that the essays he has selected contain no ideological determinants and no themes that guide the selection of observations to be recorded, rewritten, and packaged for reading consumption. Yet any summation of an individual's experiences must be culturally and ideologically constructed, as Hayden White has so compellingly demonstrated in the case of history, not to mention the decision to undergo and to reflect on such experiences in the first place.[54] Through her metacritiques of scientific discourse Haraway is able to reveal the interaction of ideologies and "objectivity." Hoagland would have us believe that science is something objective and nonpartisan, to be combined with rapture in developing nature writing. And Lyon seems to suggest that observation is a theme in itself. But the answer to, Whose science and which guiding paradigms? will reveal in whose service any given nature text has been written.

Rather than accepting the myriad definitions of nature exposed and deposed in Griffin's *Woman and Nature*, Haraway argues that

> nature emerges from this exercise [*Simians, Cyborgs, and Women*] as "coyote." This potent trickster can show us that historically specific human relations with "nature" must somehow—linguistically, ethically, scientifically, politically, technologically, and epistemologically—be imagined as genuinely social and actively relational; and yet the partners remain utterly inhomogeneous. . . . Curiously, as for people before us in Western discourses, efforts to come to linguistic terms with the non-representability, historical contingency, artefactuality, and yet spontaneity, necessity, fragility, and stunning profusions of "nature" can help us refigure the kind of persons we might be. These persons can no longer be, if they ever were, master subjects, nor alienated subjects, but—just possibly—multiple

heterogeneous, inhomogeneous, accountable, and connected human agents.[55]

A dialogic construction of human/nature interactions, one that does not attempt to posit static absolutes and hierarchical dichotomies, poses the possibility of developing a new human self-consciousness that would render superfluous most nature writing as it is currently practiced and generically prescribed. In particular, Haraway recognizes the illusory character of so much of the monological observations that pass themselves off as naturalist essays, solitary observations, and the individual (read Thoreau) "fronting nature." Additionally, Haraway warns us against the monological maneuvers that conflate human and nonhuman interests through anthropomorphic depictions of the rest of nature, as well as the foundationalist arguments that dominate the debates over environmental ethics.

Metanarratives and metacritiques add a powerful and highly self-conscious dimension to the concept of nature writing. Precisely this element of self-consciousness, the interrogation of foundational assumptions, may prove postmodernism's greatest contribution to nature writing, as well as being the reason that the proponents of a nature-writing canon so studiously avoid inclusion of anything even remotely postmodernist because their arguments cannot stand the scrutiny such a text would initiate. Gloria Anzaldúa's *Borderlands/La Frontera* (1987) may serve as a case in point. This is not nature writing per se, but it very much addresses the issues raised in the lengthy quotation from Donna Haraway. Anzaldúa begins her preface with the premise that geography and psychology are both engaged in mapping mutually interpenetrating territories, and both are dialogically constructed: "The actual physical borderland that I'm dealing with in this book is the Texas-U.S. Southwest/Mexican border. The psychological borderlands, the sexual borderlands and the spiritual borderlands are not particular to the Southwest. In fact, the Borderlands are physically present wherever two or more cultures edge each other, where people of different races occupy the same territory, where under, lower, middle and upper classes touch, where the space between two individuals shrinks with intimacy."[56] And in these borderlands are occurring "the further evolution of humankind" in intimate relationship with the lands and places of their inhabitation.

Borderlands displays an amazing range of dialogic structures, from the polyphony of Anzaldúa's switching seamlessly among English, Spanish, and various Spanglish dialects to her interweaving of the mythologies, beliefs, and practices of the Anglo, Spanish, and Indian ancestors who have blended to produce the new *mestiza*. In addition, the book mixes prose and poetry, with the two parts echoing each other. And throughout, culture and territory are developed as parallel structures defining and being defined by each other, even as both structure and are structured by human consciousness: "Indigenous like corn, like corn, the *mestiza* is a product of crossbreeding, designed for preservation under a variety of conditions. Like an ear of corn—a female seed-bearing organ—the *mestiza* is tenacious, tightly wrapped in the husks of her culture. Like kernels she clings to the cob; with thick walls and strong brace roots, she holds tight to the earth—she will survive the crossroads."[57]

Native American texts prove an impossible stumbling block to the efforts to codify nature writing, as demonstrated by Finch and Elder's and other anthologizers' difficulties in coming to terms with them.[58] For one thing, their teaching-storytelling does not admit a separation between facts and fictions; and for another, these texts, including ones by contemporary writers, do not easily admit a clear-cut division between prose and poetry. Many poetry volumes could be cited here, such as those by Linda Hogan, Paula Gunn Allen, Luci Tapahanso, Wendy Rose, and Joy Harjo. Let me use just one Native American collection of poems to suggest the ways in which poetry can present a dialogical and, in this case, feminist nature writing. *Not Vanishing* (1988), by Chrystos,[59] initiates a dialogue in its title similar to that practiced by Gloria Anzaldúa. "Not vanishing" refers both to the individual speaking through these poems as well as to the native peoples to whom she feels deep responsibility. The poems oscillate between terror and love, between the possibilities of survival and triumph that emerge from an Indian heritage and the genocidal threat that the dominant North American cultures continue to pose, and between the experiences of an individual and the relationship of those experiences to oppressed peoples and groups—natives and other people of color, women and lesbians, working-class and street people.

The opening poem, "Crazy Grandpa Whispers," establishes the inversion of sanity and insanity with regard to the speaker's native heritage and contemporary U.S. culture. The ancestral voice tells her to "take back these cities / live as your ancestors," but the speaker counters that if she listens to this voice of ecological sanity, she will be declared insane and institutionalized. But she does not reject the voice. Her conclusion suggests that at the moment the emphasis must be on survival, which is in itself subversive because it allows Crazy Grandpa's voice to continue speaking to the present and suggesting the ways out of this contemporary madness. The next poem, "You Can't Get Good Help These Daze," draws on the author's experience as a maid to warn the dominant culture that the underclass is preparing for just the kind of revolt that Crazy Grandpa recommends. In contrast, "Foolish" enacts a lunar celebration, introducing the love that can counter the terror of the two preceding poems. As with other poems in *Not Vanishing* that focus on native heritage and experiences, this one is set off from the other poems in the volume through the use of a Turtle Symbol, which refers to the concept of North America as Turtle Island. Chrystos in the introduction warns the reader: "While I am deeply spiritual, to share this with strangers would be a violation. . . . you will find no creation myths here." And indeed she retells no such traditional stories. Yet the Turtle Island symbol does invoke an extremely popular creation myth for those readers who already know it. Through this iconography, then, Chrystos is able to suggest another level of meaning for poems such as "Foolish," but only for a segment of her reading audience. For them "Foolish" can be read as a ritual poem announcing not just the survival of a people, but also the beginning of a triumph, as in midpoem the speaker chants "*Here we come Here we come Get ready to / know us Throw your doors down.*"[60] "Foolish" connects this celebration with the spring renewal of plants, implying a certain inevitability to the envisioned return of native values.

Similar arrangements of poems appear throughout *Not Vanishing.* "Today Was a Bad Day Like TB" enunciates the terror of whites who turn native spiritual practices and artifacts into tourist attractions and trinkets. The association of this experience with tuberculosis links cultural and physical disease, in much the same way that Anzaldúa depicts their interpenetration. "Poem for Lettuce" on the next page, however, humorously presents the road of revenge in terms of the speaker striking an alliance with "lettuce" by promoting carnivorous behavior. Chrystos pokes fun at people who make rigid distinctions between the human and the animal, animal life and plant life, relying on dichotomies to structure their world rather than relationships and continuities. "My Baby Brother" and "Vision: Bundle" emphasize the destruction wrought by U.S. culture first on an individual Native American and then on Native American cultures in general. Baby brother is depicted as a heroin addict who rides horses only in his drug-induced dreams, utterly separated from his heritage and his place. "Vision: Bundle" decries the destruction of native spiritual practices through imperialistic anthropology, museum displays, and unauthorized ethnographic recordings of religious rituals. Such behavior is linked to a reliance on technology and the resulting evisceration of the human spirit. Yet, despite the record of terror presented in both poems, Chrystos ends the second one with the survivor's recognition that "the only part of us they can't steal / is what we know."[61]

Finally, there is the novel. It seems utterly inappropriate in an essay relying on Bakhtinian dialogics as a key component of its methodology to ignore the genre that prompted so much of Bakhtin's theorizing. The novel, too, has a role to play in nature writing. And this role should not be limited to works that can be labeled "realism." Two novels that exemplify this point are Ursula K. Le Guin's *Always Coming Home* (1985) and Alice Walker's *The Temple of My Familiar* (1989).[62] Of course, Le Guin's novel cannot be nature writing. After all, it is science fiction set in the future. But if nature writing is defined not on the basis of some notion of objective observation, or record of immediate direct experience—whether or not it is recollected in tranquillity or agitation—but on the basis of explorations of the relationships among nature, including human interaction with and attitudes about the other parts of nature, then *Always Coming Home* is excellent nature writing. This novel is dialogical, ecological, and feminist. Le Guin develops a postmodernist structure to enable a rich interplay of intratextuality and reader interaction with the text. It contains a novel in the sense of a narrative story, but that is only part of it. This narrative need not be read linearly, as it is broken up by a series of chapters that appear to be anthropological records of the people depicted in that narrative. These in turn are shot through with a series of metanarrative chapters on "Pandora," the alleged anthropologist authoring the "nonfiction" chapters.

There is a quest, but one undertaken by a female protagonist. This quest, however, is not for a boon to bring back to one's people, but for the reunification of family, the understanding of the patrilineal and matrilineal oppositions that structure conflict in the future. But that is not the real story here; it is just the narrative. For the reader, the real story is that of the necessity and difficulty of building healthy new cultures. These would be able to retrieve the most valuable lessons of past and current peoples in order to build contemporary societies capable of regaining ecological balance. They would also be able to generate multicultural social interactions that recognize the inevitability of difference and conflict without domination or forced assimilation. Le Guin's novel requires a rethinking of relationships, something that far too much of the recognized "nature writing" has neglected to undertake.

Similarly, Alice Walker's *Temple of My Familiar* focuses on relationships, a vast array of them. And the dialogical development of this multiplotted novel relies heavily for its philosophical underpinnings on the spiritualist wing of ecological feminism. The relationships that are plotted out cannot be understood outside of an ecological framework, one that is based on feminist recognitions of multiplicity, heterogeneity, and heterarchy. The "familiar" of the title may well be interpreted as a symbol of the individual's rootedness in natural relationship, that interconnection of spirit, psyche, and place that also animates *Borderlands*. The first page of the novel sets into motion a rethinking of relationships through the comparison of the two people who pluck feathers from living birds to make costumes and "the old woman who specialized in 'found feathers' and who was poorer than the others but whose face was more peaceful." This is carried further in the presentation of the need for a return to animistic spirituality.[63] These examples just touch the surface of Walker's complexity but do suggest the dialogical and feminist, as well as nature-writing, characteristics of the text.

Donna Haraway has posited that the nature-human dialogic is the most pressing issue to work through at this moment in time. Susan Griffin has argued that this dialogic is also inextricably intertwined with the male-female dialogic. And both of these dialogics are beset by the logic of domination. Only in the past few years have literary critics even begun to concern themselves with such matters as "ecological criticism," "environmental literature," and the "genre of nature writing." Debate over such concepts is vital, if not for the future of literary studies then certainly for their social relevance. Yet, at a point when such discussion has barely overcome inertia, there are those who would seek to bring it to rest through a codification of prescriptive genre criteria that would render nature writing a dead genre, closed off, conventionalized, and, increasingly, of merely historical interest. Too much is at stake to allow this to occur. Feminists need to encourage this debate, to help introduce a set of criteria for literary evaluation largely ignored by ecological critics. At the same time, feminists need to listen to women who are calling for a reintegration of woman and nature, of humanity and nature, so that they can learn how to expand feminist theory to encompass the ecological dimensions of women's lives. This dimension can only adequately be incorporated into feminist thought through a dialogical process that recognizes that human-nature relationships and contradictions will remain throughout all social permutations.

Through a feminist dialogical intervention, not only can we blur the genre of nature writing by dissolving the absolute dichotomies being posited in order to codify it into a monological, centripetal mode of writing, we can also redefine the terms of human-nature interaction and their literary representations. Through encouraging the voicing of another nature, and learning the means by which to generate the literary criticism and analysis of such voicing, we can help to continue the feminist project of developing another mode of human behavior, one founded on relational anotherness rather than alienational otherness, an affirmative praxis so much needed in this time of negative critique.[64]

Notes

1. This essay builds on work I have undertaken elsewhere, particularly "Prolegomenon for an Ecofeminist Dialogics" in *Feminism, Bakhtin, and the Dialogic Voice*, eds. Dale M. Bauer and Susan Jaret McKinstry (Albany: State University of New York Press, 1991), 39-56; and "Ground, Pivot, Motion: Ecofeminist Theory, Dialogics, and Literary Practice," *Hypatia: A Journal of Feminist Philosophy* 6,1 (1991): 146-61. Parts of the arguments there are recapitulated here. In both, the ideas of ecofeminism are developed in greater detail than in this essay. In the former I give more attention to the aspects of Bakhtin's thought I find particularly productive for the ecofeminist project; in the latter I explore ecofeminist dialogics as a method of literary criticism in relation to contemporary women's poetry and fiction without attention to the "nature writing" debate.

2. Robert Finch and John Elder, eds., *The Norton Book of Nature Writing* (New York: Norton, 1990).

3. Ibid., 20.

4. Ibid., 26.

5. In a review of *Native American Literatures* edited by Laura Coltelli (*Studies in American Indian Literatures* 3,2 [1991]: 86-89), Arnold Krupat notes that "one of the most recent clichés is the regular reference to the term 'alienation' as applicable to the situation of some of the better-known protagonists of contemporary Native American fiction, an odd term to employ, one might think, for critics who regularly point out the problems of using Western terms for Indian literatures. . . . What Tayo or Abel or Jim Lonely feel may be something like what 'alienation' in its western history tries to denote—but of course what is interesting is how that term does not quite account for what they feel."

6. Finch and Elder, *Norton*, 828.

7. Barbara Johnson, *A World of Difference* (Baltimore: Johns Hopkins University Press, 1987), 190.

8. Max Horkheimer and Theodor W. Adorno, *Dialectic of Enlightenment*, trans. John Cumming (1972; rpt. New York: Continuum, 1990), 4.

9. Ibid., 9.

10. Constance Penley and Andrew Ross, "Cyborgs at Large: Interview with Donna Haraway," in *Technoculture*, ed. Penley and Ross (Minneapolis: University of Minnesota Press, 1991), 5.

11. M. M. Bakhtin, "Epic and Novel," in *The Dialogic Imagination: Four Essays by M. M. Bakhtin*, ed. Michael Holquist, trans. Caryl Emerson and Michael Holquist (Austin: University of Texas Press, 1981), 5.

12. Ibid., 6.

13. Ibid., 3.

14. Gary Snyder cogently criticizes the dominant attitude about order and chaos when he remarks that "it is not nature-as-chaos which threatens us, but the State's presumption that *it* has created order. Also there is an almost self-congratulatory *ignorance* of the natural world that is pervasive in Euro-American business, political, and religious circles" (*The Practice of the Wild* [San Francisco: North Point, 1990], 92-93).

15. Bakhtin, "Epic and Novel," 11.

16. Rachel Blau DuPlessis, "Breaking the Sentence; Breaking the Sequence," in *Writing beyond the Ending: Narrative Strategies of Twentieth-Century Women Writers* (Bloomington: Indiana University Press, 1985), reprinted in *Essentials of the Theory of Fiction*, ed. Michael J. Hoffman and Patrick D. Murphy (Durham, N.C.: Duke University Press, 1988),474.

17. Ibid., 487.

18. Michael Holquist, *Dialogism: Bakhtin and His World* (New York: Routledge, 1990), 72-73.

19. Ibid., 32. For readers unfamiliar with the term transgredience, Holquist defines it as "the degree of outsidedness toward the second. . . . Transgredience is reached when the *whole* existence of others is seen from outside not only their own knowledge that they are being perceived by somebody else, but from beyond their awareness that such an other even exists. . . . there is in fact no way 'I' can be completely transgredient to another *living* subject, nor can he or she be completely transgredient to me" (32-33; emphasis in original).

20. Dale M. Bauer, *Feminist Dialogics: A Theory of Failed Community* (Albany: State University of New York Press, 1988).

21. See Ynestra King, "Toward an Ecological Feminism and a Feminist Ecology," in *Machina Ex Dea: Feminist Perspectives on Technology*, ed. Joan Rothschild (New York: Pergamon, 1983), 119-20; and Karen Warren, "Feminism and Ecology: Making Connections," *Environmental Ethics* 9 (1987): 7-8.

22. For example, Patricia Clark Smith argues that much contemporary Anglo women's poetry on women relatives treats these people as being alien to the author from an individual, psychological perception of otherness ranging from "seeing the woman as suddenly unfamiliar in some way to seeing her as a monster." But, Smith claims, "The image of a woman relative as an alien being simply does not appear in American Indian women's poetry." Instead, there is "a tendency to see conflict between women as not totally a personal matter but, rather, as part of a larger whole, as a sign that one of the pair has lost touch not with just a single individual but with a complex web of relationships and reciprocities" ("Ain't Seen You Since: Dissent among Female Relatives in American Indian Women's Poetry," in *Studies in American Indian Literature*, ed. Paula Gunn Allen [New York: Modern Language Association, 1983], 112, 114, 115).

23. Ecofeminism has exploded across disciplines and politics in recent years to the point that a bibliographical note the length of this essay would fail to do justice to the literature, although it is just starting to become familiar in literary studies. Three helpful starting points that suggest the breadth of this movement would be the 230-page "Ecological Feminism" special issue of *Hypatia: A Journal of Feminist Philosophy* 6,1 (Spring 1991); *Reweaving the World: The Emergence of Ecofeminism*, ed. Irene Diamond and Gloria Feman Orenstein (San Francisco: Sierra Club, 1990); and *Healing the Wounds: The Promise of Ecofeminism*, ed. Judith Plant (Philadelphia: New Society, 1989).

24. M. M. Bakhtin, *Problems of Dostoevsky's Poetics*, ed. and trans. Caryl Emerson (Minneapolis: University of Minnesota Press, 1984). In an editor's note to appendix 2 Caryl Emerson explains Bakhtin's statement "*ja i drugoi*": "Russian distinguishes between *drugoi* (another, other person) and *chuzhoi* (alien; strange; also, the other). The English pair 'I/other,' with its intonations of alienation and opposition, has specifically been avoided here. The *another* Bakhtin has in mind is not hostile to the *I* but a necessary component of it, a friendly other, a living factor in the attempts of the *I* toward self-definition" (302).

25. Gary Saul Morson and Caryl Emerson, "Introduction," in *Rethinking Bakhtin: Extensions and Challenges*, ed. Morson and Emerson (Evanston, Ill.: Northwestern University Press, 1988), 23.

26. Mary Austin, *The Land of Little Rain* (1903; New York: Penguin, 1988).

27. Ibid., v.

28. Alice Walker, *The Temple of My Familiar* (New York: Pocket Books, 1990).

29. Austin, *Land*, x, xii.

30. Bakhtin, "Epic and Novel," 16-17.

31. Mary Austin, *Stories from the Country of Lost Borders*, ed. Marjorie Pryse (New Brunswick, N.J.: Rutgers University Press, 1987).

32. Ibid., xi.

33. Ibid., xv.

34. Holquist, *Dialogism*, 28; see also 47.

35. Austin, *Land*, 1.

36. Austin, *Stories*, xv, xix.

37. Bakhtin, *Problems*, 47. Bakhtin was clearly not ecologically minded, never himself extended any of his ideas to pertain to the human/nature dialogue, and even attempted to preclude it in some of his early writing. Perhaps this reflects in part the pernicious residues of Kantian philosophy and the antiecological attitudes prevalent throughout Marxist thought that constituted nature as always a thing-for-us, a raw material to be worked up, no different from the bourgeois attitude, both equally products of instrumental reason: "The multitudinous affinities between existents are suppressed by the single relation between the subject who bestows meaning and the meaningless object," as Horkheimer and Adorno argue (*Dialectic of Enlightenment*, 10). Bakhtin was unable to distinguish, as ecofeminists do, between speaking subjects who exercise agency and nonspeaking subjects that exercise agency, or, as Donna Haraway puts it in the interview with Penley and Ross (see note 10 of this chapter), between "speaking subjects" and "actors."

38. Austin, *Land*, 4.

39. Pryse points out that in line with Lydia Maria Child's *Hobomok* (1824) and Catharine Sedgwick's *Hope Leslie* (1827), Austin's writing shares a recognition for "alliance and sympathy between white women and Indian women," which is also reflected in "her lifelong recognition of the value of Indian culture" (Austin, *Stories*, xvi).

40. Austin, *Land*, 8.

41. Susan Griffin, *Woman and Nature: The Roaring inside Her* (New York: Harper & Row, 1978).

42. Susan Griffin, *Made from This Earth: An Anthology of Writings* (New York: Harper & Row, 1982), 82.

43. Ibid., 161.

44. Ibid., 164-65.

45. Jacques Lacan, "The Agency of the Letter in the Unconscious or Reason Since Freud," in *Ecrits*, trans. Alan Sheridan (New York: Norton, 1977), reprinted in *Critical Theory Since 1965*, ed. Hazard Adams and Leroy Searle (Tallahassee: Florida State University Press, 1986), 754.

46. Griffin, *Woman and Nature*, xv.

47. V. N. Voloshinov, *Marxism and the Philosophy of Language*, trans. Ladislav Matejka and I. R. Titunik (Cambridge, Mass.: Harvard University Press, 1986), 128.

48. Ibid., 129.

49. Griffin, *Woman and Nature*, 11.

50. Ibid., 83.

51. Ibid., 227; emphasis in the original.

52. Donna J. Haraway, *Simians, Cyborgs, and Women: The Reinvention of Nature* (New York: Routledge, 1991), 1, 2.

53. Thomas J. Lyon, ed., *This Incomperable Lande: A Book of American Nature Writing* (New York: Penguin, 1991), xv.

54. See, for example, Hayden White, *The Tropics of Discourse: Essays in Cultural Criticism* (Baltimore: Johns Hopkins University Press, 1978).

55. Haraway, *Simians, Cyborgs, and Women*, 3.

56. Gloria Anzaldúa, *Borderlands/La Frontera* (San Francisco: Spinsters/Aunt Lute, 1987), n.p.

57. Ibid., 81.

58. See the first part of this essay for Finch and Elder's treatment of Native Americans. Tom Lyon has a similar problem and ends up excluding Native Americans altogether from *This Incomperable Lande* because they had no sense of nature as a "wilderness" and, apparently, for him an inadequate distinction in their storytelling between fact and fiction (xv-xvi).

59. Chrystos, *Not Vanishing* (Vancouver: Press Gang, 1988).

60. Ibid., 3.

61. Ibid., 21.

62. Ursula K. Le Guin, *Always Coming Home* (New York: Bantam, 1986).

63. Walker, *Temple*, 145, 287-89.

64. Quite recently, the efforts of ecofeminism to work for positive critique and inclusive debate have come under attack by the social ecologist Janet Biehl in *Rethinking Ecofeminist Politics* (Boston: South End, 1991). Biehl engages in extensive negative critique of ecofeminism because so many of the individuals who use this term to define their beliefs fail to meet her criteria that feminist ecologists must adopt Murray Bookchin's Enlightenment-based, rationalistic theory of "social ecology" and its clearly delineated political program in order to be progressive. Apparently, her notion of "a free ecological society" has no more room for heterarchical difference and dissonance than did Plato's. A more helpful approach in addressing the differences between ecofeminism and social ecology can be found in an article by Mary Mellor, "Eco-Feminism and Eco-Socialism," and an interview by Valerie Kuletz with Barbara Holland-Cunz in *Capitalism, Nature, Socialism* 3,2 (1992): 43-78.

Monstrous Dialogues: Erotic Discourse and the Dialogic Constitution of the Subject in *Frankenstein*

Siobhan Craig

Mary Shelley's *Frankenstein* raises many questions about the nature of discourse and the nature of the human subject. Speech is a central concern of the novel, its frame and the filter through which all of the action passes. The verbal "confession" creates a link, an eroticized bond; through this dialogic interaction the monster attempts to constitute himself as a human subject. In this paper I explore the applicability of aspects of Michel Foucault's *History of Sexuality* to the process of self-constitution as Mary Shelley presents it. The discourse of science, the *ars scientifica* that Foucault discusses, is fundamental to consciousness in *Frankenstein*. My thesis is that the explorer in science, seeking to go beyond the boundaries of the known universe, becomes the explorer of sexuality, a transgressor of boundaries in the erotic also. *Ars scientifica* is substitutable by *ars erotica*; the discourses of science and of pleasure eventually become interchangeable. Through this eroticized discourse subjecthood comes into being.

Anne Herrmann, in *The Dialogic and Difference*, rewrites Bakhtin, positing the "female dialogic" as a process of self-constitution that, although arising from a reciprocal process, a dialogue, departs from the familiar hierarchized model of constructing the self/subject as defined in opposition to an objectified "other." The monster's self-constitution, in dialogue largely with Victor Frankenstein, remains bound by this hierarchical process and, arguably, fails because of it.[1] I maintain, however, that Shelley raises the possibility of a different, nonhierarchical, "specular" constitution of subjectivity, a potential that remains unrealized in the novel. This potential exists in Walton's exchange of letters with his sister Mrs. Saville, who is the missing half of the dialogue that makes up *Fran-*

kenstein, and in the unfinished female monster that Victor promises to create and then destroys. These two female presences are at the center of the novel but are undeveloped, unspoken, unrealized. The monster asks for a female companion "with whom I can live in the exchange of sympathies necessary for my being": I argue that the desired dialogue with the female monster represents the possibility of a successful, specular constitution of self that escapes hierarchy. Mrs. Saville is the implied but absent "reader" to whom the novel *Frankenstein* is addressed. She would complete the dialogic circle that Shelley leaves open. Does Mrs. Saville, the unspeaking and unrepresented partner, invoke the female reader of the novel? Is she—we—invoked as an accomplice in completing the aborted "specular" dialogue, a different, egalitarian constitution of subjecthood, that is implicit but not realizable, not representable?

Victor and Walton are both scientists. They both have an overwhelming, obsessive desire for knowledge that is the ostensible mainspring for all their actions. On the surface they share a passionate desire for discovery, to know "the truth." They both explore unknown realms, Victor in discovering the "spark of life," and Walton in attempting to reach the undiscovered tropical lands at the North Pole. Foucault, in *The History of Sexuality*, discusses the connections between the "will to knowledge" and sexuality, including the scientificizing of sexual discourse, the increasing development of a specialized, "impartial" and "scientific" body of "knowledge" about sexuality, that seeks to discover the "truth" of human desires and motivations. The burgeoning sexual discourse, a sort of obsessive circling around matters ostensibly taboo but actually, in discourse if not in practice, widely acknowledged, became the province of scientists. According to Foucault, scientific discourse became sexual discourse, and vice versa. What, on the surface, underlies the intense bond between Victor and Walton is their shared scientific passion. They are painted as kindred spirits in their reckless thirst for "the truth," sharing a typically Romantic desire to challenge all the boundaries they encounter, to enter forbidden and unknown territory in search of "knowledge."[2]

Their relationship is passionate and romantic in other ways as well. Almost immediately, they appear to "discover" an intense, obsessive erotic connection, albeit one that is acted out entirely through discourse. It could be argued that there is a sexual subtext throughout *Frankenstein*, that what is encoded in the scientific passions is in fact erotic passion. The unknown territory that Walton discovers is not the tropical North (in fact, he never gets there), but an area of warmth and desire where it "should" not be, where it is "alien," or even "inverted" (as in tropical heat instead of cold); that is, in a relationship with another man. The language and metaphors that are used for scientific discovery in the novel support this interpretation. Walton describes anticipation of his trip this way: "I cannot describe to you my sensations. . . . It is impossible to communicate to you a conception of the trembling sensation, half pleasurable and half fearful, with which I am preparing to depart. I am going to unexplored regions."[3] What he expects to find in this unknown place is "the region of beauty and delight . . . a land surpassing in wonder and in beauty every region hitherto discovered. . . . I feel my heart glow with an enthusiasm that elevates me to heaven" (15-16). A "burning desire" to go outside the known erotically as well as scientifically, to enter forbidden sexual territory, underlies the passion for "knowledge" and "discovery." Discovery of the "terra incognita" of illicit homosexual desire is what both Victor and Walter attain, with each other and, for Victor, also with the monster.

Transgression and obsession accompany scientific investigation. The metaphors that Victor uses to describe his early attraction to science often have to do with transgression, invasion, attaining knowledge and "entry" that is forbidden: "partially unveiled the face of Nature. . . . I had gazed upon the fortifications and impediments that seemed to keep human beings from entering the citadel of nature . . . Here were books and here were men who had penetrated deeper and knew more" (40). The "penetration" of nature's "secrets" is transgressive, a metaphoric violation of the mother, an entry into an area of sexual taboo. The dangers of erotic transgression are also underlined by some of the metaphors that Shelley uses to describe the passion for "discovery" on Victor's part. Walton's first impression of Victor is as a "shipwrecked" man: "Strange and harrowing must be his story; frightful the storm which embraced the gallant vessel on its course, and wrecked it—thus!" (31). The "storm" is perhaps a storm of desire, of obsessive and overwhelming sexual passion, as much as scientific passion. Storms are often associated with pivotal moments in Victor's story. The first impetus that starts him on the path to his transgressive and Promethean scientific discovery—the "spark of life"—comes from watching a thunderstorm's extreme destructive power. Victor is excited and fascinated by its overwhelming violence: "the thunder burst at once with a frightful loudness. . . . I remained, while the storm lasted, watching its progress with curiosity and delight . . . I had never beheld anything [a tree] so utterly destroyed" (41). Storms also frequently rage during Victor's encounters with the monster—which are, of course, themselves erotically charged. Victor's journey, both erotic and scientific, is always transgressive, involving investigation of what is forbidden, proscribed, but infinitely, obsessively, attractive. The storm of desire, with its attendant terrifying and exciting dangers, is a key image here. This sort of "perverse" or transgressive sexuality is exactly what became the primary focus of the "*scientia sexualis*" that Foucault postulates, the object of investigation, classification, definition, and endless discussion by scientists like Walton and Victor. They, in their search for the erotic unknown, remain within the scientific model: scientific discourse and sexual discourse substitute for each other.

Foucault makes a distinction between *scientia sexualis* and *ars erotica*, in which the latter's focus on pleasure is superseded by investigation, classification, a search for "truth." The distinction is not absolute, however; scientific discourse can also become a discourse of pleasure:

> And we must ask whether . . . the scientia sexualis, under the guise of its decent positivism, has not functioned, at least to a certain extent, as an ars erotica. Perhaps, this production of truth . . . multiplied, intensified, and even created its own intrinsic pleasures. . . . We have discovered a different kind of pleasure: pleasure in the truth of pleasure, the pleasure of knowing that truth, of discovering and exposing it, the fascination of seeing it and telling it, of captivating and capturing others by it, of confiding it in secret, of luring it out in the open . . . The most important elements of an erotic art linked to our knowledge about sexuality are not to be sought in . . . the lyricism of the orgasm . . . but in this multiplication and intensification of pleasures connected to the production of the truth about sex. . . . The anguish of answering questions and the delights of having one's words interpreted; all the stories told to oneself and to others, so much curiosity, so many confidences . . . the profusion of sexual fantasies and the right to whisper them to whoever is able to hear them; in short, the formidable "pleasure of analysis." (71)

In the conversations between Victor and Walton in *Frankenstein*, discourse, between these two quintessential scientists, does become an erotic activity in which pleasure is sought out and cultivated. "The truth" is investigated through the "delights" of verbal connection, a confessional, eroticized bond. The explorer in science becomes the explorer of sexuality, the creator of a scientificized *ars erotica* in which the erotic medium is not genital sex, but the eventually interchangeable discourses of science and pleasure.

Throughout *Frankenstein*, and especially in the Victor-Walton and Victor-monster relationships, speech, "confession," is the deeply desired erotic act that binds speaker and listener in a profoundly satisfying mutual attainment of pleasure. Speech is an intense desire and need, almost a physical sensation. Walton's desire for speech with Victor becomes increasingly intense as he waits for Victor to recover his strength. The discursive bond begins with Walton's telling his story—"confessing"—to Victor: "I was easily led by the sympathy which he evinced, to use the language of my heart; to give utterance to the burning ardor of my soul"

(28). The "burning ardor" here leads to a physical and psychic bond between the two that is described as "warming." The description of the beginning of Victor's "confession" that immediately follows this is perhaps less joyous, somewhat agonized, but unquestionably erotic. Walton is observing him: "My voice quivered and failed me . . . a groan burst from his heaving breast. . . . Such words, you may imagine, strongly excited my curiosity, but the paroxysm of grief that had seized the stranger overcame his weakened powers . . . he appeared to despise himself for being the slave of passion" (28). Walton's "curiosity" here—a word associated, of course, with scientific "discovery"—appears to be a code word for desire, in keeping with the substitution of scientific for erotic discourse.

The eroticization of discourse, speech as an erotic medium and bond, is also paramount in the interactions between Victor and the monster. The first real encounter in which speech between them is possible—after the monster has learned language—takes place on the alpine glacier at Chamonix. The isolation and the extremity of the landscape are important here, as they are in the interactions between Victor and Walton on the arctic ice sheet. In both cases, the couple is physically as well as metaphorically outside the everyday, the "known" world, at the margin, and this is one of the things that makes "discovery" in all its meanings possible. The monster is the incarnation of Victor's "discovery," of his transgression and his desire to go "beyond," to and past the margins of acceptable experience. Again, in Victor's relationship with the monster, science and pleasure are conflated. The monster is the incarnation of Victor's transgressive erotic desire, both as its object and as a projection of himself, a "creation" that is, in a sense, still a part of Victor.

As with Walton, confessional speech is what binds Victor and the monster. Speech is intensely desired; it in itself appears to be the focus of the monster's desire. He begs Victor repeatedly to listen to his story: "Listen to my tale. . . . But hear me. . . . Listen to me, Frankenstein, and so on." Victor at first adamantly refuses, and appears to allow no possibility of compromise. He capitulates, however, without explanation: "He led the way across the ice: I followed" (101). Victor desires the discursive act as much as the monster does: his passivity in "following" him (the Latin root of "seduction"—literally, "being led"—comes to mind here) as well as the sudden surrender of hostility allow the discursive bond to enact itself. Victor's responses on several occasions when he catches sight of the monster reveal the intensity of his own desire: "A mist came over my eyes, and I felt a faintness seize me" (98). The monster's threat to Victor when he destroys the female monster he had started to create makes the implicit eroticism of their relationship even clearer: "Remember, I shall be with you on your wedding night" (168). The monster verbalizes the indissoluble bond between himself and Victor: "Thy creature, to whom thou art bound by ties only dissoluble by the annihilation of one of us" (99). Both these statements are, I think, an exchange of vows of sorts, an acknowledgement of the obsessive nature and the primacy of their bond. A kind of symbolic marriage takes place between Victor and the monster, beginning from the moment when Victor willingly follows the monster into a hut and consents to hear his story. They establish their erotic-discursive bond on the glacier at Chamonix, and from this moment they are, in a sense, pledged exclusively to each other. Victor could never be part of a "normal" heterosexual marriage, as the monster could not find happiness with his Eve, because both are already "coupled," linked in all-consuming passion, and their bond has already been discursively consummated, through confessional speech. They have had their wedding night.

Speech and the erotic-discursive bond are also extremely important in *Frankenstein* for other reasons. The human subject itself is constituted through the dialogic relationship with another person, through discourse. This emerges clearly in Walton's sense of himself before he meets Victor. He passionately desires "to discover" on his journey to the "terra incognita" of tropical (and, again, erotic) heat, but his sense of his own being as he undertakes the journey is incomplete. He has a strong need for a "friend": "I have one want which I have never yet been able to satisfy; and the absence of the object of which I now feel as a severe evil. I have no friend" (19). Walton can feel no joy in life because he lacks this "friend"; nothing really seems to have meaning for him because his life is unshared. He needs another person, "a man who could sympathize with me; whose eyes would reply to mine" (19). Walton's self is only semi-formed, not fully constituted, and he feels an acute sense of lack. The other person, the "friend," is needed to complete the process of constitution as a subject. Victor, when he and Walton begin the eagerly awaited conversation, puts it this way: "I agree 'with you,' replied the stranger; 'we are un-fashioned creatures, but half made-up, if one wiser, better, dearer than ourselves—such as a friend ought to be—do not lend his aid to perfectionate our weak and faulty natures' " (28). It is important that this definition of self can be accomplished only through a dialogue, through mutual recognition and acknowledgment, through interaction. The loved "friend's" eyes "reply"; it is a process in which both parties must participate equally, and willingly. This is what, for Walton, banishes the feeling of loneliness, of incompleteness, of purposelessness and unreality, of the inauthenticity of one's own experience. The intense erotic desire for the discursive bond, for verbal connection to another person is, therefore, also a desire for the completion of self, for the attainment of subjecthood. The desire to "discover," to go beyond what is known, in both the scientific and erotic discourses, is also a desire to "discover" a completed self, to attain subjecthood through the eroticized discursive link.

Shelley's problematization of the constitution of individual subjecthood through a dialogic process is a central focus in *Frankenstein*. Herrmann, in *The Dialogic and Difference*, takes up precisely this point in her attempt to redefine the Bakhtinian concept of the dialogic in feminist terms. She posits the "female dialogic" as a process of self-constitution that, while it arises from a reciprocal process, a dialogue, departs from the familiar hierarchized male model of constructing the self/subject as defined in opposition to an objectified "other." In the self/other (male/female) and subject/object (male/female) oppositions, hierarchy is an intrinsic part of any construction of self/subject, while in a "specular" model, in which the subject is defined as female, this hierarchy is deconstructed. Herrmann defines the unhierarchized dialogic this way: "The dialogic names the discursive relation between two subjects, understood as a dialogue in which the subject constitutes itself without the annihilation or assimilation of the other. This dialogue posits itself as a struggle between the two subjects' respective discourses" (6). According to Herrmann, the dialogic allows an escape from the hierarchized binary oppositions that define alterity: "The dialogic disrupts that hierarchy by positing the other as another subject rather than as an object" (7). The Bakhtinian theory of dialogism, however, ignores (or, as Herrmann puts it, "represses") gender as a defining element in the discursive power struggle. Herrmann turns to the work of Luce Irigaray, in particular to her concept of "specularity," in an attempt to reintroduce gender: "Specularity . . . infuses the dialogic with a notion of gender by imagining the constitution of the subject as female. The specular subject constitutes itself simultaneously as subject and object, as woman and the 'other woman': that is, woman's own otherness in language and the other women of her sex" (7). Herrmann posits the notion of specularity as, in its definition of woman as subject(s), also deconstructing the power relationships implicit in the model of alterity, through which the female is constituted as other and object in relation to the one/subject. It is important that the specular female dialogic does not simply reverse this inherent power relationship, substituting woman as the valorized term, or just add in gender as an additional element. The concept of alterity and the subject/object relationship are fundamentally redefined.

In *Frankenstein*, the possibility of an unhierarchized dialogic constitution of self is nullified in the relationship between Victor and the monster. They are locked into a relationship based on alterity. Annihilation or assimilation are apparently the only two directions that their reciprocal constitution of self can take. The monster's relationship to Victor is complex because of his double role: he is both another, a separate person/being, and a component of Victor, a projection of the parts of Victor's self that Victor wants to exteriorize. In both his aspects, however, the monster is, in a sense, "feminized." He takes, unwillingly, the role of other and object as his part in the dialogue that constitutes Victor as self and subject, and is assigned the female role in the male/female opposition that is implicit in these interdependent categories. Self/other, subject/object, and male/female are concepts that inevitably imply hierarchy, as Herrmann points out. The monster is constituted dialogically along with Victor—to the extent that he is Victor's projection, he is even constituted as part of Victor—in a mutual and reciprocal process. Reciprocity does not, however, imply equality. Within the subject/object model of self-definition through alterity, equality would be possible only through sameness, or identity: difference can only be conceived of in hierarchical terms. The monster is defined by Victor (and by almost everyone else he encounters) only through this kind of otherness. He is constituted in terms of Victor, as the embodiment of alterity relative to Victor. Even though Victor is the creator, the monster is the primal and subhuman being: violent and terrifyingly, mysteriously powerful, disruptive, close to nature (though, paradoxically, his origins are unnatural) and able to live in symbiosis with the natural world, where humans would perish. The monster is always other, the dark side of the human, just as women are, within the hierarchized oppositional framework that the dialogic would seek to undermine.

Although Victor and the monster are locked into a relationship based on alterity, with its inevitable hierarchization, the power relationship between them sometimes appears to shift, even to reverse itself. In their pivotal conversation on the glacier at Chamonix, the monster discusses the hierarchical relationship between himself and Victor, promising obedience, willing subjugation, if Victor fulfills what the monster sees as the responsibilities arising from his position within their hierarchy: "I am thy creature, and I will be even mild and docile to my natural lord and king, if thou wilt also perform thy part, the which thou owest me" (100). Here, the monster appears to provisionally accept his place as other, his position in the reciprocal process of hierarchization relative to Victor. He also has just reminded Victor, however, how easily he could overpower him physically: "Remember, thou hast made me more powerful than thyself; my height is superior to thine; my joints more supple" (100). He goes on to elaborate his threat of hierarchical reversal, comparing himself to Milton's Satan, who rebelled against his creator, as the monster does: "Remember, that I am thy creature; I ought to be thy Adam; but I am rather the fallen angel" (100). Immediately after this conversation, an actual reversal in hierarchy does occur: Victor abandons his fulminating professions of hate and intransigent hostility, suddenly "surrenders," is led or "seduced," and meekly follows the monster to his hut, where the discursive bond between them is first enacted. From this moment on, Victor often takes the role of apparent subordinate, and the monster that of master. This is perhaps most explicit in the scene in which the monster berates Victor for destroying the female, whose creation is almost completed. He addresses Victor as "Slave!" and continues: "You are my creator, but I am your master;—obey!" (167). In the last section of the novel Victor, in his obsessive pursuit of the monster, follows in his track, his every movement determined by the monster, who also keeps him alive by leaving food for him. The power relationship here is evident in a message the monster leaves for Victor: " 'My reign is not yet over,' (these words were legible in one of the inscriptions;) 'you live, and my power is complete. Follow me' " (204). The monster here directly reverses his earlier statement offering subjugation; by speaking of his "reign" and "power" he is taking for himself the role of "lord and king."

The erotic overtones in Victor's "surrendering" agency and power to the monster are unmistakable. The obsessive chase, in which the monster participates by providing "clues" to his whereabouts as well as sustenance for Victor throughout, underlines the indissoluble primacy of their bond, the intensity of desire that links them. Victor's rhetoric of hate and vengeance here, as at many points throughout the novel, is easily readable as erotic passion: "I strained my sight . . . and uttered a wild cry of ecstasy when I distinguished a sledge, and the distorted proportions of a well-known form within. Oh! with what a burning gush did hope revisit my heart! warm tears filled my eyes, which I hastily wiped away, that they might not intercept the view" (207). The hierarchical relationship between the monster and Victor, therefore, is not static: it can shift, even reverse itself. These reversals, however, intensify the obsessive erotic link between them. Through discourse they come together in desire, in reciprocal constitution of self. Their relationship always remains one of alterity: the subject and object, one and other, reciprocally constitute each other as such. Even though the position of each term relative to the other may reverse, as in the monster's appropriation and Victor's concession of agency, leading or "seduction," the basic nature of their relationship is unchanged.

The dialogic process by which the self is constituted through connection with another—through passionately desired erotic-discursive connection, in *Frankenstein*—has failed for the monster and has only entrapped him in a less-than-human, "feminized" role. Though tied to

Victor through the indissoluble bonds of symbolic paternity and symbolic marriage, he feels essentially alone, because the dialogic relationship with Victor has not resulted in his being "seen" as a separate self, a true subject—which would have made it possible for him to truly become those things—but instead has meant entrapment in the subject/object dichotomy. Because of being trapped in inequality, in the hierarchized model of selfhood based on alterity, the monster feels incomplete in himself. This is expressed when he discusses the origin of his "vices": "My vices are the children of a forced solitude that I abhor; and my virtues will necessarily arise when I live in communion with an equal. I shall feel the affections of a sensitive being, and become linked to the chain of existence and events, from which I am now excluded" (147).

The monster's "vices"—notably, I think, his embrace of violence—are exactly what mark him as other, as embodiment of the dark side, and are perceived by him as caused by inequality and lack of connection. He is outside the "chain of being" because he is not a "being" in the fullest sense, largely because Victor has not been "sensitive," has not "seen" him. Victor, by objectifying and hierarchizing, has denied the monster the equal relationship he needs to construct a self that feels complete and has so condemned him to the "vices" of less-than-human otherness. What the monster is at this point insisting that Victor do is make up for the objectification and hierarchy. He is insisting that Victor provide him with a new opportunity to form the "true" dialogic relationship, try again what failed so miserably between them. Because Victor did not hold up his side of the dialogue, did not do what he should have done to allow a mutual process of constitution of subjecthood to occur, it is his "duty" to pay the monster back by giving him a new "being" with whom to attempt it. The monster is very clear about what he perceives as Victor's responsibility in this situation. He says: "Do your duty towards me, and I will do mine towards you" (99) and "I demand it of you as a right which you must not refuse to concede" (144).

By demanding that Victor create a female monster as his companion, the monster is searching for a way out of the trap of hierarchized oppositions, looking for a new kind of dialogic out of which to construct the self. It is important that he envisions the female monster as his equal. He is not attempting to maintain the hierarchy, simply substituting himself as the male/subject/self, but to subvert it in a fundamental way. He says, "My companion will be of the same nature as myself"; that is, not other or object, but another subject, an equal partner in the dialogue that will constitute them both as such (146). He sees that the model of hierarchy and alterity denies "true" subjecthood—that is, subjecthood based on a dialogic of equality—to both sides. The monster says, "You must create a female for me, with whom I can live in the interchange of sympathies necessary for my being" (144). The only way the monster sees achieving "being" as possible is through a different model. He, unlike Victor, can envision a subject/subject relationship, without the necessity for objectification or inequality, or the "absorption" and "annihilation" to which Herrmann refers.

The female monster, destroyed violently by Victor before she is fully created, represents, I think, an unrealized and unexplored potential that underlies all of *Frankenstein*. Shelley may be positing a relationship that very much resembles Herrmann's conception of the female dialogic. The two monsters would both be female in a sense, the male monster having been feminized through his position in his relationship of alterity with regard to Victor. Both would be symbolically female, but, in their own dialogic relation, neither would be feminized because neither would take the role of other/object/woman. The unrealized potential that the female monster would carry within her is the overturning of the hierarchized model of self-constitution that is based on alterity and inequality. The dialogic process by which a reciprocal constitution of self would occur would be specular, in which equality does not presuppose sameness, and difference does not imply hierarchy. In her discussion of specularity, Herrmann quotes Luce Irigaray: "We live by two beyond all mirages, images, and mirrors. Between us, one is not the 'real' and the other her copy. . . . we relate to each other without simulacrum. Our resemblance does without semblances" (25). Between the male and female monsters, this relationship could occur: they would be "the same"—both monsters and both female, whether physically or symbolically—and also different, but difference would not mean the hierarchized alterity that defines the bond between Victor and the male monster. Sameness would not lead to absorption or difference to annihilation. Herrmann puts it this way: "not as the 'other,' not as another 'one,' but as the simultaneity of subject and object in a state of reciprocity" (24). The male monster never gets to live this different kind of "being" and subjecthood in *Frankenstein*; it remains only suggested as a possibility, never actualized. The unrealized possibility of the dismembered female monster underlies all of the "coupling" that does happen in the novel, however, and opens the door to an awareness of a new kind of subject.

The dialogue that is the frame of the novel, the dialogue that contains and glosses all the others, also contains an unrealized potential to escape the model of self-constitution based on hierarchized alterity. Mrs. Saville, Walton's enigmatic sister, is the designated recipient, the envisioned reader, of the letters that make up *Frankenstein*. Again, the possibility that she represents, like that of the female monster, is only suggested, never explored. The dialogic circle is incomplete, left open. The female presence of Mrs. Saville, though crucial to the structure of the novel, is only alluded to, not represented. Mrs. Saville's name is suggestive, presents interesting possibilities. Contained in the name, perhaps, is the French word *savoir*, to know. Does Mrs. Saville "know" something that cannot be represented, that can only be suggested by its absence, but that is crucial in opening a way out of the subject/object trap that Victor and the monster are imprisoned in? Her name also suggests "save" and "savage"—is she symbolically linked to the "savages" in *Frankenstein*, the male monster and the dismembered ("dis-remembered"—i.e., repressed?) female monster. Could she be a "savior," a path to the specular self-definition that the male monster envisions but, because of Victor's murderous destruction of his longed-for dialogic partner, can never attain?

Mrs. Saville is an unspoken, undeveloped female presence at the heart of *Frankenstein*. The entire book is "addressed"—literally, as letters—to a woman reader who is absent, but who is also always present because she is half of the dialogue. Letters (like novels?) are written "to" a reader. *Frankenstein* is a novel about speech, discourse, the erotic-dialogic connection that constitutes the self. Could it also be a novel about "reading," about an unrealized, perhaps unrepresentable, female consciousness that—to borrow some terminology from reader reception theory—could actualize the areas of indeterminacy that Shelley has built into the dialogic circle of the novel? Throughout *Frankenstein*, we, the readers, are frequently reminded that we are reading. The complex structure of the novel, the multiple voices-within-voices that filter the action, although an integral part of the "story," function at times almost as an estrangement or distancing device. The way in which this is typically accomplished is by suddenly drawing attention to this structure with its many levels of mediation, pulling the reader away from absorption in the "action," emphasizing that this is a story, a narrative. The processes of narration and of reception are emphasized; we are reminded of the presence of a listener, and therefore, perhaps, of our own analogous presence as readers. There are several instances of this in Victor's narrative. For example, just before he recounts the monster's first murder—at a moment when tension is building, when the reader is increasingly caught up in the suspense of impending tragedy—Victor interrupts himself to address Walton directly: "I fear, my friend, that I will render myself tedious by dwelling on these preliminary circumstances" (75). The presumptive reader's presence, our avid involvement in a suspenseful narrative, is teasingly evoked by Victor's ironic apology to Walton for "tediousness." Any illusion of self-contained "reality" is suspended, and the layers of mediation are emphasized; we are reminded once again of the constructedness of the novel, that it is a story, a narrative, and that we are reading it.

The omnipresence of Mrs. Saville continually foregrounds the process of reading. She is frequently addressed directly, as the designated reader of the manuscript, a break into the self-sufficiency of the narrative that creates a distancing effect very much like that produced by Victor's direct addresses to Walton. At the end of Victor's story, for example, the first utterance in Walton's own "voice" is a direct address to his sister, in which he evokes her as reader. "You have read this strange and terrific story, Margaret; and do you not feel your blood congeal with horror" (209). Mrs. Saville, though a vitally important figure in *Frankenstein*, is not a "character" in any conventional sense; it is *as a reader* that she is present throughout the novel. Does Mrs. Saville, the unspeaking and unrepresented partner, the "reader" and the presumptive completer of the epistolatory dialogue, invoke the female reader of the novel *Frankenstein*? Perhaps we, the readers, are being invited to take part in the discursive intercourse of the novel, to become dialogic participants, albeit in a voyeuristic fashion. (We are, after all, reading someone else's mail.) If discourse is by definition erotic in *Frankenstein*, if it is in the words themselves that eroticism inheres, we as readers of the letters, as well as Mrs. Saville as their addressee, are drawn into desire, into involvement in the dialogue. We are also, perhaps, "explorers," engaged, like Walton and Victor, in a transgressive process of "discovery." Walton and Victor discover their "terra incognita," the "inverted" continent of illicit desire, and the dialogic constitution of self. Perhaps the female reader will, instead, "discover" the dialogue that the monster passionately seeks but is denied because Victor dismembers his dialogic partner. Are we all—Mrs. Saville, the women who read *Frankenstein*, and the female author, Mary Shelley, herself—invoked as accomplices in "completing" the aborted specular dialogic (the constitution of equal subjects) that is implicit but not realized, not representable, in the novel? The "crime" that is continually referred to in *Frankenstein* but never defined could in fact be Victor's "murder"—his violent rending, drowning, dismemberment—of the specular potential implied in the female monster. The unexplored presence of Mrs. Saville—the unrepresentable female presence in general—will perhaps rectify this "crime" against the human subject by envisioning an as yet not actualizable other way, a process of self-constitution that is free of hierarchy.

Notes

1. Anne Herrmann, *The Dialogic and Difference: "An/Other Woman" in Virginia*

Woolf and Christa Wolf (New York: Columbia University Press, 1989). Subsequent quotations from this work will be cited by author and page number in the text.

2. Michael Foucault, *The History of Sexuality*, vol. 1 (New York: Vintage, 1978), 71. Subsequent quotations from this work will be cited by author and page number in the text.

3. Mary Shelley, *Frankenstein* (New York: Oxford University Press, 1969), 21. Subsequent quotations from this work will be cited by page number in the text.

Desire and Temptation: Dialogism and the Carnivalesque in Category Romances

Eleanor Ty

Critics who have examined women's category romances have pointed out their generally negative and harmful effects. Readers of these romances are thought to be vapid housewives who passively consume these texts and who unquestionably imbibe the ideological construction of the "ideal" woman that these romances offer. In the last few years, a number of scholars have speculated on the reasons why romances have continued to be so popular despite our living in the post-1960s feminist liberation era. That romances provide emotional involvement without risk;[1] that they facilitate women's "disappearing act," or the "desire to obliterate the consciousness of the self as a physical presence";[2] that they provide the reader with "the sensations evoked by emotional nurturance and physical satisfaction" and "reinforce . . . her sense of self;"[3] and that they provide women with the fantasy of escape from their tedious roles in real life[4] have been suggested as possible reasons why these novels are so widely read by women. The answer is likely an amalgamation of all these conjectures, but I want to demonstrate why it is possible that these and other often conflicting theories are all applicable. Using Mikhail Bakhtin's notions of dialogism and the carnivalesque to look at a selected number of these books, I argue that these romances reveal a structure based on a compelling system of oppositions—between writer, text, and reader; between fantasy and reality; between freedom and restraint; between submission and rebellion.[5] In addition, examining this much-maligned genre is worthwhile because it shows some of the complexities and the tensions inherent in the construction of female subjectivity in our society today.

Though the romances are formulaic, there are some slight differences depending on the lines and on the dates of composition or publication.[6] Among readers of romances, it is well known that Harlequin's original Romance series is tamer and more conventional than the Harlequin Presents, which was started later. I use examples from recent Harlequin Presents, from Silhouette Desires and Harlequin Temptations, the latter two considered the sexier and racier lines for the contemporary reader.[7] Bakhtin's notion of "double-voiced discourse," where language "serves two speakers at the same time and expresses simultaneously two different intentions: the direct intention of the character who is speaking, and the refracted intention of the author," is particularly useful for my reading of these category romances.[8] Dialogism highlights otherness and differences while at the same time it is based on conversation and exchange. [9] I want to demonstrate that dialogics and double discourse become effective ways of dealing with the contradictory and ambivalent nature of the production and reception of romances. Neither the writers nor most readers are helpless victims of patriarchy or the dominant ideology but rather are involved in a system that involves power, which Michel Foucault defines as a "multiplicity of force relations" in "ceaseless struggles and confrontations."[10] Obvious exercisers of power are the editors, publishers, and other "gatekeepers" of the romance industry.[11] But authors and, to a lesser extent, readers also exercise power in what materials they select and how the love story is handled. In fact, Radway, Thurston, and Frenier credit readers' changing taste and their disgust with rape scenes and bodice rippers for the near-disappearance of such from romances written today.[12] One author even has her heroine, who is an editor, reject a romance manuscript written by a man because the love scenes are actually "enforced rape"and because the "sexual passages" are "entirely one-sided and completely without pleasure for its female victim."[13] This commentary on the preferences of female readers is particularly interesting because it is a self-conscious dialogue between the author, who herself is known for her rather sadistic and cruel heroes, and her readers.[14] It is a public acknowledgment of the author's awareness of the changing values and inclinations of her readers.

Another sense of Bakhtin's dialogic that is useful here is the interplay of voices in a text. According to Bakhtin, unlike the epic or the lyric poem, the novel does not use a repressive, authoritarian single voice, but a variety of voices, which he calls "heteroglossia."[15] Bakhtin is particularly attracted to the novel because it flaunts or displays a "variety of discourses, knowledge of which other genres seek to *suppress*."[16] For Bakhtin, "literariness," or what he calls "novelness" is "the study of any cultural activity that has treated language as dialogic."[17] Because of its dialogic nature, then, a genre such as romance, which today is considered a form of mass culture, would be studied for its *literariness* in Bakhtin's sense of the term. In contemporary romances, one often sees numerous conflicting discourses at work. Analyzing the different discursive practices helps explain the ideologies that are shaping the imaginations and beliefs of a reported one-fourth of adult American women.[18] These discourses stem from a wide range of sources such as advertising, women's magazines, Freudian and popular psychology, Hollywood movies, classical literature, hit songs, theology, tour and travel brochures, television, gothic novels, and one developed and only found in the genre, which I shall call the romance discourse. In romances often the language of the "high"and "low"are brought together and relativized, creating a "hybrid" discourse. Stallybrass and White explain that these terms depend on perspective:

> It would be wrong to imply that "high" and "low" in this context are equal and symmetrical terms. When we talk of high discourses—literature, philosophy, statecraft, the languages of the Church and the University—and contrast them to the low discourses of a peasantry, colonized peoples, we already have two "highs" and two "lows."[19]

Hybridization, as the word suggests, "produces new combinations and strange instabilities in a given semiotic system. It therefore generates the possibility of shifting *the very terms of the system itself*, by erasing and interrogating the relationships which constitute it."[20]

An example of hybridization is the description of sex and lovemaking in romances. Stallybrass and White borrow from Bakhtin's vocabulary of "classical" and "grotesque" in their exploration of high/low symbolism, which I shall use here. In Bakhtin, the "classical body" denotes the "inherent form of high official culture," while the "grotesque" suggests impurity, "heterogeneity, masking, protuberant distension, disproportion, exorbitancy, . . . a focus upon gaps, orifices and symbolic filth . . . physical needs and pleasures of the 'lower bodily stratum,' materiality and parody."[21] The sexual act itself, focusing on the material body, the flesh, and oral and anal orifices, seems to come from the "low" but in romances, becomes metamorphosed into "high" art. "Classical" language is used instead of the "grotesque," so that the genitals, the lower, bodily pleasures, are transformed into distanced, spiritual, aesthetic expressions of beauty. Orgasm is described in lyrical prose:

> Time, reality, lost all meaning. Nothing existed but the two of them, locked together in a moonlit room with only the sound of their whispered voices and their sighs of pleasure. He was wind and she was fire, he sweeping through her, touching her, marking her while she burned deep into the walls of his very soul. And he gave himself to her without hesitation. . . .

> He felt the first wave sweep through her and paced his movements to heighten and prolong the crest. He was rewarded with a soft cry as she arched strongly against him as the crescendo built and built, then broke, spilling through her with rippling shivers that he felt as clearly as though they were his own. [22]

This "hybrid" language borrows from poetic discourse the "moonlit room," the metaphor of the "wind" and "fire"; from pseudo-philosophy, "walls of his very soul"; from music or art, "movements," "crest," "crescendo." It transforms the physical, bodily pleasures into a pure, sentimental encounter acceptable to most female, bourgeois, conservative readers. Through this discourse, sex not only becomes a quasi-religious, elevating, transcending experience, but it no longer is forbidden, dirty, or "low."

This transformation through discourse has both positive and negative effects. On the affirmative side, romances provide readers with the articulation of female sexuality and desire. It is the closest thing we have to an *ars erotica*, which Foucault says occurs when

> truth is drawn from pleasure itself, understood as a practice and accumulated as experience; pleasure is not considered in relation to an absolute law of the permitted and the forbidden, nor by reference to a criterion of utility, but first and foremost in relation to itself; it is experienced as pleasure, evaluated in terms of its intensity, its specific quality, its duration, its reverberations in the body and the soul. [23]

The pleasure is significant because it is female centered, where woman is no longer the object of the gaze but coagent, if not subject of the action. In other popular media, such as art, cinema, and magazines, critics have pointed out that women are more often the object than the subject of erotic experience.[24] Romances provide a place for the legitimization and expression of female as sexual being. This attention to woman's desire aligns romances with radical French feminists who clamor for the recognition of female sexuality.[25] But, as Jan Cohn points out, "unlike radical feminism," romances settle for "unradical solutions."[26] Though they succeed in creating a "hybrid" discourse that provides women with erotic expression, romances still subscribe to the traditional answer of love and marriage as the solution to women's psychological, social, and economic problems. Sexuality in romances is also dependent on heterosexual relations and the phallus, as only with the virile hero is the heroine able to attain her full sexual being.

Nevertheless, the significance of the sex scenes and the sexual aspect of romances cannot be stressed enough. Romances have been disparagingly called soft porn for women, but the sex scenes in romances are erotica rather than pornography. One way the two have been differentiated is that "erotica involves mutuality and reciprocity while pornography involves dominance and violence."[27] A woman's sexual satisfaction is the focus of romances but, as Carol Thurston points out,

> overtly sexual excerpts . . . cannot alone spell out the necessary and sufficient conditions that make a romance erotic, because they are lifted out of the stream of events and out of the context of the relationship in which they take place. Women romance readers seem to derive a sustained level of sexual awareness and pleasure from the tension built into the development of this loving relationship *over time*, and it is the process of conflict and resolution that takes place between two wills and bodies that creates the necessary tension to turn the entire story into a psychogenic stimulus.[28]

Thurston emphasizes the development of tension in the relationship as well as the time element. But I believe that the pleasure is also literary and is brought about by the interplay of different discursive practices. Bakhtin's notion of dialogism is important because of its emphasis on everyday speech utterances and their links with the social and cultural world.[29] Dialogism does not set literature in opposition to life but assumes relations between all speech activities. What sets the literary text apart from other discourses is that it manifests "the *highest* degree" of internal organization, according to Michael Holquist.[30] In the case of sex scenes in romances, research has shown that males are "more aroused by the pictorial stimuli and females by the literary and imaginary stimuli," and that females are "more sexually stimulated by stories in which mental processes beyond the purely sensory are engaged."[31] Romance authors and readers recognize the importance of the literary, which in turn is dependent upon and interacts dialogically with myths, culture, and language.

In romances, unlike in pornography for males, desire is never expressed in explicit, scientific, or crude terms. Expressed in poetic prose, it is inextricably linked with mythical, elemental forces; with the post-Freudian idea of repressed emotions; and with the liberal humanist notion of the awakening of one's being or selfhood.

> Behind Carla, Luke's nostrils flared as he once again drank in the scent of her, flowers and warmth and elemental promises she shouldn't keep. Not with him. . . . Yet he wanted her the way he wanted life itself. [32]

> For an instant reality had slipped and he had been looking at the shadowed image of a woman to possess and be possessed by, beyond the restraints of the imagination, a woman who made him feel lean and hungry again,

> greedy for things that he had thought he had successfully put aside as a young man's fantasy.[33]

> Jeremy . . . considered the fact that he'd never had any trouble resisting a woman before. No matter how seductively she behaved or how beautiful she was, he'd maintained his perspective. But Maddy got to him without even half trying; and that terrified him. At an early age, he'd learned what happens to a man who allowed a woman too much power over his emotions, and he'd sworn that no female would ever get that close to him. But Maddy cut through his defenses as if they weren't there. . . . Maddy also had the capability of warming a dark, cold place in his soul, a place that before she'd entered his life, had always resisted touching.[34]

In these three romances, the desire that the hero feels for the woman goes against his reason or preconceived plan of life. The woman is associated with a powerful force that seems to be beyond his control. She represents "elemental promises" (Elizabeth Lowell), the fantasy image "beyond the restraints of the imagination" (Susan Napier), or the only being capable of "warming a dark, cold place in his soul" (Joyce Thies). As in many other cases in these novels, the response the male feels is unwanted by his conscious self because of its impracticality. The woman awakens feelings he has deliberately buried in order to survive in the world. Representative of an unsettling force, the woman exhibits qualities that can be linked with Julia Kristeva's notion of the semiotic, the heterogeneous pulses associated with the maternal and the preverbal.

Although the subject of Kristeva's work is the problem of language, her emphasis on the destabilizing force of the semiotic and the marginal in linguistics is useful here. According to Kristeva's theory, the semiotic *chora* is the "heterogeneous, disruptive dimension of language, that which can never be caught up in the closure of traditional linguistic theory."[35] While the symbolic is associated with language and the law of the Father, the semiotic is linked with the rhythmic, the intonational, "articulated by flow and marks: facilitation, energy transfers, the cutting up of the corporeal and social continuum as well as that of signifying material."[36] In romances, women are often connected with forces that are inexplicable in the everyday world or through symbolic language. They evoke feelings that the hero has repressed in the predominantly masculine world that he lives in. In the passages cited, the women possess disturbing powers that force the hero to acknowledge an aspect of himself he wishes to forget about, "as a young man's fantasy" (Napier), for instance. They also often move the hero not by traditional use of language, but through gestures, looks, and intonations, which are akin to Kristeva's semiotic realm.

This affinity between the qualities of the heroines of romances and those Kristeva describes in her theory of the semiotic is important and can be viewed both positively and negatively by feminist critics. On the one hand, women are again marginalized into the dark other of mythology and culture. As Hélène Cixous has pointed out, dualities of sun/moon, head/heart, father/mother, and so on are "*hierarchized* oppositions" that privilege the first term.[37] Judith Butler says of Kristeva's semiotic:

> Although the semiotic is a possibility of language that escapes the paternal law, it remains inevitably within or, indeed, beneath the territory of that law. Hence, poetic language and the pleasures of maternity constitute local displacements of the paternal law, temporary subversions which finally submit to that against which they initially rebel.[38]

It is true that romances affirm the authority of paternal law. Yet they also bring to the fore the power and the subversive possibilities of the feminine. Every story can be seen as a repetition of the same female victory. Male resistance, when present, is ineffectual in each case because the hero eventually concedes to the female. To read romances positively would be to see them as works that celebrate the force and energies of woman. Cynics may want to reduce this force to mere lust, but, as I have tried to show, desire and the sexual act itself are imbued with language that elicit the complexities of myth, fantasy, and popular Freudian psychoanalysis. In addition, the yielding of the hero does not mean a loss to his masculine selfhood but is usually depicted as advantageous to both the woman and the man. The acknowledgment of the other or his semiotic side often makes him a more complete or finer person.

> Then Luke looked down in Carla's clear eyes. He felt something shimmer through him like sunrise, transforming him, freeing him from darkness of the past, giving him a vision of a future more beautiful than his hungry dream. He wanted to tell Carla all that he saw . . . a man and a woman sharing and building and creating together, giving back to life the gift it had given them.[39]

> "But it's not just physical," he added, searching for words. "It's a wholeness. A oneness. I told you that night that I felt as if I'd been shaken to the core of my soul. That's what it was like. Shattering and humbling. Reverent."[40]

The union, then, is usually a recognition of the limitations of the initial vision of the hero, and sometimes, of the heroine. For the heroine, marriage at the end of the romance is paradoxically both a submission and a triumph. She surrenders herself, sometimes giving her virginal body to the hero. But the giving and its consequences are described in language that is idealistic, perhaps slightly melodramatic, and at times almost sacred or worshipful. It is giving with distinct emotional and spiritual returns.

Perhaps it is too facile and rather unfair to generalize, to dismiss all romance heroines as representative types of one sort or another. Recent romances deliberately jumble the polar categories of angel and whore, the innocent sweet girl and the sexy vamp. Some attempts are being made to make heroines psychologically complex rather than one-sided:

> He stood there staring at her, wondering how she could be hard and soft at the same time, knowing she was. She was so different. Whether she was being quiet and vulnerable or vocal and insistent, he wanted her.[41]

If a woman does become a Madonna by the end of the romance, she had to be an Eve to get there. Most of the Desire and Temptation heroines are wonderful temptress figures, extraordinarily good in bed, yet are depicted as warm, generous, and sympathetic.

> The thought of having her all to himself sent a jolt of anticipation through him. . . . They spent a great deal of time with each other. It was just that he wanted more. He wanted her night and day, day after day. She lived in his mind, and a longing for her constantly ate at his gut. He'd experienced these symptoms with a woman only once before, and never this fiercely.[42]

One optimistic development of recent romances is that authors and booksellers, in response to complaints from readers, are unscrambling age-old codes that defined the traditional "good woman." The conventional virginal heroine of the 1960s and 1970s used to be set off against an older, more sophisticated, manipulative, and sometimes deceitful "other" woman, but the better romances today do not have such obvious distinctions between the Snow White and the wicked stepmother figures. Instead, recent romance heroines are creative amalgamations of what Virginia Woolf calls the "Angel of the House" and the professional woman who might be involved in business, art, community work, or even science.[43] In other words, they come not only from the pages of *Redbook* and *Good Housekeeping*, but also from such women's magazines as *Vogue*, *Ms.*, *Cosmopolitan*, and *Working Woman*. They incorporate a diversity of ideologies put forth by the media, the popular culture, and the feminist movement.

This mixed ideal of woman can, however, create problems in characterization. The interplay of discourses or heteroglossia can sometimes add to the confusion of what woman is. For instance, the depiction of the protagonists often shows how women are divided between the ideology of the "natural" woman and the notion of women as glamorous products of bourgeois capitalism. Part of the difficulty stems from the ideal man in romances. The hero is usually suave, debonair, handsome, and very rich.

> Daniel Bishop was quite as formally beautiful as his dining-room. And he was tall, . . . with broad shoulders made sleek by the sophisticated cut of his dark jacket. A dazzling white shirt with a hint of silk stripe accentuated the tanned skin and blue-black hair streaked with silver. His waist and hips were tapering, suggesting a greyhound leanness beneath the custom-tailored elegance of his clothes, a lethal grace. A dark wine-red tie and a discreet gleam of gold at the pristine cuffs provided the only touches of colour about his person . . . except for those extraordinary sapphire eyes.[44]

This is the verbal rendition of the photographs found in modern-day magazines such as *GQ*, *Esquire*, or *Vanity Fair*. The description borrows from the discourse of the fashion industry and advertising: "sophisticated cut," "hint of silk stripe," "custom-tailored elegance," and "dark wine-red tie." Heroines fall for these men, but they themselves have to be "natural," or at least not overly concerned about their makeup and clothes.

For this reason, one favorite scenario of the rags-to-riches or Cinderella story used to be the shopping expedition initiated and financed by the hero. The heroine reluctantly allows her employer—or husband, in the case of a marriage-of-convenience story—to buy her clothes that accentuate her innate beauty.

> "Try it on," Hal suggested persuasively.
> Laurel wanted to shake her head, to tell him that she couldn't let him buy her such a dress. It was the sort of dress a man would buy for the woman he loved and, tormented by her uneasy conscience, she knew she could never accept it from Hal. . . .
> The dress fitted perfectly as she had known it would, and for a long moment she stared disbelievingly at her own reflection in the mirror, swaying slightly so that the delicate material swirled sensuously round her like a pale mist. . . .
> . . . She knew that never before had she looked so good, so feminine, and she felt a thrill of excitement as she watched his expression change, warming to a look so frankly sensuous and approving that it was almost a physical caress.[45]

A contradiction in this type of romance arises because the heroine is often set off against the scheming, materialistic other woman who has disappointed the hero. He finds the heroine enticing precisely because she is unworldly, simple, and without guile. Yet in this scene, the wearing of the elegant designer dress transforms the ordinary girl into a desirable woman in the hero's eyes. The passage moves from the discourse of the morally scrupulous Puritan—"her uneasy conscience"—to the cosmopolitan shopper, as it is the dress that makes her look so good, so feminine, and makes her feel the "thrill of excitement." The various borrowed discourses reveal the different, sometimes competing, ideologies at work in romances. They have inherited but also themselves perpetuate the conflicting myths of woman from other media such as advertising and magazines. According to these, only by purchasing a certain hair color or brand of jeans can the "natural you" be brought out. Dress, particularly for women, is still an important system of signs and a means of symbolic communication. Woolf remarked that "there is much to support the view that it is clothes that wear us and not we them; we may make them take the mould of arm or breast, but they mould our hearts, our brains, our tongues to their liking."[46] That romances have such elaborate scenarios about shopping and clothes is an indication of the importance society still places on women's appearance. These scenes highlight the ambivalence and perhaps confusion women feel about their looks, their weight, and their bodies. As long as the fashion and advertising industries continue to make people believe that women are what they look, and men are what they do, this uncertainty felt by women about their identities will continue. Some present-day romances deliberately minimize physical descriptions and emphasize the personality of the character instead: "It was a strong face . . . the face of a woman accustomed to making her own decisions and carrying them out, the face of a woman who did not rely on men to smooth her way in the world."[47] Most, however, are not radical enough to depart from the physiology of the relatively attractive average white woman.

Another important Bakhtinian concept that is significant in looking at romances is the carnivalesque. Developed most fully in *Rabelais and His World*, the carnival as Bakhtin presents it is a world of "topsy-turvy, of heteroglot exuberance, of ceaseless overrunning and excess where all is mixed, hybrid, ritually degraded and defiled."[48] Bakhtin writes:

> As opposed to the official feast, one might say that carnival celebrates temporary liberation from the prevailing truth of the established order; it marks the suspension of all hierarchical rank, privileges, norms and prohibitions. Carnival was the true feast of time, the feast of becoming, change and renewal.[49]

I use this notion of liberation, or what Stallybrass and White call "transgression," to describe both the world of the category romance and the experience of reading these novels. For the world of the romance, like that of Bakhtin's carnival, is also topsy-turvy and exaggerated, located both outside and inside ordinary, civilized space. It may not always be filled with the disrespectful, parodic laughter that Bakhtin sees as part of the carnival, but it is full of inversions and the disregard of certain social prohibitions. It disrupts traditional boundaries of the mythic, the legendary, and the real by deliberately conflating these realms into one. In its celebration of what society and law see as unstable and negative, it can be read as a protest, albeit limited, of the established order.

Theatricality, masks, multiple figures, and role playing are essential parts of the carnival, as they are in many romances. Disguise and mistaken identities prevail in a large number of category romances. The most overt manifestation of this theme is the revelation and often self-discovery of the virgin heroine; that is, the wide-eyed innocent girl awakens or is actually a fiery, sexually responsive woman. But in romances, appearances are not trustworthy in more ways than one. Through the thematization of multiple roles and disguises, the difficulty of becoming a female subject is explored or at least suggested. The notion of the female self is seen to be complex and elusive. As characters in the romance narrative don costumes, so do readers as they put on their other bodies and read the novels for two to three hours. This act has been seen as a denial of reality or a form of escapism, but I think that what women are reenacting is either the fantasy or the nightmare of their "other" or "multiple" selves. To read these plots constructively is to see them as signs of acknowledgment or recognition from both readers and writers of the multiple roles women are forced to play in society.

That all their lives women have had to play parts—the professional or career woman, mother, sister, nurturer, cook, housekeeper, wife, sex object—becomes evident in the sometimes amusing, but sometimes near-schizophrenic stories of heroines who become inadvertently deceitful. The plots of duplicity are evident from titles such as *The Counterfeit Secretary* and *Bittersweet Betrayal*,[50] but countless other romances are about women who either have to pretend to be or are mistaken for somebody else. Innocuous office clerks are actually computer experts, spies, or bodyguards; kind and generous girls are erroneously taken for their scheming twin sisters; a nurse is thought to be a hooker; a waitress is actually a rich corporate worker, and so on.[51] Such plots reveal women's fascination with theatricality and role playing. Through disguise and masks, the heroines live in a carnival-like fantasy with two or more identities at the same time. Often in these novels, the question of who is the "real" woman that the hero loves has ontological implications for women in general. Significantly, what these novels show is the difficulty for a woman of ascertaining identity or achieving subjectivity. More than just providing excitement for a bored audience, the repetition of these plots demonstrates a yearning for the suspension of the hierarchies associated with the quotidian; for the chance, however temporary, of living in a Bakhtinian upside-down world without regard for social restrictions. In these stories, women can lead exciting, adventurous lives as the other self, while maintaining their respectability through their traditional, everyday counterparts.

An interesting variation of the role-playing and disguise motif is the romance of the frog princess or hidden beauty. In these stories, the hero starts off by believing erroneously that the heroine is plain, dowdy, or older or younger than she really is. Despite this belief, the hero falls in love with her, not for her physical attributes but for her disposition. In the face of so much emphasis on the physical attractiveness of women in certain occupations as portrayed in TV, magazines, and advertising, this choice seems to be the ultimate test of character for the modern-day hero. He gratifies a woman's fantasy of being loved for her intrinsic self or character, rather than for her outward appearance or sexual allure. As in Chaucer's "Wife of Bath's Tale," however, the woman's loveliness or fairness is a reward or bonus the hero receives after he makes his decision. Paradoxically, as in Charlotte Brontë's *Jane Eyre*, at times the man literally has to be rendered blind before he can see the woman's desirable qualities. The blind hero appears in such romances as Emma Goldrick's *If Love Be Blind*, Joan Bramsch's *At Nightfall*, Annette Broadrick's *Choices*, and Binnie Syril's *Out of Darkness*.[52] That a plot involving a sightless hero is so fascinating to women writers and readers is revealing.

The most obvious reason that comes to mind for the plot's popularity is a woman's desire for dominance or power. The hero's blindness temporarily makes him physically weaker than the heroine. He becomes more reliant on the woman for transportation, companionship, and, sometimes, food. But in these novels the heroines never take advantage of the situation to render the hero pathetic and helpless. In fact, the independence of the hero is often emphasized. The more likely explanation is that the blindness again creates a particular kind of Bakhtinian carnival world for the heroines. Blindness establishes a realm where normal everyday rules can no longer apply. It gives women a chance to explore the possibility of creating rules anew, configuring a new domestic space both literally—by moving furniture around—and figuratively—in the concept and organization of the household. More importantly, the hero's blindness allows the woman to ignore society's obsession with the beautiful woman ideal, which is largely a visual presentation. She does not have to comply with custom or fashion because he cannot see her.

One could read the situation negatively, as Patricia Spacks does with *Jane Eyre*: "Rochester, even crippled, remains the strong male on whom a woman can safely and happily depend, to whom she will willingly submit."[53] But looking at these novels dialogically, one could also say that they enable both authors and readers to explore male/female relationships that are not based on the male's visual pleasure or desire. Instead, in these romances, other qualities of the heroine have to be emphasized: her strength, adaptability, warmth, compassion, humor, and perseverance. These romances are unwilling to carry through with their radical potentials, however. In most stories, the heroes eventually regain their sight and discover, to their great surprise, that the woman they have fallen in love with is beautiful after all. These novels end with the conventional foundation of male desire, which, more likely than not, is still based largely on visual pleasure.

The necessity for closure and stability in romances reveals much about the needs of women in our society. Marriage seems to be a mandatory ending of which many feminists are critical. Cohn says, for instance, that "love and marriage become means for appropriating the power and dominance neither the real world nor even the conventional surface plot will allow."[54] Critics of the genre equate the novels' endings with readers' objectives or their ultimate fantasies, but I think that regarding the goal of marriage, even the most unconscious readers of romances are in some ways "resisting readers," to borrow Judith Fetterley's phrase.[55] Thurston's research shows that more than 70 percent of romance readers are married,[56] so that even if romances affirm the values of the institution of marriage, they do not actually "sell" it. Angela Miles documents lesbians who read Harlequins,[57] further complicating the question of female desire, compulsive heterosexuality, and male-dominated relationships in romances, which could be explored further. My point is that the pleasure of the text stems not from the final proposal of marriage, but from the repetition and predictability of the formula: from the intimate and detailed account of the fulfillment of the heroine's sexual desires, and from the knowledge that however tumultuous and full of conflicts the heroine's adventures may be, she will emerge unscathed and triumphant. As in comedy, the formal resolution is sometimes rather strained, achieved only by sacrificing the finer details of plot and character. This closure, however, seems to be a necessary counterbalance to the sense of fragmentation or schizophrenic split felt by heroines—and, in turn, by the readers—in the center section of the novel where they search for who they really are. The formality of marriage is a signal of the return to normalcy, to civilized space. It marks the end of the carnival or the topsy-turvy world.

Finally, romances, like the gothic novel, "assume the primacy of feeling, and the pleasure of exercising it vicariously." Both "gain their effect by encouraging particularly strong emotional responses from their readers."[58] Romances are not really about falling in love; rather, they are systematic attempts to create a mood in which a woman's pleasure and desire for transgression are explored in reassuringly predictable ways. They provide a space wherein a complex union of emotions and states—the spiritual and the sensual, the sublime and the earthly, enthrallment and ecstasy—can be played out. A dialogic reading of these novels reveals twentieth-century women's obsession with identity and subjectivity and demonstrates their paradoxical yearning for selfhood and for being free of this self at certain times. The genre's inconsistencies betray the unresolved conflicts between the romantic and bourgeois ideologies that underlie it and make it functional. If romances do not work for some readers in our cynical postmodern age, it may be because in some ways this genre seeks the impossible. Romances, like fairy tales, ask that we believe in fantasies that our practical, daytime selves have rejected or no longer believe in.

> And suddenly she knew without a shadow of a doubt where she had seen him before. He was the man in her dreams, the one she had first begun to know when she had changed from girl into woman; the one who had haunted her all these years; the one she put into every book she wrote. This was her pirate—fierce, tender, passionate and proud.[59]

Notes

1. Angela Miles, "Confessions of a Harlequin Reader: The Myth of Male Mothers," in *The Hysterical Male: New Feminist Theory*, ed. Arthur Kroker and Marilouise Kroker (Montreal: New World Perspectives, 1991), 101.

2. Tania Modleski, *Loving with a Vengeance: Mass-Produced Fantasies for Women* (Hamden, Conn.: Archon, 1982), 36-37.

3. Janice Radway, *Reading the Romance: Women, Patriarchy, and Popular Literature* (Chapel Hill: University of North Carolina Press, 1984), 113.

4. Margaret Ann Jensen, *Love's $weet Return: The Harlequin Story* (Toronto: Women's Press, 1984), chap. 4.

5. It is very difficult to do a thorough research of these romances as six novels are produced per month in each of the Silhouette Desire and the Harlequin Temptation lines alone.

6. See Mariam Darce Frenier, *Good-Bye Heathcliff: Changing Heroes, Heroines, Roles, and Values in Women's Category Romances* (Westport, Conn.: Greenwood, 1988), who examines the difference in heroes and heroines of romances over the course of the 1970s and 1980s.

7. This contemporary reader is not the vapid housewife, but an educated and, more often than not, working woman. In both the 1973 survey of British readers of Mills and Boon romances and a 1985 survey of U.S. romance readers, only one-third are full-time "housewives." The majority of these readers either have high-school diplomas or some

college/university education, according to Carol Thurston, *The Romance Revolution: Erotic Novels for Women and the Quest for a New Sexual Identity* (Urbana: University of Illinois Press, 1987), 115, 119.

8. M. M. Bakhtin, *The Dialogic Imagination: Four Essays by M. M. Bakhtin*, ed. Michael Holquist (Austin: University of Texas Press, 1981), 324.

9. Michael Holquist, *Dialogism: Bakhtin and His World* (London: Routledge, 1990), 40-41.

10. Michel Foucault, *The History of Sexuality: An Introduction*, trans. Robert Hurley, vol. 1 (New York: Vintage, 1990), 92.

11. "Gatekeeper" is used to "designate the person or persons who function to filter from the mass of information being generated the fewer specific items that are passed on to the public." Thurston uses this term to refer to the agents, editors, and market analyzers who decide what to allow through the "gate" (*Romance Revolution*, 166, 182 n. 1).

12. See Radway's chapter "The Failed Romance," in *Reading the Romance*; Thurston's "Romancing Women Readers," in *The Romance Revolution*; and Frenier's "Under American Influence: Category Romances in the 1980's," in *Good-Bye Heathcliff*. All three agree that the violence and physical brutality that were characteristic of the romances of the 1970s have lessened or are disappearing.

13. Penny Jordan, *Desire for Revenge*, Harlequin Presents #978 (Toronto: Harlequin Books, 1987), 76-77.

14. *Rendez-vous* 6 (April 1985) commented about *The Only One*: "Our hero is a little less cruel than the usual type we see from Ms. (Penny) Jordan." Quoted by Thurston, *Romance Revolution*, 14 n. 5.

15. Bakhtin, *Dialogic Imagination*, 332.

16. Holquist, *Dialogism*, 72; emphasis in the original.

17. Ibid., 68.

18. Some statistics, according to Thurston, *Romance Revolution*: By 1984, some 20 million or one out of four adult women in the United States were reading romances at an average rate of four or more per month (vii, 3); by 1985 paperback romance novels accounted for about 40 percent of all mass-market paperback books published in the United States, which accounted for close to a half-billion dollars in annual sales (16).

19. Peter Stallybrass and Allon White, *The Politics and Poetics of Transgression* (Ithaca, N.Y.: Cornell University Press, 1986), 4.

20. Ibid., 58; emphasis in the original.

21. Ibid., 21, 23.

22. Naomi Horton, *The Ideal Man*, Silhouette Desire #518 (New York: Silhouette Books, 1989), 156-57.

23. Foucault, *History of Sexuality*, 57. Foucault believes that China, Japan, India, Rome, and the Arab-Moslem societies are endowed with an *ars erotica*, Western culture with a *scientia sexualis* (58).

24. In his study of the nude in art history, John Berger, *Ways of Seeing* (New York: Viking, 1973; 47), notes that "men look at women. Women watch themselves being looked at." Similarly, Laura Mulvey, in "Visual Pleasure and Narrative Cinema" (*Screen* 16, 3 [Autumn 1975]: 6-18), notes that in mainstream film, the spectator's unconscious is formed by the dominant order, which is patriarchal. The on-screen female functions as icon; she is an erotic object both for characters in the filmic narrative and for spectators in the cinema.

25. For instance, Luce Irigaray, *This Sex Which Is Not One*, trans. Catherine Porter (Ithaca, N.Y.: Cornell University Press, 1985; 95), links sexuality to discourse. She says that woman "is not a subject," so long as she cannot disrupt through her speech, her desire, *her* pleasure, the operation of the language that lays down the law, the prevailing organization

of power. . . . So there is, *for women*, no possible law for their pleasure. No more than there is any possible discourse" (emphasis in the original).

26. Jan Cohn, *Romance and the Erotics of Property: Mass-Market Fiction for Women* (Durham, N.C.: Duke University Press, 1988), 171. Cohn argues that in romances, economic power is given to the heroine only through marriage to the hero, and that sexual pleasure is repeatedly conflated with economic gratification.

27. As quoted by Thurston, *Romance Revolution*, 159.

28. Ibid., 154; emphasis in the original.

29. See Bakhtin, *Dialogic Imagination*, 262-63.

30. Holquist, *Dialogism*, 85; emphasis in the original.

31. See Thurston, *Romance Revolution*, 157.

32. Elizabeth Lowell, *Fire and Rain*, Silhouette Desire #546 (New York: Silhouette Books, 1990), 72.

33. Susan Napier, *The Love Conspiracy,* Harlequin Presents #1252 (Toronto: Harlequin Books, 1990), 75.

34. Joyce Thies, *Mountain Man*, Silhouette Desire #511 (New York: Silhouette Books, 1989), 70-71.

35. Toril Moi, *Sexual/Textual Politics: Feminist Literary Theory* (London: Methuen, 1985), 162.

36. Julia Kristeva, *Revolution in Poetic Language*, trans. Margaret Waller (New York: Columbia University Press, 1984), 40.

37. Hélène Cixous, "Sorties," in *New French Feminisms: An Anthology*, ed. Elaine Marks and Isabelle de Courtivron (New York: Schocken, 1981), 91; emphasis in the original.

38. Judith Butler, *Gender Trouble: Feminism and the Subversion of Identity* (New York: Routledge, 1990), 88.

39. Elizabeth Lowell, *Fire and Rain*, 186.

40. Diana Palmer, *His Girl Friday*, Silhouette Desire #528 (New York: Silhouette Books, 1989), 177.

41. Barbara Delinsky, *Montana Man*, Harlequin Temptation #280 (Toronto: Harlequin Books, 1989), 152.

42. Jenny McGuire, *Christmas Wishes*, Harlequin Temptation #232 (Toronto: Harlequin Books, 1988), 170.

43. Virginia Woolf, "Professions for Women," in *Virginia Woolf: Women and Writing* (London: Women's Press, 1979), 60.

44. Susan Napier, *The Love Conspiracy*, 29.

45. Kate Walker, *Chase the Dawn*, Harlequin Presents #1196 (Toronto: Harlequin Books, 1988), 62.

46. Virginia Woolf, *Orlando: A Biography* (London: Granada, 1977), 117.

47. Jayne Ann Krentz, *The Pirate*, Harlequin Temptation #277 (Toronto: Harlequin Books, 1990), 28.

48. Stallybrass and White, *Politics and Poetics*, 8. Stallybrass and White note that Bakhtin is "self-consciously utopian and lyrical about carnival and grotesque realism" even though the carnival itself, because it is a licensed festivity, may not be "*intrinsically* radical"(14; emphasis in the original).

49. M. M. Bakhtin, *Rabelais and His World*, trans. Hélène Iswolsky (Cambridge, Mass.: MIT Press, 1968), 10.

50. Susan Napier, *The Counterfeit Secretary*, Harlequin Presents #924 (Toronto: Harlequin Books, 1986); Suzanne Ashley, *Bittersweet Betrayal*, Silhouette Special Edition #556 (New York: Silhouette Books, 1989).

51. These plots are found in the following romances: Ashley, *Bittersweet Betrayal*; Glenda Sanders, *The All-American Male*, Harlequin Temptation #277 (Toronto: Harlequin Books, 1989); Roberta Leigh, *Not Without Love*, Harlequin Presents #1217 (Toronto: Harlequin Books, 1989); Emma Goldrick, *And Blow Your House Down*, Harlequin Presents #688 (Toronto: Harlequin Books, 1983); Kate Walker, *Chase the Dawn*.

52. Emma Goldrick, *If Love Be Blind*, Harlequin Presents #1035 (Toronto: Harlequin Books, 1989); Joan Bramsch, *At Nightfall*, Bantam Loveswept #88 (New York: Bantam Books, 1985); Annette Broadrick, *Choices*, Silhouette Desire #283 (New York: Silhouette Books, 1986); and Binnie Syril, *Out of Darkness*, Harlequin Temptation #276 (Toronto: Harlequin Books, 1989).

53. Patricia Meyer Spacks, *The Female Imagination* (New York: Knopf, 1975), 66.

54. Cohn, *Romance and the Erotics of Property*, 9.

55. Judith Fetterley, *The Resisting Reader: A Feminist Approach to American Fiction* (Bloomington: Indiana University Press, 1978).

56. Thurston, *Romance Revolution*, 116.

57. Miles, "Confessions of a Harlequin Reader," 130 n. 53.

58. Elizabeth R. Napier, *The Failure of Gothic: Problems of Disjunction in an Eighteenth-Century Literary Form* (Oxford: Clarendon, 1987), 26.

59. Krentz, *The Pirate*, 102.

Is Bakhtin a Feminist or Just Another Dead White Male? A Celebration of Feminist Possibilities in Manuel Puig's *Kiss of the Spider Woman*

Denise Heikinen

Mikhail Bakhtin's theory of dialogism has been embraced by several feminist critics for its ability to provide a platform for marginalized feminine voices to be heard above the din of the monologic, authoritative, and hegemonic voice. Dale Bauer, for instance, applies dialogism to expose the dominant community's attempt to subvert and silence females. In the four novels she analyzes in *Feminist Dialogics: A Theory of Failed Community*, Bauer maintains that this attempt at silencing produces a counterpoint effect of trivializing the dominant patriarchal attitudes. The authoritative voice's efforts to suppress merely call attention to other voices, thus opening a dialogue out of which readers become aware of possibilities and alternatives. Julia Kristeva, too, appropriates Bakhtin's dialogism for feminist purposes by emphasizing the contextual interplay of ideology and language. And Sandra Boschetto, though noting that Bakhtin himself never alluded to feminism by name, nevertheless freely extends his ideas about the unofficial voice to include a feminist perspective in her analysis of a Puig novel.

Indeed, Bakhtin's theories of dialogism and heteroglossia, in which meaning emerges on the borders of conflict, seem so tailor-made for feminist criticism that many might assume that Bakhtin himself expressed feminist ideas by name. Such is not the case, however, and some critics are calling attention to Bakhtin's glaring omission of any mention of feminist voices. Wayne Booth, for instance, in "Freedom of Interpretation: Bakhtin and the Challenge of Feminist Criticism," expressed initial dismay over Bakhtin's apparent lack of a feminist conscience in his treatment of Rabelais. And as Diane Price Herndl notes, Bakhtin never specifically mentions females in his analysis of marginalized dialects and speech genres, nor does he include any female writers among his many examples of heteroglossia in the novel. Why, she wonders, would Bakhtin mention Henry Fielding or Charles Dickens but not Jane Austen or George Sand? This is especially problematic when we consider that Bakhtin, though living an isolated life, some of it in exile, nevertheless was extremely well read and familiar with a large body of literature. Both Herndl and Booth conclude that Bakhtin was made deaf to alternative feminist voices by the authoritative voice of his time, but they are also quick to add that this glaring silence doesn't negate the power and usefulness of dialogism for feminism. In fact, Herndl asserts that one lesson of dialogism is that feminists must remember to remain dialogic in their philosophies; that is, we must allow for multiple feminisms, rather than attempt to impose any one authoritative feminism over others.

Kay Halasek echoes similar sentiments in 'Feminism and Bakhtin: Dialogic Reading in the Academy":

> In other words, Bakhtin (like all of us) falls victim to the ideology of his language, and what his language and ideology omit is (among other things) gender. In theory, Bakhtin provides space for other, unnamed, stratifying languages to take shape and to gain power within any given sociohistorical period when he suggests that groups, circles of thinkers or writers—even individuals—are capable of creating and enacting a stratifying language.[1]

Halasek reminds us that all of the earlier-mentioned feminist critics have appropriated some portion of Bakhtin's work and extended it into a feminist consciousness. For instance, Herndl's work allows for multiple feminisms. And in Halasek's case, Bakhtin teaches her to read "internally persuasively"—even against the grain of Bakhtin's authoritative voice—thus becoming more critically aware. None of these critics is contorting or apologizing for Bakhtin's dialogism in any way to accomplish their ends. In fact, Bakhtin admonished readers to adapt his words to their own intents in one of his most-quoted passages from *The Dialogic Imagination*:

> [Language] lies on the borderline between oneself and the other. The word in language is half someone else's. It becomes "one's own" only when the speaker populates it with his own intentions, his own accent, when he appropriates the word, adapting it to his own semantic and expressive intention. Prior to this moment of appropriation, the word does not exist in a neutral and personal language . . . but rather it exists in other people's mouths, in other people's intentions: it is from there that one must take the word and make it one's own.[2]

It is in this spirit of extension and appropriation of the dialogic word into a feminist realm—a realm into which Bakhtin personally never ventured—that we need to view the following Bakhtinian/feminist reading of Manuel Puig's *Kiss of the Spider Woman*. I here apply a feminist criticism to a novel that emphasizes the influence language has on the development of the self. Alienated voices, similar to those Bauer describes in the novels she treats, also speak out in Puig's *Kiss*, and, as Bauer notes about her examples, the dominant community is anxious to suppress them. I believe Puig's emphasis is not so much on the message of these other voices, however, as on the role that language plays in helping to form those voices, the process through which our notions of the self emerge—notions that delineate definitions and attitudes about gender and sexuality.

To suggest that Puig's novel is a vehicle for a feminist inquiry needs further explanation. After all, one might assume at least the necessity of female characters in order to build such a case. But Puig's lack of "real" female characters—that is, other than those fabricated by Hollywood movie scriptwriters or recalled from the memories of the imprisoned male characters—allows us more freedom to explore the impact of language on the development of the self in general, before we take it into the consciousness of the gendered self. Similarly, in this case at least, Bakhtin's peculiar silence about *gender* allows us to explore the dimensions and definitions of that word. I should note that, though Bakhtin never specifically referred to a gendered world in his many descriptions of heteroglossia, he also seldom defined any word too definitively, preferring more general terms such as official, government, or religious language. He might have unconsciously avoided using a word such as feminism, believing that all "ism" words indicate what Milan Kundera calls "totalitarian kitsch," an acceptance of a "categorical agreement of being." As Kitsch, such "ism" words too easily give in to stabilizing hegemonic forces and partake in what Herndl describes as the "relentless attack (in the guise of 'critique') on other feminist criticisms with different points of view."[3] For Bakhtin this results in a breakdown of dialogue, which by its interplay of words should encourage change, potential, flux, becoming, emerging—rather than stasis.

Dale Bauer's contention is that the community that inhibits intersubjective communication fails because it is destructive "of the self."[4] And the self, as Bakhtin notes, is developed only through dialogue with the other:

> I achieve self-consciousness, I become myself only by revealing myself to another, through another and with another's help. The most important acts, constitutive of self-consciousness, are determined by their relation to

> another consciousness (a "thou"). Cutting oneself off, isolating oneself, closing oneself off, those are the basic reasons for loss of self. . . . I cannot do without the other; I cannot become myself without the other; I must find myself in the other, finding the other in me (in mutual reflection and perception).[5]

Being "(both internal and external)" can only be defined in terms of one's relationship to the other, and that relationship is developed through the "profound communication" on the borders of dialogue.

Unlike the four novels Bauer analyzes, Puig's writing techniques—a mixture of kitsch (Hollywood B movie plots), narrator-free dialogue, silences, and footnotes—downplay the intervention or judgment of the author and allow readers to turn their own disciplined gaze on a community to examine familiar language that becomes "defamiliarized" because it is taken out of context. We begin to appreciate the power of the context of language as well as its content.

Possibilities for alternative voices emerge when Puig's readers realize how the dominant communities—whether they be right-wing governments, Marxist opposition, or even heterosexuality—fail their members by attempting to deny alternative interpretations. Puig's novel exposes the flimsy tactics that the dominant culture uses to insure conformity of public opinion, thus making the alternative countervoices seem, if not better, perhaps as valid as the dominant voice. This carnivalizing of the dominant official voice, in turn, allows us to laugh at fear.

In *Kiss*, a prison cell becomes a microcosm of the outside world by which readers can gaze at society in isolation and magnification, as if under a microscope's lens. Two men are thrown together for daring to oppose the dominant culture, one for his Marxist politics and the other for his homosexuality. These two characters are supposedly representative of marginalized "other voices," and yet we come to see that their views on gender relations, at least, are remarkably similar to the community they have offended. Though one is a Marxist espousing socialist principles of equality, even he expresses the dominant view that women are sex objects or, at best, helpmates for the cause. The other, condemned for his homosexuality, has also bought into the myth that women should be subservient to men. In fact, he wishes he were a female so he could sacrifice himself for a "real" man because he longs to be a martyr. The two characters, removed from the influence of the outside world as they are, begin to question how their ideas were formed. It is out of their dialogue that new consciousnesses develop for the characters.

At the same time the readers develop an awareness of language's role in shaping the self. As Bakhtin tells us, the self does not emerge in isolation from others but as a response or reaction to others. The "I" can only be defined in terms of its relationship to "Thou" (or other), and that relationship is developed through dialogue. Language serves two purposes: it is the glue that binds the diversity of its members into a community and also the mirror that reflects those members to each other. Through discourse the members learn who they are. And just as the prisoners are released by dialogue, we, too, can celebrate the possibilities of other voices rather than repress them. We, too, can change rather than be trapped by monologic ideas about gender relations.

In *Kiss*, Molina, the homosexual convicted of "perversion," passes the time by telling the plots of his favorite B movies to Valentin, a macho political prisoner. Interwoven within the telling of the movies are editorial interruptions by Valentin. Taken out of the context of "normal" everyday society as they are and inserted into the confines of a prison cell, the contrasting characters cast carnivalesque shadows under the harsh scrutiny of the bare prison lightbulb. Furthermore, readers view the scene without comment, and therefore guidance, from an omniscient narrator. The unguided reader, not oriented to eyeing segments of society cut up and exposed in this manner, becomes confused and disconcerted. As Bauer contends, however, such confusion is necessary before we can begin to look at conventions in a new light:

> "Confused" is the focal term: we are meant to be unsettled by these dialogues between fools and accepted languages, just as we are meant to be unsettled by feminist criticism which seeks to shake up the critical communities which do not acknowledge the excluded margins. What Bakhtin might teach us, then, is to conceive of the discourses within the novel as objects, as ideologemes which require interpretation and revision and which involve us in what Gabriele Schwab calls the "vertiginous undertow" of language. In fact, such "prose wisdom" allows us to see that no language is universal. Bakhtin calls this study of stupidity and incomprehension "a basic (and extremely interesting) problem in the history of the novel."[6]

Confusion reigns in *Kiss of the Spider Woman* for both characters and readers. The readers hear the voices of the popular movies, not in the original uncut visual version, but retold by Molina and edited with Marxist commentary by Valentin. Ironically, these cinematographic techniques first make readers feel like passive moviegoers but eventually force us to become active consciousness developers, as Bakhtin describes, rather than mere witnesses. Puig presents each official and unofficial voice in a documentarylike nonjudgmental style, so readers have to grapple with the issues themselves, just as the prisoners do. Interruptions of pain or sleep or silence throw readers from one voice to another without smooth transitions or commentary by the author. Furthermore, the readers can't always decide which is official and which is unofficial because the voices seem to switch positions often. Readers first laugh at the overly romantic movies and the pedantic footnotes that describe research on homosexuality, yet at the same time we manage to find value and serious content in them. We come to see that each voice has an official and unofficial component—both are madness and reason simultaneously—but we are only able to notice these oxymoronic situations because Puig presents them to us out of context.

The movies are about romantic love frustrated by mysterious or pathetic circumstances. Gustavo Pellon notes that the popular movies provide a "consistent and unambiguous" "paradigm of the world" into which Molina, and eventually Valentin, escapes. This narrative strategy, as Pellon tells us, "demands the formation of a double vision on the part of the reader."[7] Readers alternate between accepting this kitsch as the characters' only form of escape and rejecting it for betraying a false sense of reality. Puig doesn't editorialize about the simplemindedness of the B movies. On the contrary, he respects both kitsch and the intellectual footnotes, but he doesn't want to add his voice into the mix. Obviously Puig's position is not neutral, but neither is it vocal. His nonstance leaves us with the problem of finding our own way out of his tangled web of this juxtaposition of "reason" and "madness." Reading Puig, then, as an "internally persuasive reader" is less of a problem because Puig's authoritative stance is so unclear.

As a homosexual prisoner, Molina reminds us of the roles of both Foucault's madman and Bakhtin's fool or clown, whose laughter enables literature to "put its questions to life," as David Patterson tells us.[8] Molina, a male character who would rather be a woman, provides the impetus for a new feminist consciousness for another character, Valentin, and ultimately, and more importantly, for the readers. Besides contrasting the "official" against the mad, Puig's carnivalesque style pits one "madness" against another "madness" (or reasonableness against reasonableness), until we can recognize the possibility that reason resides within both contrary madnesses. *Kiss* casts us into a confusing tangle of many familiar voices where we are forced to unravel the knot in a new light, much as Valentin and Molina are forced to dispel or confront the shadows they encounter under the stark light of their prison cell. Our consciousness is also gradually developed in much the same way as Valentin's—out of confusion:

> "I want to think about my woman, there's something I'm not

understanding, and I want to think about it. I don't know if that's happened to you, you feel like you're about to understand something, you're on the point of untangling the knot and if you don't begin pulling the right thread . . . you'll lose it."[9]

The Panther Woman movie serves as an example of the kind of double-vision that emerges from Puig's double-voiced perspective. Already, we have irony with the mere choice of movie-plot teller. Molina, considered a pervert by official society, is the one who swallows the romantic notions of the official voice of society that reinforces the official discourse of male superiority. So a "madman" becomes the spokesperson for "reasonable" official society. We see, in this B movie, Foucault's association of sex with power as expressed through the selection of discourse that has informed Molina's notion of the ideal relationship between the sexes. Because it is presented to us (and to the character Valentin) out of context, however, that is, in a prison cell, with interruptions by prisoner dialogue, and through a "mad" viewer's translation—we are informed by another voice within the same movie about the falsehoods of such official doctrine. We feel ourselves choosing a voice, or at least recognizing that we have alternatives, seemingly without Puig's encouragement.

Molina attempts to tell the plot of his favorite movie to Valentin, who is willing to be an audience only because he is captive; his attitude toward such romantic movies is one of scorn because they ignore what he considers to be political realities. Molina, therefore, is never able to develop the plot very far without a comment or question from Valentin, whose purpose is to poke holes in Molina's blind fascination with romance. For instance, when Molina explains that a woman with catlike features is sketching a panther at the zoo, Valentin immediately asks why the caged animal can't smell her. We are told "there's a big slab of meat in the cage" that "blocks out any smell from outside." And, later, Molina says that the animal is watching the woman, but moviegoers can't tell if he's anxious to make a meal out of her or if "he's driven by some other, still uglier instinct" (3).

The telling of the movie is constantly manipulated by Puig in this way so that both the original message of the movie, which reflects and encourages a distorted attitude toward the sexes, and Molina's possible intention for telling it—to seduce Valentin for sex and/or information that he can trade for freedom—come to be overridden by a new understanding of the movie for the readers. The same movie that first seems laughable takes on a new and serious voice. Even the slab of meat in the cage indicates that a different discourse is, or can be, operating here. We can view it as propaganda fed to males by the dominant culture, which prevents them from acknowledging women as other than "meat" to be devoured or subjugated. And on another level, the meat for the caged animal (a male) can also be a sign that the male is not allowed to acknowledge the woman caged within him.

Other inside and outside voices struggle against each other throughout this movie and the novel. The movie is no longer an empty-headed pastime. Nor does it belong only in the realm of the dominant culture; alternative interpretations begin to present themselves. Just as the panther at the zoo is caged, the cat woman is "wrapped up inside herself, lost in that world she carries inside her, that she's just beginning to discover" (4). We see the meat as the official discourse of society, and the readers and Valentin begin to identify with both the trapped woman and the caged animal. Now none of us scoffs as we once did.

Valentin's sexism begins to waver as we watch his consciousness develop during the telling of the films. At first, Valentin refers to the cat woman as a "real piece" (5), and he asks if an architect's assistant is a "dog" (6). But the movie plots start to work on Valentin's consciousness until he succeeds in grabbing hold of that tangled ball of yarn and unknots it. His eventual epiphany regarding his definition of what it means to be a man could not have occurred to the same person who earlier had equated women to a "piece" or a "dog." A new consciousness is developing in the character of Valentin, and it develops, in part, in response to movie plots aimed at maintaining the dominant role of men over women. The very attempt at denying a voice to women only emphasizes it. Finally, Valentin hesitatingly offers the following definition of a man:

> "Mmm . . . his not taking any crap . . . from anyone, not even the powers that be. . . . But no, it's more than that. Not taking any crap is one thing, but not the most important. What really makes a man is a lot more, it has to do with not humiliating someone else with an order, or a tip. Even more, it's . . . not letting the person next to you feel degraded, feel bad." (63)

The movie, which reflects the dominant voices of society regarding gender relations, had informed Molina's perception of reality. Now the same movie is affecting Valentin's perceptions in a different way, however, because he has to color in the details himself from Molina's account of the movie. The readers get the movie filtered not only through Molina but through Valentin as well, and within the context of the stark empty cell. Ironically, the more distance we have from the original showing, the more we are able to see the carnivalesque double-voicedness of the movie close-up. The caged animal looms large as society's selection and organization of order and normalcy. But what society portrays as reasonable repression of madness, we begin to see as mad repression of reasonableness.

Molina does not change as much as Valentin, possibly because he is contaminated by the first showing. When he discusses why he wants to be a woman he tells Valentin it is "because I know what the score is myself and I've got it all clear in my head." Yet, when Valentin accuses him of half inventing the picture, Molina retorts:

> "No, I'm not inventing. I swear, but some things, to round them out for you, so you can see them the way I'm seeing them . . . well to some extent I have to embroider a little." (18)

This embroidery is also what society does when it attempts to cage us in a romantic web of monologic discourse. Valentin begins to realize that even his political rhetoric has woven a romantic web around him that has caged him as much as any physical cell. The readers see the deception also. We are reminded of William Wordsworth's definition of reality—and Bakhtin's definition of self—as "half perceived and half created." These perceptions are not formed within the confines of the individual psyche but rather where language intersects the self and the other. Robert Stam explains Bakhtin's emphasis on the importance of language to our self-perceptions and self-identities:

> Even when looking within oneself, one looks in and through the eyes of the other; one needs the other's gaze to constitute oneself as self. Even the apparently simple act of looking in the mirror, for Bakhtin, is complexly dialogical, implying an intricate intersection of perspectives and consciousnesses. To look at ourselves in the mirror is to oversee the reflection of our life in the plane of consciousness of others; it is to see and apprehend ourselves through the imagined eyes of our parents, our brothers and sisters, through the supportive look of our friends or the hostile regard of our enemies, as well as through the more abstract panoptical "eyes" of mass-mediated culture, with its implicit norms of fashion and acceptable appearance.[10]

As Bakhtin tells us, our concept of self is attained through dialogue with outside influences, but if we choose not to question authority, we give up responsibility for any part in our own authorship and succumb to the will of the dominant culture. This point is never more clear than when we hear Molina tell the plot of a German World War II film that Valentin immediately recognizes as a Nazi propaganda film. Molina had chosen to ignore the politics of the film and tried to appreciate it only for its romantic story of a French singer who falls in love with her German officer/captor, a situation that appeals to Molina's notion of woman as martyr. The French woman joins the German cause but falters when she overhears her lover impose the death penalty on a French Jew. To convince his lover that his action was warranted, the German officer shows her a propaganda film that depicts the condemned man as a monster. The French woman then becomes even more determined to embrace her German captor because she has supposedly seen the truth. The fallacy that one propaganda film can defend the action in another propaganda film seems lost on Molina, who swallows the ruse too.

All the movie plot tellings are repeatedly interrupted by the realization of prison, so that what was once familiar to Molina within the context of a so-called free society becomes unfamiliar within the prison setting. Ironically, whereas Molina was imprisoned by the monologic discourse of the movies when he was on the outside, Valentin, aided by a confusion that is further exacerbated by physical sickness and its accompanying disorientation, begins to build with these movies a freeing consciousness within the confines of the physical prison. He, at least, begins to understand that only when we interact in a dialogic manner with the heteroglossia of society can we develop a healthy consciousness.

Valentin's new awareness is not limited to the kitsch that Molina is so fond of. He also recognizes that the intellectual and political rhetoric he consumed on the outside in the hopes of freeing society also is representative of another dominant view aimed at conformity and stasis. He never gives his politics up, but he acknowledges its subjectivity so that he is free once again to love his former lover, Marta, a bourgeois, though he knows he will probably never see her again. Increased capacity to love is the result of releasing caged minds—both for Valentin and for the readers.

Kiss readers are especially challenged when they come upon footnotes in Puig's novel. People who might immediately see through the fallacy of propaganda films often exhibit an unquestioning attitude toward footnotes and other academic language. Their presence lends most texts an air of authority and documentation. Yet the use of footnotes in a novel is carnivalesque, and we notice a similar defamiliarization and carnivalization occurring in them as in the B movies.

The footnotes report on the scientific and nonscientific causes of the "deviant" behavior of homosexuality in an official-sounding textbook-like voice, giving them a factual ring. Their juxtaposition within a fictional novel with a "real" homosexual character, however, compounds the carnivalesqueness of the footnotes, which encourages us to laugh at them at first. Why study footnotes about homosexuals, like specimens in a lab, when the real character is in front of us on the pages of the novel?

One footnote entry, which goes on for two pages of small print, reports on the findings and theories of such known and unknown authorities as J. L. Simmons, J. C. Flugel, Freud, Marcuse, Dennis Altman, and Theodore Rozak. The reader is confused and struggles to relate the comments not only to each other, but also within the context of the novel. The context offers no help, however. The asterisk for this footnote refers the reader back to a conversation between Molina and Valentin, but the asterisk is placed at Molina's turn at the dialogue, which is marked by an ellipsis indicating that he is silent.

We can't dismiss the footnotes altogether, if only because they seem to make about as much sense as anything else in the novel when taken out of context. We can easily agree with Francine R. Masiello who says that "language emerges as the central protagonist" in *Kiss of the Spider Woman.*[11] Power resides within the context of the discourse as much as in its content. We are being asked to question how we come to form our selves; we are being asked to take another look at heteroglossia—the language of life—and decide what makes us accept some of it and deny the rest.

At the same time we begin to sense the influence individuals can wield in order to change society. Change, flux, becoming—this is the sought-after goal of dialogue. Bakhtin maintained that just as individuals need society as a reference point for their own identity, society also needs the individual—the other—before it can form its collective stand. Meaning emerges through dialogue between society and the other, and meaning should never be static. As Katerina Clark and Michael Holquist explain, "Dialogism . . . celebrates alterity. . . . As the world needs my alterity to give it meaning, I need the authority of others to define, or author, my self."[12]

Puig's characters begin the novel not only in a real physical prison but in one made of the language of the dominant culture. Only Valentin is able to break out of the prison within him by releasing the woman caged deep within his psyche. Like the zombie in one of Molina's movies, he finally ceases to be "a pawn of someone else's perversity" (212). Molina seems to maintain his repressed notions about what constitutes proper gender roles, but his presence serves as a vehicle for truth for Valentin and a reminder of the importance of dialogue. In this respect Molina becomes the martyr he always wanted to be. In addition, Molina's insistence on being someone else's pawn leads to his "real" martyrdom at the end of the novel.

Puig's readers can hear the voices of people imprisoned by their social language that defines gender relations, and, more important, they can begin to change that language. As Bauer contends:

> Language is not merely a prison house; it does not only cage human potential (although it does that, too), but also produces eruptions of force which do not always follow the norms or conventions that language

> commands. The very language which restricts human intercourse produces occasions for its own disruption and critique.[13]

As Valentin's consciousness changes, the footnotes, too, become more accepting of homosexuality, no longer referring to it as a deviant lifestyle; and finally they seem to call our attention to bisexuality. Here, we become more aware of the presence of the author, especially if we know that Puig himself was bisexual. The emphasis is not aimed at getting the reader to accept or reject any particular belief, however; indeed, that would run counter to Puig's message that no official discourse is unified, reasonable, or official, though it may seem so within the context it is presented. Therefore, we must look to create a dialogue between ourselves and the heteroglossia of society in order to separate the reasonable from the mad. In this way, we learn to partake in a celebration of possibilities.

Here, too, Halasek's caution that we should read against the grain, or as internally persuasive readers, allows us to empower our own values and language rather than the authority of either the official discourse of the footnotes or Puig's authority as the author. In fact, in an interview before his death Puig insisted his motivation for the footnotes was merely educational. He was concerned that his Latin American audience was not properly informed about homosexual matters; therefore, he added the footnotes because they offered what he assumed was an objective account of ideas about the subject. Apparently, if we are to believe him, he had no intention of confusing readers or of parodying the convention of footnotes but merely included them as a public service. Yet the realization that footnotes are accorded value merely by convention must occur to many readers as we encounter them in this parodied position. By extension, then, we can question other language genres as well.

The police who follow Molina after his release from prison write the last such genre of the novel in the form of the "observation" notes, detailing the activities of the newly released Molina. Their so-called objective descriptions of the "subject," devoid of all resemblance to the "real" Molina we have come to know, speak volumes about the importance of context in language, as well as the significance of dialogue in order to know another. Mere empirical observation notes don't capture the true self, the one developed through dialogue and interaction with other beings.

As a dialogic reading of Puig's novel demonstrates, Bakhtin has made remarkable contributions to critical, literary, and linguistic theory. And to that list we may confidently add feminist theory. Bakhtin is not just another dead white guy because he failed to consciously include gender among the many kinds of language genres. As the works of Booth, Boschetto, Halasek, Herndl, Kristeva, and others already attest, we can extend dialogism to include feminist critiques by appropriating the languages of others and making them our own, allowing us to read internally persuasively rather than authoritatively, and allowing for a plurality of feminisms instead of one. Furthermore, we can do it without apologizing for Bakhtin or making excuses for him. His theories allow for such development of divergent selves if we seek meaning at the ever-changing borders of language and context.

Notes

1. Kay Halasek, "Feminism and Bakhtin: Dialogic Reading in the Academy," 66.
2. M. M. Bakhtin, *The Dialogic Imagination*, 292.
3. Diane Price Herndl, "The Dilemmas of a Feminine Dialogic," *Feminism, Bakhtin, and the Dialogic*, 20.
4. Dale M. Bauer, *Feminist Dialogics: A Theory of Failed Community*, xvii.
5. See Tzvetan Todorov, *Mikhail Bakhtin: The Dialogical Principle*, 96.
6. Bauer, *Feminist Dialogics*, 13.
7. Gustavo Pellon, "Manuel Puig's Contradictory Strategy: Kitsch Paradigms Versus Paradigmatic Structure in *El beso de la mujer arana* and *Publis Angelical*," 186, 193.
8. David Patterson, *Literature and Spirit: Essays on Bakhtin and His Contemporaries*, 25.
9. Manuel Puig, *Kiss of the Spider Woman*, 37. Quotations from this work will be cited by page number in the text.
10. Robert Stam, *Subversive Pleasures: Bakhtin, Cultural Criticism, and Film*, 5.
11. Francine R. Masiello, "Jail House Flicks: Projections by Manuel Puig," 23.
12. Katerina Clark and Michael Holquist, *Mikhail Bakhtin*, 65.
13. Bauer, *Feminist Dialogics*, xiii.

Bibliography

Bakhtin, M. M. *The Dialogic Imagination: Four Essays by M. M. Bakhtin*, ed. Michael Holquist, trans. Caryl Emerson and Michael Holquist. Austin: University of Texas Press, 1981.

Bauer, Dale M. *Feminist Dialogics: A Theory of Failed Community*. Albany: State University of New York Press, 1988.

Booth, Wayne. "Freedom of Interpretation: Bakhtin and the Challenge of Feminist Criticism." *Critical Inquiry* 9 (1982): 45-76.

Boschetto, Sandra M. "Female Scripts and Intertextual Traces in Manuel Puig's *Eternal Curse on the Reader of These Pages*." *LCHLL* (1986): 73-85.

Clark, Katerina, and Michael Holquist. *Mikhail Bakhtin*. Cambridge, Mass.: Harvard University Press, 1984.

Foster, David William. *Alternate Voices in the Contemporary Latin American Narrative*. Columbia: University of Missouri Press, 1985.

Foucault, Michel. "The Order of Discourse." In *Untying the Text: A Post-Structuralist Anthology*, ed. R. Young. New York: Routledge, 1981. 221-33.

Halasek, Kay. "Feminism and Bakhtin: Dialogic Reading in the Academy." *Rhetoric Society Quarterly* 22 (Winter 1992): 63-75.

Herndl, Diane Price. "The Dilemmas of a Feminine Dialogic." In *Feminism, Bakhtin, and the Dialogic*, ed. Dale M. Bauer and Susan Jaret McKinstry. Albany: State University of New York Press, 1991. 7-24.

Kristeva, Julia. "Word, Dialogue, and Novel." In *The Kristeva Reader*, ed. Toril Moi, trans. Alice Jardine, Thomas Gora, and Leon S. Roudiez. New York: Columbia University Press, 1986. 34-61.

Kundera, Milan. *The Unbearable Lightness of Being*, trans. Michael Henry Heim. New York: Harper & Row, 1984.

La Capra, Dominick. *Rethinking Intellectual History: Texts, Contexts, Language*. Ithaca, N.Y.: Cornell University Press, 1983.

Masiello, Francine R. "Jail House Flicks: Projections by Manuel Puig." *Symposium* 32 (Spring 1978): 15-24.

Patterson, David. *Literature and Spirit: Essays on Bakhtin and His Contemporaries*. Lexington: University of Kentucky Press, 1985.

Pellon, Gustavo. "Manuel Puig's Contradictory Strategy: Kitsch Paradigms Versus Paradigmatic Structure in *El beso de la mujer arana* and *Publis Angelical*." *Symposium* 37 (Fall 1983): 186-201.

Puig, Manuel. *Kiss of the Spider Woman*, trans. Thomas Colche. New York: Vintage, 1979.

Stam, Robert. *Subversive Pleasures: Bakhtin, Cultural Criticism, and Film*. Baltimore: Johns Hopkins University Press, 1989.

Todorov, Tzvetan. *Mikhail Bakhtin: The Dialogical Principle*, trans. Wlad Godzich. Minneapolis: University of Minnesota Press, 1984.

The Ideological Intervention of Ambiguities in the Marriage Plot: Who Fails Marianne in Austen's *Sense and Sensibility*?

Julie A. Shaffer

Since the novel's original publication in 1811, those writing about *Sense and Sensibility* have agreed that the work is thorough in its attacks on the target of its criticism, and, although opinions have differed on what the target of the novel's indictment might be, critics for the past forty years or so by and large agree in one respect: the novel's indictments of its target are undermined by the novel's retaining the appeal of one of its heroines, Marianne, and of the approach to life she embraces. Such readings are limited, I would argue, not so much because of what each identifies as the target of the novel's attacks, but rather because the critical assumptions informing these readings insist on treating the ambiguity of the retained appeal of Marianne and her early views of life as undermining the project of the book as a whole. Recuperating the ambiguous attachment to Marianne and her way of life as meaningful to the novel's overall project must prove more satisfying, and, as I argue, uniting the interests of feminist criticism with a Bakhtinian view of novels as dialogic discourse makes such a recuperation possible. Before offering such an approach, I will outline the two major positions that critical thought on *Sense and Sensibility* has taken recently, as my discussion will to a great extent progress in dialogue with this discourse surrounding the novel.

The more traditional approach has viewed the novel as offering sense and sensibility as competing approaches to life and as teaching readers that it is better to embrace sense—or, rather, to temper sensibility with sense, to control and restrain strong feeling by a judicious recognition that indulging and revealing the emotions is harmful, especially for females.[1] This approach treats the novel as a satire of Marianne, its misguided proponent of sensibility, and by extension, of women who embrace the tenets of sensibility along with the view of romantic love it provides and so mislead themselves about the actual conditions of the world. The ambiguities that undermine the target of the novel's attacks so identified stem from the novel's apparent ambivalence toward its moral lesson. While clearly showing Marianne to be wrong to be guided by sensibility in a world in which those who grant primacy to the emotions suffer from doing so, Austen makes the misguided Marianne sympathetic, her stress on the emotions appealing.[2] As a result, by the novel's conclusion, when Marianne has become self-chastened and less emotionally demonstrative and has been granted the reserved, older, flannel-waistcoated Brandon as a husband rather than the flamboyantly attractive Willoughby, it has been easy to conclude that Marianne, like Milton's Satan, has perhaps been made more engaging than Austen wished so that the only way she could make the story's point is to betray the sympathy for Marianne that she has all too successfully elicited.[3]

Feminist readings, the other recent main critical trend on this novel, focus not on the text's critique of Marianne and her sensibility, but on its critique of the patriarchal society in which the two heroines live; such readings, too, however, have argued that ambiguities in the text undermine the text's proto-feminist project. Mary Poovey, for instance, argues that much of the novel indicts conditions that leave women like Marianne and Elinor dependent and powerless but that the novel's concluding with their weddings weakens its critique of the patriarchal power structure it depicts. She explains that this conclusion retains and recuperates fantasies offering romantic love as a consolation to women for their powerless position, embraceable because it is represented as outside or beyond ideology, rather than part of that very ideology that leaves them powerless. The problem is that the fantasy of "romantic relationships [of the kind that sensibility's marriage plot promises] . . . cannot provide women with more than the kind of temporary and imaginative consolation that serves to defuse criticism of the very institutions that make such consolation necessary" (Poovey, 237). The recuperation of romantic love in the novel's closure, that is, weakens the work's otherwise wide-ranging ideological critique of patriarchal society; it feeds fantasies that defuse the more useful reactions Poovey sees the text as encouraging toward institutions that leave women in need of consolation. Her argument thus suggests that any ideological critique of patriarchal society that appears within the marriage plot will be undermined precisely by the form in which it is couched, a conclusion shared by other critics of the marriage plot, who have found that form by its very nature inimicable to projects designed to launch such a critique.[4]

For many reasons, recuperating the ambiguous attachment to Marianne and sensibility's approach to life might be more satisfying than decrying it as harmful to the book as a whole. Assuming that retaining that appeal was unintentional requires one to conclude that the ambiguities stem from a failure on Austen's part. Readings not assuming such authorial lack of control, however, seem more useful. Treating the romance plot as of necessity undermining any critique of patriarchy seems a little more satisfying; here, at least, the fault in the ideological project gets identified as lying with the form, rather than with the author. All the same, dismissing this whole plot form as useless for feminist critique is problematic. Given that women writers throughout much of the eighteenth and nineteenth centuries have been understood to have been by and large constrained to use the marriage plot form, arraigning that form as useless implies that these writers had no means within fiction to signal their critical stance toward the reigning ideology. As I have argued elsewhere, such a conclusion is overly dismissive of the critiques of patriarchal ideology that are provided within the marriage plot form and successfully evident.[5]

A model of interpretation capable of viewing ambiguities as serving the meaning of a novel might not only provide a more satisfying reading of this particular novel than those seeing it as self-undermining but might also lead to understanding the way that (proto-)feminist messages *have* successfully been couched within the marriage plot. Developing such readings would require new ways of reading satire, parody, and other literary genres capable of criticizing their target, however that target be identified. Conventional readings of such genres require privileging the voice or norms informing the critical impulse over whatever has been included as its target, after all—such readings seem invited by any desire to identify stability in the critique. The limitations of this kind of reading are highlighted by the case of *Sense and Sensibility*; regardless of what one identifies as the privileged norm and as the target of the critique in this novel, stability is undermined by the retained appeal of sensibility and its romantic marriage plot.

A better mode of reading *Sense and Sensibility*, at least, would avoid privileging one term over another so as to remain better able to deal with the ambiguities that arise from the retained appeal of sensibility and what it has to offer. A mode of reading refusing to privilege one term over the other should, by extension, also prove useful for reading other novels of a satiric or critical impulse, especially those in which ambivalence seems to undermine the hegemony of the norm by which these novels' critique can be performed.

Bakhtin's definition of novelistic discourse, most thoroughly elaborated in the essays comprising *The Dialogic Imagination*, provides a means toward that mode of reading, one that makes it possible to recognize the multidimensional thrust of the criticism in Austen's text and others similarly unstable in their critique.[6] Bakhtinian theory on the dialogic nature of novelistic discourse enables readings that recognize the propriety of ambiguities in novels because the theory treats such ambiguities, or lack of stability of privileged terms, as central to what makes the discourse of a novel dialogic—or *novelistic*, a term that Bakhtin uses interchangeably with "dialogic." As Bakhtin argues, novels are made up of different languages, each ideologically saturated and conveying the ideology—worldview, or "idea-system"[7]—of a particular speaking person, the speaking person itself viewed as ideologically rather than psychologically constituted and motivated. Rather than conveying one ideology or worldview at the expense of others, what Bakhtin identifies as true novels bring ideologically saturated languages into dialogic contact with one another.[8] Although some ideologies are treated as ideology-free "truth" or "reality" outside novels, the dialogic contacts that occur between languages by means of novelistic discourse turn languages into *images* of languages that allow all ideologies to become relativized, reified, so that all can be held up for examination and exposed as ideology. These dialogic confrontations thus make it possible to question the value of ideologies elsewhere granted an unquestioned authority.

The usefulness of Bakhtinian theory for dealing with the ambiguities in *Sense and Sensibility* becomes clear as soon as one recognizes that sense and sensibility in Austen's novel, comprising opposing worldviews as they do, represent ideologically saturated languages, in the Bakhtinian sense of the word, of the sort capable of entering into a dialogic relationship. Rather than reading for a stable direction in the novel's critique, one that privileges one term over the other, intervening in conventional readings by way of Bakhtinian theory then makes it possible to see the thrust of the novel's critique as bidirectional, as ideologically reifying both sense and sensibility, and as thereby questioning the value of embracing either term and the worldview or ideology these terms represent as "natural," or as giving the best means of approaching the social, economic, and emotional conditions that get termed "reality" and so treated as unassailable and unchangeable.

Such a reading will enable us to see that because the novel does retain the appeal of sensibility—because Marianne, when emotionally engaged, remains so sympathetic—the critique in this novel becomes double-edged: it not only reveals the limitations in Marianne's approach to the world but also suggests that there are limitations to the world with which Marianne is left after giving up her illusions. In *Sense and Sensibility*, the most obvious target of deauthorization has been Marianne's sensibility, but as Bakhtin's theory of the dialogic nature of novelistic discourse makes clear, every language drawn into the discourse of a novel gets confronted and challenged by all other languages involved: every language, with its underlying ideology, thereby becomes relativized. The bidirectional critique not only reveals Marianne, with her "excess of sensibility,"[9] to be misguided, but, by retaining the appeal of that sensibility and so questioning the value of consensual reality, it also destabilizes the grounds upon which the authority of *that* version of reality is based, suggesting that it too is an ideological construct like any other. By bringing the sisters' differing versions of the world into dialogic contact in a way that foregrounds the limitations of both, the destabilizing critique in this novel enacts a battle between the conflicting ideological constructs or competing versions of social experience offered within the novel.[10] Recognizing the heroines' approaches as dialogically illuminating the ideological basis of each thus allows a reading that sees the ambiguities in the text's treatment of sensibility as central, rather than detrimental, to the novel's critique of the characters' approaches to those conditions of the world that both characters and readers encounter.

Because this novel so clearly focuses on problems for women inherent in the patriarchal society represented, and because it does so within the framework of a plot form generally considered to disable feminist critiques of the dominant ideology, to avoid addressing these issues deriving from a variety of interests in feminist theory would require neglecting much of what both informs this text and makes it problematic. Bringing the questions raised by feminist criticism together with Bakhtinian theory enables a reading that focuses on the marriage plot within which the dialogic nature of this novel is framed to recognize that the romance or marriage plot of sensibility itself becomes as involved in the novel's project of ideological foregrounding as are all other languages or worldviews in the text, rather than being destructive of the text's project of ideological interrogation or outside it altogether. Bringing feminist interests to bear on a Bakhtinian approach to this novel thus provides a means for understanding the ways in which formulating critiques of patriarchal or other oppressive ideologies within the marriage plot structure need not be seen as compromising that critique. Combining feminist and Bakhtinian theory will allow us to see that in *Sense and Sensibility*, closure in the conventional conclusion of romance plots of sensibility—the heroines' marriages—is vital to the ideological project that works itself out through the novel's bidirectional critique of the heroines' differing approaches to their world and their marriage plots, an ideological project that includes a critique not only of romance plots and what they have to offer, but of the dominant ideology as well.

Given the centrality of the romance plot as a principal voice in the dialogics of *Sense and Sensibility*, my discussion of necessity concentrates on this plot and on the approach to the conditions of the world for which it argues as though in response to other potential participants in dialogue. The ideology most readily embraced by sense—the dominant ideology, as it is represented in the text—constitutes another principal voice in the dialogic discourse of this novel; because the text indicts this ideology and because these indictments provide part of the context against which the language of sensibility and its romance plot speak, before I address what sensibility and its romance plot have to say, I first outline those indictments of the ideology against which it sounds. In doing so, I concentrate specifically on the text's critique of the conditions for women inherent in this ideology; progressing as it does through its heroines' marriage plots, all indictments of the dominant ideology (and of sensibility as well) are, after all, refracted through an attention to the heroines in their movement toward marriage. As a result of this focus within the novel, its exploration of the limitations of the dominant ideology becomes a focus on the effect the dominant ideology has on women—young marriageable women especially. I demonstrate, then, that through its heroines' marriage plots the novel uses its ambiguities to construct an intervention into, or disruption of, a naturalization of an ideology that leaves women, in particular, disadvantaged.

Readers have long noted that the novel indicts characters like John and Fanny Dashwood for their selfish greed and Willoughby for his conventional rakish villainy, but what has remained less obvious is the novel's indictment of the system that both sanctions the attitudes and behaviors of the Willoughbys and John Dashwoods of this world and leaves women like Elinor and Marianne dependent on such people for their welfare and happiness. In fact, the novel reveals forcefully that while the patrilineal, patriarchal basis of this society places men in positions both of power and responsibility and leaves women in many ways dependent on men for their welfare, that society allows and even countenances betrayals of the women it should protect. Claudia Johnson's recent treatment of the novel explains clearly the ways in which the novel does indict this society, and, although she does not then focus on the ways the novel's treatment of sensibility enhances this indictment, her argument is worth summarizing here.

Johnson argues that by revealing the ways that society accepts flaws in those in power, *Sense and Sensibility* "assails the dominant ideology of its time."[11] She explains that "property, marriage, family"—the institutions that maintain the structure of society—give John and Fanny Dashwood,

Willoughby, and Edward Ferrars power. By virtue of their "supposed . . . benevolizing" effects—effects that justify their position in the patriarchal system—these institutions should inspire those in power to protect others' welfare, but, as the novel demonstrates, they "actually enforce avarice, shiftlessness" (49). As property owners and family, John and Fanny should provide for the nearly entirely dispossessed Dashwoods but instead virtually abandon them, using as an excuse their concern for their immediate family: providing for these women in accordance with John's father's dying wishes would be robbing their son. And as almost-certain heirs to estates, Willoughby and Edward should be developing qualities that will enable them to fulfill the responsibilities of heads of estates, but instead they are left idle, free to court women they have no intention of marrying, with little concern about the repercussions for anyone but themselves.[12] As Johnson explains, such faults "are described as the effects of established and accepted social practices for men of family, not as aberrations from them" (58)—as accepted elements of the dominant ideology, that is, the "reality" to which Marianne needs to adjust.

If the novel shows that society leaves women like Mrs. Dashwood and her daughters at the mercy rather than under the protection of men like John Dashwood, Willoughby, and Edward Ferrars, it does so in part to underline their powerlessness. The novel makes it clear that because Elinor and Marianne are poor and neither protected nor supported by extended family, they, like the second Eliza, are in many ways defenseless against men like Willoughby. High social status or fortune would render them less dependent, more powerful, in the way that some single women in the novel are—Mrs. Ferrars and Willoughby's aunt, for instance (Johnson, 70). Because it revolves around its heroines' marriage plots, the novel suggests that the best mode by which women such as Elinor and Marianne can improve their lot when they lack fortune, status, and the protection of the wealthier members of their family is through marriage, which at least can place women in a position of relative safety, and perhaps power, at least while the husband lives, and if they remain faithful.[13] But the same circumstances that render women dependent and hence in need of the relative power and protection that marriage can bring makes it difficult for them to form good marriages—marriages capable of leaving them economically secure, at least.

Such is particularly obvious in Marianne's and Elinor's cases. Their actual marital expectations should be no better than those of any women in that era with no fortune or aristocratic name to increase her appeal in a highly competitive marriage market.[14] The novel's early narration of the Dashwoods' reversal of fortune, along with Fanny and John's insistence that Edward cannot marry Elinor because she has neither fortune nor rank, stress the Dashwood sisters' low appeal on the marriage market. Their dispositions and physical attractiveness draw men like Edward and Willoughby but cannot break down the barriers that make the women unacceptable as daughters-in-law to people like Mrs. Ferrars or as wives to men like Willoughby. And as John Dashwood makes clear, the sisters' chances of marrying men of fortune decrease once they start to lose their looks. After Marianne's illness has caused her to lose her "bloom," John Dashwood questions "whether [she] *now*, will marry a man worth more than five or six hundred a-year" (227; emphasis in the original).

Even were the sisters' chances on the marriage market good, John Dashwood's characterization of this market implies that women are valued in this society primarily as ornaments and bearers of fortune and status rather than for intrinsic qualities of personality. His views make clear that on this market, female beauty is a commodity that brings a predictable price. So too are the rank and fortune that women bear; Elinor's, according to John and Fanny Dashwood and Mrs. Ferrars, are inadequate exchanges for a husband of Edward Ferrars's rank. In "realistic" terms, disposition and even moral uprightness in women have little bearing compared to rank and fortune: Mrs. Ferrars finds both Lucy Steele and Elinor equally objectionable as daughters-in-law because of their poverty and low social standing; she is unable to differentiate between them in terms of moral worth.[15]

By providing the stories of women betrayed by those in positions of power and by revealing that their society values women more for the wealth and position they bring than for their innate virtues, *Sense and Sensibility* demonstrates why women such as Elinor and Marianne might be dissatisfied with the conditions of the world that comprise "reality" within this novel. And at the same time that it shows this version of reality to be inadequate for women, the novel develops the appeal of sensibility by suggesting that it imaginatively satisfies precisely those needs that reality does not meet. Because the novel progresses primarily through its heroines' marriage plots, it develops the appeal of sensibility and the limitations of reality through the different way that each ideology treats marriage-directed heterosexual relationships. Moving by the conventions of sensibility but unsuccessful, Marianne's marriage plot should underline the limitations of sensibility. Moving by a recognition of the contingencies of reality as it is represented in this book and successful, Elinor's marriage plot should convince readers that recognizing reality and accommodating oneself to it honorably can lead to happiness in ways that Marianne's approach cannot.[16] Marianne's failed marriage plot remains more attractive than Elinor's despite its failure, however, which suggests that sensibility offers women something that reality cannot, despite sensibility's being, finally, unrealistic, as critics have pointed out in their identification of the novel's ambiguities.[17]

Reasons why Marianne and Willoughby's relationship remains appealing are not hard to identify, given an understanding of the conditions of Marianne's world, for which her relationship with Willoughby offers compensatory fantasies. It is, in fact, the depiction of the conditions of that world that provides the dialogizing context within the novel, one that makes the appeal of Marianne's fantasies so apparent. In this, the conditions of that world operate similarly to a foil, except that foils are not bidirectional; they operate statically, without entering into the dialogic interaction that occurs as different languages within a text interanimate and thereby allow for an ideological critique of one another, as is the case in the relationship between the depiction of Marianne's world unadorned by the fantasies of sensibility on the one hand, and, on the other, the fantasies in which Marianne prefers to dwell.

The relationship between Marianne and Willoughby garners and retains appeal, then, because Willoughby is personally attractive, more than any other man in the book. The Dashwoods first meet him when he carries the injured Marianne home, and while Mrs. Dashwood is grateful to him for helping her daughter, it is clear that "the influence of [Willoughby's] youth, beauty, and elegance" adds to her feelings for him. His "uncommon handsome[ness]" along with his "manly beauty and more than common gracefulness" (42) are rendered more appealing by comparison to the lesser attractions of the other men in the novel, men who mobilize the language, or set of assumptions—the approach to the world—against which sensibility responds. Of Edward, Elinor says, "His person can hardly be called handsome, till the expression of his eyes, . . . and the general sweetness of his countenance, is perceived. At present, I know him so well, that I think him really handsome; or at least, almost so" (20). Others have been harsher, calling Edward "an unpleasant shadow," "spineless," and chronically depressed.[18] Brandon hardly fares better, getting called a "vacuum" and "depressing."[19] Against the listlessness and average looks of the other male characters in the novel that fit into and represent the world of sense, Willoughby's appeal and the appeal of what he comes to represent only increase.

Although I am loathe to downplay the very real appeal of Willoughby's beauty and grace, as doing so would downplay this novel's affirmation (here at least) of women's desire for sexually attractive mates, Willoughby's physicality satisfies only part of the appeal of Marianne's relationship with him. Much of the rest derives from other sorts of fantasies it validates and satisfies—fantasies of escape from the problematic details of most people's lives as they are impinged upon by what gets represented in this novel as reality. Comprised as Marianne and Willoughby's relationship is of their attentiveness to one another only, this relationship suggests that love relationships can be so all-consuming that attention to the rest of the world is unnecessary. The fantasy of an all-absorbing passion is especially appealing when an attention to the world entails an attention to one's very limited expectations in that world, such as are Marianne's. It is true that Brandon has been presented as a potential suitor for Marianne throughout the novel, and this undercuts John Dashwood's stress on the hopelessness of her marital expectations; the willingness of the even more appealing Willoughby to enter into a public relationship with her, however, argues that a woman like Marianne, if lively and attractive enough, need not heed the bothersome concerns that control the lives of most women. Marianne and Willoughby's relationship acts out a fantasy in which passion is so strong that, beside it, problematic details of life fade into unimportance.

This element of the relationship's appeal is related to another fantasy seemingly substantiated by the passionate love Willoughby holds for Marianne, a fantasy granting personal power and value to individuals normally most powerless and most devalued—women not financially independent. For a man as physically, financially, and socially attractive as Willoughby to be as attentive as he is to a portionless woman like Marianne suggests that, despite evidence to the contrary, even a fairly poor woman such as Marianne has power over her situation, simply because her personal attributes make her desirable: she can attract the love of a man who will marry her and thereby improve her status. Furthermore, the fantasy of a man like Willoughby loving a woman like Marianne attentively, simply for who she is, validates her need both to be loved and to be treated as important for her own sake.[20] Willoughby's loving her with a devotion that ignores the rest of the world in the way that he seems to while in Barton at least provides a fantasy that there are men who can recognize women to be so worthwhile in and of themselves that they need nothing besides a woman's own, dear self—and her love—to bring them happiness. It is an ego-bolstering fantasy bound to appeal to women in a society in which people like John Dashwood and Mrs. Ferrars treat them so differently.

The appeal of this relationship also stems from one other fiction of personal power it presents as possible: it treats the plot lines of lovers' relationships as though lovers are the controlling center of the story of which they are hero and heroine, thereby granting great power to the lovers themselves. Marianne and Willoughby frequently ignore social propriety, as though they think that they alone control the outcome of their relationship. They act so in going to Allenham alone together to see property that is not yet Willoughby's, not recognizing that doing so could compromise either's situation: Marianne could lose her reputation for purity, and Willoughby could, one assumes, lose his inheritance were his aunt to discover this episode and disapprove. Their apparent belief that others' opinions cannot affect them, along with their relative socioeconomic positions, makes their relationship resemble much heroine-centered sentimental fiction of the era, fiction organized around the motif of the Cinderella story—a story that ultimately empowers lovers, female lovers especially, and that can therefore be seen as just as dialogically responsive to ideologies that leave female lovers unempowered as are Marianne's own fantasies of sensibility.[21]

The Cinderella story, especially as it appears in its eighteenth-century novelistic form, can be summarized as follows: Man from upper classes and/or a wealthy family falls in love with a woman either with no money or of a lower social status—a woman who has only her personal attributes to recommend her. The lovers' adherence to their love for one another ultimately prevails, causing any obstacles that have arisen to give way before it. Finally, the male protagonist's refusal to give up his beloved makes those who object to the match reconsider and realize that despite the heroine's low social and/or economic status, she is so valuable in and of herself that they should welcome her marriage to the male protagonist.[22] This trajectory, then, suggests that lovers with sensibility, armed only with a steadfast love for one another, will be empowered by the virtues of their sensibility to prevail against any obstacles to their happiness.

Willoughby's being heir to wealth and position along with Marianne's fall from such a position into poverty makes the two resemble the protagonists of the Cinderella story, which invites the reader to believe their story will follow the conventional trajectory of such stories, succeeding despite Willoughby's and Marianne's social and economic differences because of the power of lovers and love over the power of economics. Their story shares with Cinderella stories its stress on the value of the emotions, its apparent denial of the importance or power of the social and economic differences between the lovers—obstacles that conventional Cinderella stories address, even if only to deny them as important in relationships between people of sensibility, the people posited by these stories as the most admirable.

Although Marianne and Willoughby's relationship grows in appeal once it enters into dialogue with the language of reality, in which Marianne's worth is left unrecognized and she is left disempowered, *Sense and Sensibility* clearly demonstrates that Marianne is foolish to be seduced either by Willoughby's beauty, gracefulness, and attentiveness or by the appeal of romance with him because the worldview such a seduction entails is at odds with and powerless before the majority ideology, the consensual views of proper modes of human interaction and appropriate views of women. While Marianne adheres to the fantasies made available by sensibility, she remains "internally persuaded," as Bakhtin would say, of the value and viability of sensibility's view of the world; as long as she remains so, however, she is unable to recognize that this sense of the world is not internally persuasive for others, especially against the authority of the view of the world and of human relations to which others lend their ideological ear, so to speak.

For Marianne to lose her heart to Willoughby, then, is for her to believe, unrealistically, that the ideology of sensibility is internally persuasive enough for others that it *can* win out over their worldly concerns; it is to deny Willoughby's connection with the more authoritative consensual view of the world that causes him to need money to remain good-humored; and it is to be too naive to realize that no matter how worthwhile she is as defined by the language of sensibility, Willoughby may want to support his life-style more than he will want to enter her view of affairs and sacrifice his worldly comforts to marry a woman in her financial situation. For Marianne to believe in the possibility of the relationship allows her to dwell in self-bolstering fantasies, but Willoughby's subsequent actions prove that believing the relationship can follow the model promised by the discourse of the romance fiction of sensibility is, finally, to embrace a minority view of the world not adequately persuasive to those capable of gaining from the normative view of human interaction. And as the novel shows, for her to lose her heart to Willoughby is not only to be unrealistic; doing so also means leaving herself open both to heartbreak and illness and to the potential for the kind of scandal and tragedy suffered by the two Elizas.

Those very elements of Marianne's life that make her approach to her relationship with Willoughby unrealistic, however, ultimately also strengthen its appeal. Marianne's beliefs about her relationship with Willoughby are unrealistic, but they are so precisely in a way that compensates for the inadequacies of the reality that her behavior to Willoughby denies. The conflict between sensibility and reality—the dialogic confrontation between the two—thus indicts this reality by exposing it as so inadequate at meeting women's needs that women like Marianne become drawn to the kinds of consoling fantasies that sensibility provides. The novel suggests further that one of the main problems with this reality is that it is so inadequate at meeting women's needs that it increases the appeal of fantasies that ultimately render women more likely to suffer at the hands of those who in reality do have power—men like Willoughby.

If Marianne's approach to life and relationships is both challenged and rendered more appealing by reality, it is also both challenged and rendered more appealing by Elinor's relationship with Edward, that relationship supposedly moving more realistically because attentive to the contingencies of the material conditions of the world in which the heroines dwell. Elinor and Edward's relationship moves, in fact, as though it is speech with others' responses in mind, speech aware of itself as a participant in a dialogue, what Bakhtin has called "words with a sidelong glance."[23] Such is the nature, as Bakhtin explains, of every novelistic utterance, in which "every word is directed toward an *answer* and cannot escape the profound influence of the answering word that it anticipates" (*DI*, 280). This relationship, then, moves as though it is an utterance in response to, or expecting the response of, Marianne and Willoughby's relationship; it moves in direct opposition to that relationship, and hence in opposition to the romanticized relationships found in the conventional sentimental fiction on which Marianne models her life.[24] As such, Elinor and Edward's courtship works as a dialogic response to Marianne and Willoughby's—one able to aid in revealing the ideology behind each relationship in a way that ultimately shows the appeal of Marianne's approach, even as it treats that approach as unrealistic and misguided. In addition, however, and precisely because it moves in apparent direct response to Marianne's, Elinor's courtship plot loses its ability to claim a better connection with the contingencies of reality, because it becomes, by inclusion in this dialogue, clearly a fictive construct, as much as Marianne's is a fictive construct of that heroine's mind. The fictiveness of this better connection with reality is revealed by its plot's moving so precisely in opposition, in every point, to Marianne's.

While Elinor and Edward's courtship ostensibly offers the book's exemplary relationship, one based on emotions and backed up by a realistic sense of the world, it does not engage interest as successfully as Willoughby and Marianne's, especially because it enters into dialogue with theirs in every particular, as though fantasy were being rebuked by a realism that unwittingly made fantasy all the more appealing. Edward, for instance, is much less appealing than Willoughby, and his physical plainness, comparative or absolute, prevents him from satisfying female desires for attractive mates that are satisfied by fantasies of union with men like Willoughby. He is also unappealingly listless, especially in comparison with Willoughby, which prevents him from satisfying the needs or desires met by fantasies of relationships with men capable of being the energetic lover that Willoughby has been. Edward's listlessness and restraint toward Elinor can of course be explained by his remaining engaged to Lucy Steele throughout most of the story, but, however understandable that restraint may be, it prevents Edward from capturing the interest of female readers who want vicariously to experience the feeling of inspiring the kind of love and devotion that Marianne seems to inspire in Willoughby in the early part of their relationship. Edward remains unappealing too because he is primarily absent from the book except through others' reports of him. Elinor defends Edward as having valuable qualities to Marianne and so to readers as well, but because knowledge of him remains secondhand and because his good qualities are fairly unremarkable, he cannot appear as attractive as the more spirited Willoughby. It is difficult to become caught up in a courtship when one of the main participants remains unengaging because primarily absent.

This courtship also remains unappealing because its plot line revolves around Elinor and Edward's passivity and restraint rather than the kind of passionate interaction that comprises Marianne and Willoughby's early courtship. Elinor and Edward's love story consists of their having to wait, give up hope, and, for most of the book, master their apparently ill-fated love for one another. There is no appropriate action either can take to bring them together as they might were they hero and heroine in a conventional novel of sensibility. Elinor could tell Edward that Lucy is scheming, spiteful, and money hungry, but doing so would hardly help her situation; even if it did not reflect badly on her, it still would not take care of their other obstacle, Mrs. Ferrars.

And Edward can do little more than Elinor. For most of the story he does not know that Lucy is manipulative and malicious, so for him to leave her would make him appear fickle and irresponsible rather than heroic; such an act would reflect as badly on him as Elinor's informing on Lucy would reflect on *her*. Instead, he submits to his misguided commitment to Lucy, a stance that might make him seem admirable if it did not involve his having been duped into thinking her in love with him, which she clearly is not; she easily transfers her "affections" to Edward's brother when Mrs. Ferrars disinherits Edward, after all. He could confront his mother with his love for Elinor, as the hero of a novel of sensibility might, but then Mrs. Ferrars would no doubt cut him off from his inheritance precisely as she does for his saying he will marry Lucy. Even if such an action rendered Edward more appealing to readers, it would not rid the lovers of an obstacle as it might in a conventional novel of sensibility, for Mrs. Ferrars is shown to be influenced more by obsequiousness such as Lucy's than by the power of love. Rather than being able to find a way of acting that befits a passionate hero of a novel of sensibility, Edward remains in the feminized passive position of having to wait and hope that circumstances turn out well—a position as unappealing for men as for women.

Obstacles to Edward and Elinor's union finally do disappear, but neither because the heroine is so heroic, so innately worthwhile that everyone finally recognizes her personal value nor because their love is so powerful that all obstacles bend before it. In the end, they finally are able to marry only because Lucy's sister tells Fanny about Lucy and Edward's secret engagement. This of course precipitates a series of events concluding in Lucy's leaving the disinherited Edward for the now apparently wealthy Robert, which has as a side effect Mrs. Ferrars's realizing that she cannot control her sons. Mrs. Ferrars then simply stops being an obstacle to Elinor and Edward's union. Her doing so is in no way a response to Edward and Elinor, and does not therefore include a recognition of Elinor's innate worth and power as a beloved in the way it might in conventional romanticized courtship plots.

Because the resolution comes about in a way that has very little to do with Edward's heroic qualities or Elinor's worth, their story comes across not as the story of a courtship, but rather as an antilove story, a story accidentally ending in marriage for reasons that have little to do with either of its ostensible protagonists. Even the action that allows for the successful resolution of their love story, Lucy's sister's blurting out the secret of Lucy and Edward's engagement, is centered elsewhere. Elinor and Edward ultimately appear to be minor characters in the plot line that begins with their attraction to one another and concludes with their wedding. Their experience suggests, in fact, that relationships can depend as much on chance as on love, and that in the marriage plot, the ostensible hero and heroine can have very small parts to play, even if the main event in the plot concerns them more than anyone else. Although conventional marriage plots in novels of sensibility typically give power to the hero and heroine and although their resolution typically depends on the hero's and heroine's actions, *Sense and Sensibility* shows that action can be misguided or even irrelevant, and that innate qualities can go unvalued.

Elinor and Edward's courtship plot, then, offers a version of the marriage plot that disempowers lovers—and that thereby conflicts directly with Marianne and Willoughby's early relationship and so more clearly seems a counterpart in a dialogue into which Marianne and Willoughby's relationship also enters. Because the resolution of Elinor and Edward's problems does not satisfyingly prove that all obstacles will give way before them, the plot line of their relationship cannot offer the fantasy of the power of the self and passion that engages readers who find Willoughby and Marianne's relationship appealing. By revealing that love has little sway in reality—in this case, this period's patrilinear society as it is depicted within the realism of the novel—Elinor and Edward's courtship shows how misguided Marianne is to ascribe to fictions that grant power to women and to love. By proceeding as response to Marianne's courtship plot, the fictiveness of the supposedly realistic courtship plot becomes foregrounded, undermining its claim to realism. In effect, the dialogic interaction between the two plots questions the extent to which it is possible to construct a plot that *is* realistic.

But the question is not simply one of aesthetics, of successful mimesis; it is also ideological, as Bakhtin makes clear is always the case with discourse. This interaction makes possible the novel's ability to question the extent to which what gets identified as reality, both inside this novel and outside—in that world occupied by readers who recognize Elinor's world as representing reality—can be claimed to be any more than fictive construct—any more, in fact, than any ideological construct overly naturalized. The dialogic interaction between the two versions of reality or social experience figured forth in this novel begins to impinge on the extranovelistic world; its ideological critique pulls the extranovelistic world into its novelistic discourse to reify "reality" and initiate an examination of its limitations.

The project of undermining any easy acceptance of the ideology-free nature of what gets identified as reality is furthered by the fact that this novel counters women's disempowerment in "reality" with sensibility's fantasies of female empowerment. Through this encounter, the novel both reveals the inadequacy of "reality" for women like the Dashwood sisters and makes it easy to understand the appeal of any fiction that provides a version of social experience that treats women like Marianne as equal in power to women like Mrs. Ferrars. As the sisters' marriage plots dialogically interanimate each other, they reveal that although Marianne's may move unrealistically, Elinor's moves by an overpowerful ideology that has limited value only and that therefore deserves deauthorization. And this revelation is furthered by the particular form that the novel uses to conclude its heroines' intertwined marriage plots.

If one regards *Sense and Sensibility* primarily as providing a conduct-booklike lesson that women should not subscribe to the versions of social experience provided by sensibility, one could argue that the conclusion of the novel tries, at least, to continue the lesson the novel means to provide. Such an argument might suggest that the novel reveals that sensibility is unrealistic in order to demonstrate that although it promises personal happiness to those without finance or status such as Elinor and Marianne, using it as a guide to one's life can lead one away from the kinds of happiness available to women who live in worlds in which the best men are Brandons and Edwards, not Willoughbys. Elinor's marriage plot ends successfully, after all; she, with her attention to the actual nature of the world in which she moves, ends up with a man who values her as well as she could wish. And although Brandon is not as dashing as Willoughby, he does finally become the object of love Marianne so desires. Were Marianne to retain her belief that only those whose emotions are unrestrained are worthwhile, she would miss out on happiness with a man whom the more realistic Elinor has always recognized as valuable; she would miss out on the happiness that the novel claims both heroines finally find. Only because Marianne finally sees that sensibility is appealing but harmful does she finally recognize the kinds of satisfaction that Elinor has always recognized as available in the "real" world, after all. Because the realistic Elinor gets to marry the man she has always loved and because Marianne too finds happiness once she gives up the fantasies of sensibility, the novel seems to disarm the appeal of sensibility by showing that happiness is most easily achieved by those who do not live by the fantasies that sensibility provides.

The two heroines' weddings, however, are treated so peculiarly that it becomes impossible to conclude that the novel's intent is an unproblematic rejection of sensibility for its leading away from realistic happiness. As Poovey points out, both women's marriages appear ultimately to confirm the romantic fictions at the base of sensibility and thereby highly complicate any sense that this novel disarms the desirability of what sensibility promises. Although Elinor's relationship with Edward does not progress by the rules of romantic sensibility, its happy conclusion comes about for reasons that have little to do with "sense," with restraining emotion. The relationship finally gives Elinor the kind of happiness that sensibility promises: a man so drawn to her that he will repudiate fortune to be able to marry her, and who is satisfied with treating her as the greatest source of his happiness. Elinor's story's conclusion in marriage thus predicates her reward as the fulfillment of her emotions and the kind of female empowerment that comes from a man's seeing a woman as of greater value than his material inheritance.

Marianne's situation seems at first to operate similarly. The passage is worth examining:

> Marianne Dashwood was born to an extraordinary fate. She was born to discover the falsehood of her own opinions, and to counteract, by her conduct, her most favourite maxims. She was born to overcome an affection formed so late in life as at seventeen, and with no sentiment superior to strong esteem and lively friendship, voluntarily to give her hand to another!—and *that* other, a man . . . whom, two years before, she had considered too old to be married,—and who still sought the constitutional safeguard of a flannel waistcoat! . . .
>
> Colonel Brandon was now as happy as all those who best loved him believed he deserved to be; in Marianne he was consoled for every past

> affliction; her regard and her society restored his mind to animation and his spirits to cheerfulness . . . Marianne found her happiness in forming his. (*SS*, 378-79)

The source of Marianne's happiness, like Elinor's, appears to be in her emotions' fulfillment; her situation, along with Elinor's, thus seems to argue that female happiness does indeed come from indulging the emotions, despite what the rest of the book has ostensibly tried to assert.

Yet while these wedding conclusions appear finally to validate the romantic fantasies at the base of sensibility, Marianne's does so in a way that is highly problematic. Much of what is problematic inheres in the way the narrator describes both Marianne's newfound love for Brandon and the nature of their marriage. Typically, a wedding comes across as a heroine's happy ending in part because it celebrates some kind of public recognition of her worth; the wedding can then be taken as her reward for having matured or for the innate virtue that has caused her lover to remain faithful to her in spite of obstacles thrown in their way. Marianne *does* undergo emotional growth; she learns to give up her romantic illusions, something that novels of the early nineteenth century, Austen's and others', conventionally celebrate.[25]

The tone in the quoted passage, however, makes it difficult to see the wedding as a reward. The sarcasm and exaggeration make the passage come across as an authorial sneer mocking Marianne and reveling in her having had to relinquish her romantic illusions. The tone suggests that, although convention requires that Marianne's story be concluded with a wedding, the wedding might well be considered a punishment for Marianne's former flaws rather than a reward for her growth. This marriage seems more like punishment when compared to the kinds of marriages Austen's heroines typically enter. The reason Marianne marries Brandon, for instance—because she feels esteem and friendship for him but "no [superior] sentiment"—implies she has given up on any kind of romantic love. The narrator asserts that Marianne does grow to love Brandon later: "Marianne['s] . . . whole heart became, in time, as much devoted to her husband as it had once been to Willoughby" (*SS*, 379). All the same, the nature of their relationship when they wed seems inadequate. No other Austen heroine is asked to give up love as a prime reason for marrying, whatever other humiliations or suffering she may undergo.

Worse, Marianne and Brandon's relationship is portrayed as lacking in the interchange of ideas and of complementary personalities that comprise the appealing marriages in Austen's other novels. In *Pride and Prejudice*, for example, Elizabeth realizes that marrying Darcy would be "to the advantage of both; by her ease and liveliness, his mind might have been softened, his manners improved, and from his judgment, information, and knowledge of the world, she must have received benefit of greater importance."[26] In *Sense and Sensibility*, however, the reader is told that in Marianne's new relationship with Brandon, "Marianne found her happiness in forming his"; their relationship is a hierarchy in which Marianne derives happiness apparently only from serving her mate. The reader is told nothing of what Brandon does in this relationship and is therefore left believing that he passively accepts her devotion. Male-centered fantasy as this is, it cannot come across as satisfying union to most women, who feel the claims of their own desire for attention, love, and recognition.[27] It certainly cannot satisfy readers who are drawn to Marianne's relationship with Willoughby because Willoughby has been lovingly attentive to Marianne apparently solely because he has recognized her innate worth.

Marianne's "extraordinary fate" is of course to reverse her opinions completely; it is thus logical to expect that her marital relationship will be a reversal of her relationship with Willoughby. There should be no surprise then, that the relationship entails her giving up her desire for an attractive lover, along with her desire to be empowered and to garner recognition of her importance for her own sake. The tone in the passage about Marianne's marriage to Brandon along with Marianne's having to give up everything she had previously wanted furthers the sense that this conclusion is Marianne's punishment, that this denial of everything she had previously wanted is just what she deserves for having indulged her sensibility.

Readers who go along with the ostensible didactic message of this novel, however—the message that an indulged sensibility is bad—become implicated in this punishment; as long as one believes Marianne has been bad in wanting the kinds of things she has wanted, one must see her as deserving punishment and as having to give up her previous desires before she can be seen as moral. Because the tone in the passage and the depiction of the relationship elicit pity and sympathy for Marianne, however, they compromise the desires one might have to feel that Marianne really deserves what she gets; Tanner and Mudrick's reactions are cases in point. This conclusion in a dissatisfying marriage thus places readers on the side of romantic fictions—makes sensibility internally persuasive to them—rather than leaving them in the strictly moral position for which the novel ostensibly argues when it is seen as didactically directed against an indulged sensibility. The nature of the relationship, then, adds to this novel's stress on the appeal of what sensibility offers.

By claiming that Marianne is in fact happy in this marriage, this conclusion argues that there is happiness in the "real" world, even if this happiness is not as attractive as that which sensibility promises to provide. For the conclusion to assure its audience that Marianne can love a man who is not obviously appealing is for it to leave the reader with the lesson that it is possible to find happiness in a world of lowered expectations. This lesson in realism is worth learning; all the same, being allowed to believe that one's fantasies are in fact possible is bound to make female readers, at least, happier than learning that they must resign themselves to the kinds of happiness available in the real world in which they find their needs only incompletely met.[28] And the novel's including those fantasies highlights the inadequate, unsatisfying nature of this real world for women.

The ending of this novel thus makes clear that the happiness made available by the world in which Marianne and Elinor live is not as satisfying as it could be. But the world in which those characters move is mimetic of what readers generally identify as "reality"; it is in fact coextensive with the conditions of the world in which readers too live, especially Austen's early-nineteenth-century middle-class reading public. And by making clear that the happiness the heroines' world makes possible is not satisfying, this conclusion furthers the novel's indictment of what it portrays as reality; a world in which women are primarily powerless and are valued mainly for the fortune and rank they bring rather than for intrinsic qualities of personality. The strength of the appeal of sensibility in *Sense and Sensibility* thus derives from the need that women like Marianne and Elinor, disempowered by patriarchy, have for fantasies of value and power, even if only power through love. Because in "reality" women have little power and are little valued, and because the fantasies provided by sensibility argue that women are valuable and can garner power by being lovable, the dialogic confrontation between sensibility and "reality" in *Sense and Sensibility*, furthered as it is in this conclusion, permits readers to recognize how fully women might desire the fantasies that sensibility provides—how inadequate the conditions are in the extraliterary world that makes literary fantasies empowering women so appealing.

By preserving the appeal of sensibility and its marriage plot and by foregrounding the limitations of the "reality" that tempt women like Marianne to subscribe to such fantasies, the dialogic confrontation between sensibility and the actual conditions of the world in which these heroines move not only proves sensibility to be unrealistic but disarms the authority of what the novel represents as a reality that readers will recognize as fitting their assumptions of ideology-free reality as well. The dialogic interaction showing the limitations of this reality reifies "reality" as an object to be examined; that is, it thus exposes this version of reality as just an ideology like any other—one as limited as sensibility. By doing so, and by revealing that this reality leaves women in need of fantasy, rather than defusing critiques of the dominant ideology, *Sense and Sensibility* demands that we see this ideology as both too powerful and too harmful to warrant its having garnered authority for so long. As such, this novel's dialogic discourse argues that continuing to embrace "reality" is fully as harmful as subscribing to or being internally persuaded by the fantasies that sensibility provides. By revealing that both fantasy and the patriarchical version of reality are limited ideologies, *Sense and Sensibility* thus uses its dialogic nature to dramatize the view that women like Marianne are caught in a double-bind situation; they live in an inadequate reality from which they are unable to escape except through fantasies that may make them incapable of taking advantage of the limited satisfaction that can be theirs in this patrilinear, patriarchical society.

Notes

1. *Sense and Sensibility*'s first reviewers found that it provided a "useful moral," an "excellent lesson" in "many sober and salutary maxims for the conduct of life." From an unsigned review in *Critical Review*, February 1812, and an unsigned notice in *British Critic*, May 1812, both cited in B. C. Southam's two-volume *Jane Austen: The Critical Heritage* (New York: Barnes & Noble, 1968), 1:35, 40. More recent critics also read the book as intending to provide a moral lesson; see, for instance, Marvin Mudrick, *Jane Austen: Irony as Defense and Discovery* (Princeton, N.J.: Princeton University Press, 1952), 60-93, and Marilyn Butler, *Jane Austen and the War of Ideas* (Oxford: Clarendon, 1975), 182-96. Subsequent references to these works will be cited by author and page number in the text and notes.

2. One way the novel increases Marianne's appeal is by making her come more to life than her right-thinking sister Elinor, whom Mark Twain called a "wax figure" (quoted in Southam, 2:75). Mary Poovey points out in *The Proper Lady and the Woman Writer* (Chicago: University of Chicago Press, 1984) that the novel neither "exclude[s] passion . . . nor . . . so completely qualif[ies] it as to undermine its power." She argues that "Austen attempts to bend the imaginative engagement [passion] elicits in the reader to the service of moral education," which she does by using strategies of containment that prevent the appeal of passion from being overpowering (187). She argues that the closure of the novel disarms the uneasiness that the reader might feel from sensibility's garnering the appeal that it does, explaining that "[Austen's] turn to aesthetic closure enables her to dismiss many of the problems her own divided sympathies have introduced" (193). That readers like Mudrick feel that the problems have not been adequately dismissed suggests that the conclusion neither disarms this uneasiness nor undermines the appeal of sensibility as fully as Poovey thinks. Future references to Poovey's work will be cited by author and page number in the text.

3. Marvin Mudrick makes this point (91-93), as does Tony Tanner in *Jane Austen* (London: MacMillan, 1986), 100-101.

4. See Rachel Blau DuPlessis's *Writing beyond the Ending* (Bloomington: Indiana University Press, 1984), along with Joseph A. Boone's "Modernist Maneuverings in the Marriage Plot: Breaking Ideologies of Gender and Genre in James' *The Golden Bowl*," *PMLA* 101 (1986): 374-88, and his "Wedlock as Deadlock and Beyond: Closure and the Victorian Marriage Ideal," *Mosaic* 17 (1984): 65-81.

5. For a more extensive discussion on this issue, see my "Not Subordinate: Empowering Women in the Marriage Plot—The Novels of Frances Burney, Maria Edgeworth, and Jane Austen," *Criticism* 34 (1992): 51-74.

6. Mikhail Bakhtin, *The Dialogic Imagination*, ed. Michael Holquist, trans. Caryl Emerson and Michael Holquist (Austin: University of Texas Press, 1981). References to this work will be cited in the text as *DI*.

7. Holquist, in his glossary to *The Dialogic Imagination*, notes that " 'Ideology' in Russian is simply an idea-system" rather than the more purely "politically oriented English [-language]" use of the word (429). The term I have used here, *worldview*, may give a closer sense of the Russian meaning as Holquist defines it. Because Bakhtin's use of the word does carry political overtones, and because it is the term that Holquist and Emerson use in their translation of *The Dialogic Imagination*, throughout the rest of the chapter, I have generally retained the word *ideology*.

8. Not all texts conventionally called novels consist equally of novelistic discourse; only those that move in a way that can be considered dialogic can be called true novels, according to Bakhtin. What is problematic here, of course, is that recognizing the dialogic nature of a novel—the true novelistic nature of a novel—depends to a great extent on readers' perceptions of that novel, and their ability to argue, on the one hand, that a novel is novelistic, or, on the other, that it is monoglossic or univocal. By extension of the argument, however, works progressing through novelistic discourse need not be restricted to the conventional parameters of the novel genre—individual works normally classed within other genres themselves can be true novels, according to Bakhtin's definition. His discussion of these issues recurs throughout *The Dialogic Imagination* and *Problems of Dostoevsky's Poetics*, trans. R. W. Rotsel (Ann Arbor: University of Michigan Press, 1973).

9. Jane Austen, *Sense and Sensibility* [1811], vol. 1 of *The Works of Jane Austen*, ed. R. W. Chapman (London: Oxford University Press, 1926), 7. Subsequent quotations from this novel are cited in the text as *SS*.

10. While Marianne's and Elinor's versions of social experience are not the only two offered in the novel—obviously John Dashwood and Lucy Steele approach "reality" rather differently than either heroine—theirs are the two made most appealing, the two that compete most directly and most compellingly for the reader's assent and approval, and, as such, the two on which the novel concentrates. Because the novel brings in these other versions of social experience, the critique in the book can be seen as more than bidirectional; it illuminates the variety or variances in the ideological underpinnings of *each* of these different characters. Rather than discuss each of the variances of ideologies the novel's dialogic discourse illuminates, however, I will focus on the ways the heroines' plots interilluminate the ideological underpinnings of the romance plot and of what gets accepted as ideology-free reality by almost all the characters.

11. Claudia Johnson, *Jane Austen* (Chicago: University of Chicago Press, 1988), 50. Subsequent references to this work are cited by author and page number in the text and notes. It is possible to argue that Austen's novels assail those who abuse the institutions that support the ideology without assailing the ideology itself; such an argument would work best in novels in which there are enough honorable and benevolent characters who act responsibly in positions of power to argue that the system itself is viable because it works more often than not. As soon as a novel suggests that there are more people who abuse the institutions empowering them than there are responsible people, however, that novel should be seen as casting doubts on the viability of the entire system, the entire ideology—even if the wedding concluding the novel marries the heroine into wealth and high social status, a conclusion that seems to reconfirm the value of the ideology itself by accepting that what it values can be seen as reward.

12. Willoughby's hard-hearted selfishness is obvious, Edward's less so. Edward, however, is not much better than Willoughby: he courts Elinor's love while engaged to Lucy Steele, figuring that he was "doing no injury to anybody but [him]self" (*SS*, 368; Johnson, 58).

13. The reservations in this sentence about the extent to which marriage can protect women are borne out by the stories of the first Eliza and Mrs. Dashwood. The first Eliza arguably forfeits her right to be protected by marriage by her adultery, although Brandon's account of her experience suggests those who forced her to marry against her will to a husband who "provoke[d] inconstancy" (*SS*, 206) are really to blame—that marriage itself and the way it is carried out for her constitute the original betrayal. Mrs. Dashwood's case is different. She loses the protection that marriage should provide not through any fault of her husband's or her own, but because the property had already been willed away from her own family and because John, her husband's son from a previous marriage, reneges on his promise to provide for the woman.

14. For a discussion of the period's marriage market, see Poovey, chap. 1.

15. The novel in fact suggests that women interested in succeeding in the "real" world must leave morality such as Elinor's behind. That Lucy wins perhaps the most lucrative match in the book and finally does win Mrs. Ferrars's admiration demonstrates that women can enter into positions of power by manipulation in a way that the less manipulative and more moral cannot. This constitutes the site of another conflict between ideologies, between John Dashwood and Mrs. Ferrars's view of how humans and their worth are defined, on the one hand, and Marianne and Elinor's, on the other. John Dashwood and Mrs. Ferrars clearly define people by their social and economic status, but Marianne and Elinor define people primarily as moral, perhaps psychological, beings, whose worth depends on innate traits rather than on externals such as accidents of birth. See Nancy Armstrong, *Desire and Domestic Fiction* (New York: Oxford University Press, 1986) for a discussion of the ways that views of what constitutes the human changed during the eighteenth century.

16. I stress that Elinor's accommodation to the dominant ideology is honorable to differentiate her approach from that of Lucy Steele. Clearly Lucy is more realistic than Elinor in some respects; Lucy is able to see that being honorable has little to do with the dominant ideology and so is able to manipulate others and appearances so as to best succeed in the terms of that ideology—terms of finance and position.

17. Critics who have made this argument include Mudrick (93) and Jean Kennard, *Victims of Convention* (Hamden, Conn.: Archon, 1978), 29-30. Subsequent references to Kennard are cited by author and page number in the text.

18. Mark Twain, quoted in Southam, 2:75: Phelps, quoted in Southam, 2:75; Poovey, 185.

19. Mudrick, 88; Phelps, quoted in Southam, 2:75.

20. Janice Radway, in *Reading the Romance: Women, Patriarchy, and Popular Literature* (Chapel Hill: University of North Carolina Press, 1984), a work on modern-day romance novels and their readers, suggests that our society creates needs in women for love and recognition that it cannot itself meet. She explains that many modern-day romance-novel readers turn to these novels to have their needs met vicariously. Although her work deals with women of the second half of the twentieth century, there is no reason to believe that women in Austen's period did not also have needs for love and recognition that could be met only through fantasies of women-centered love stories.

21. This kind of fiction might also be called the Pamela story, for Samuel Richardson's 1740 *Pamela*, 2 vols. (London: Dent, 1942), is arguably the era's prototype of the Cinderella heroine and might be seen as most immediately influencing subsequent writers of that time. I will, however, follow the lead of Henrietta Ten Harmsel's *Jane Austen: A Study in Fictional Conventions* (The Hague: Mouton, 1964), 62; D. W. Harding's "Regulated Ha-

tred: An Aspect of the Work of Jane Austen," *Scrutiny* 8 (1940): 355; and J. M. S. Tompkins's *The Popular Novel in England, 1770-1800* (Lincoln: University of Nebraska Press, 1961), 34—all of which refer to this kind of story as the Cinderella story.

22. Frances Burney's 1782 *Cecilia* (London: Virago, 1986) is one example of such a text. It is worth noting that, in a variation on this eighteenth-century novelistic motif, the heroine is merely thought, throughout most of her story, to have no money, to be from a low social status, or indeed to be illegitimate, and only discovered after she has been chosen and long cherished by her male protagonist to have all that he and his friends could desire—wealth, birth, and position. The underlying fantasy in either case is that a woman's value, along with her power and lovability, derive from her innate qualities, rather than through accidents of birth. Burney's 1778 *Evelina* (London: Oxford University Press, 1968) and Charlotte Smith's 1788 *Emmeline, or the Orphan of the Castle* (London: Oxford University Press, 1971) provide two examples of this variation. Both Evelina and Emmeline turn out to be aristocratic once the details of each heroine's birth is discovered, but their value as women is established through most of each novel as residing in their *virtuousness*. The aristocratic birth and wealth they are discovered as possessing becomes a bonus—a material reward for the heroines and their lovers for recognizing true value in woman.

23. Bakhtin is quoted by Gary Saul Morson, "Who Speaks for Bakhtin?" in *Bakhtin: Essays and Dialogues on His Work*, ed. Morson (Chicago: University of Chicago Press, 1986), 3.

24. Although not as explicit as Austen's 1818 *Northanger Abbey* in suggesting that its misguided heroine derives her illusions from novels, *Sense and Sensibility* is clear enough in its suggestion that Marianne has learned how heroines of novels of sensibility are supposed to behave and that she consciously models her own behavior accordingly. In many instances, she is described as believing that it would be unforgivable if she did not act like such heroines. When Willoughby first leaves the Dashwood family for London, for example, the reader is told that "Marianne would have thought herself inexcusable had she been able to sleep at all the first night. . . . She would have been ashamed to look her family in the face the next morning. . . . She was awake the whole night, and she wept the greatest part of it. . . . Her sensibility was potent enough!" (83)

25. See, for instance, Charlotte Lennox's 1752 *The Female Quixote* (London: Pandora-Routledge, 1986). A commonplace of Austen criticism is that her novels are about the heroines' social and moral education, and that their wedding conclusions signify a reward for and recognition of the heroines' growth. See Evelyn Hinz, "Hierogamy vs. Wedlock: Types of Marriage Plots and Their Relationship to Genres of Prose Fiction," *PMLA* 91 (1976): 903; Julia Prewitt Brown, *Jane Austen's Novels: Social Change and Literary Form* (Cambridge, Mass.: Harvard University Press, 1979), chap. 1; and Kennard, *Victims of Convention*.

26. Jane Austen, *Pride and Prejudice* [1813], vol. 2 of *The Works of Jane Austen*, 312.

27. This part of the novel comes across as distasteful to male readers as well; this conclusion leads Mudrick, for instance, to claim that Austen betrays her lively heroine (93).

28. Brown finds that although dying of love, the tragedy Marianne had expected, does not come to pass, living with lowered expectations is worse. Brown asserts that "there is a horror in this conclusion that we may not wish to contemplate. It is not the conclusion of a writer who lacks courage" (63). Radway's *Reading the Romance* explores the reasons why modern-day romance-novel readers also prefer novels providing fantasies of complete happiness to those providing supposedly happy conclusions in which characters accept lives of lowered expectations.

The Chronotope of the Asylum: *Jane Eyre*, Feminism, and Bakhtinian Theory

Suzanne Rosenthal Shumway

I

Today the task of the feminist literary critic is no longer simply a matter of pointing out the ways in which women have been (mis)represented in various works of literature. Instead, current feminist literary theory demands that we reexamine the very basis of narrative itself, paying close attention to the inconsistencies that are often obscured by a self-censoring phallocentric text. For example, in *Alice Doesn't: Feminism, Semiotics, Cinema*, Teresa de Lauretis exhorts the feminist critic to create ways of seeing that attempt to "oppose the simply totalizing closure of final statements . . . ; to seek out contradictions, heterogeneity, ruptures in the fabric of representation so thinly stretched—if powerful—to contain excess, division, difference, resistance."[1] By searching for the chinks in a narrative system specifically designed to contain and control chaos and disorder, de Lauretis suggests, the feminist critic can unearth what we might provisionally call the feminine element of narrative.

This is precisely the task undertaken by Leslie W. Rabine in *Reading the Romantic Heroine: Text, History, Ideology*. Rabine analyzes various romantic narratives in an attempt to reveal the feminine presence hidden beneath the overt masculine narrative. She explains that "the dominant masculine voice of traditional romantic narrative imposes a totalizing structure on romantic narrative and represses an independent feminine other." This feminine other, Rabine continues, opposes and disrupts the unity of masculine discourse and thus "belongs to that textual process . . . which is not monolinear, which does not seek a return to oneness and identity, and which tolerates gaps, lacks and difference."[2]

Rabine's revealing study of the romantic narrative attempts to locate the feminine other in the text at the level of narrative. According to Rabine, hidden within the masculine narrative, obscured by its logic and by what I would term its authoritative narcissism, we can find a subverted feminine narrative, an antinarrative that exists in opposition to the narrative proper. That this feminine element can indeed be revealed through analysis is evidenced by the powerful readings Rabine's approach provides. Her chapter on Charlotte Brontës *Shirley* (chapter 5), for example, skillfully examines the novel's competing narratives and succeeds in making sense out of what many critics have discounted as a failed attempt at a historical novel.

Suppose, however, we shift our focus to examine not the narratives within a text, but rather the utterances that make up the text. Is it possible, in other words, to theorize and locate the feminine other not only at the level of plot, but at the level of the word as well?

Such an enterprise must rely on Bakhtinian theory as well as feminist theory. Indeed, feminist literary theory can appropriate Bakhtin's work to produce a powerful analytic tool with which to examine novelistic texts, because both theoretical systems valorize heterogeneity and diversity; feminism and Bakhtinian theory share a concern for the oppressed and marginalized others created by the hegemony of dominant, authoritarian, and "internally persuasive" languages. This celebration of diversity—of heterogeneity (feminist theory) and of heteroglossia (Bakhtinian theory)—allows for a rich dialogue between the two theoretical systems.

For example, in "Discourse in the Novel," Bakhtin describes the novel as a "diversity of social speech types (sometimes even diversity of languages) and a diversity of individual voices, artistically organized."[3] Predominant among these voices are two opposing sets of forces: the centripetal forces of language, which, endorsed by the dominant and dominating culture, work toward unifying and stabilizing meaning; and the centrifugal forces of language, which attempt to undo this unification and stability, releasing language from its bondage to unity by introducing multiplicity. Both the centripetal and the centrifugal forces of language exist against a larger backdrop of heteroglossia, that is, against the "social diversity of speech types"(263). Centrifugal language attempts to return to this heteroglossia, and centripetal language attempts to order it, to structure and stabilize it. In Bakhtin's stylistic analysis of the novel, these two forces of language are constantly doing battle: "Alongside the centripetal forces, the centrifugal forces of language carry on their uninterrupted work; alongside verbal-ideological centralization and unification, the uninterrupted processes of decentralization and disunification go forward" (272). In general, most utterances in the novel contain elements of both centripetal and centrifugal language: "Every concrete utterance of a speaking subject serves as a point where centrifugal as well as centripetal forces are brought to bear" (272).

Feminist theory embraces many of the same assumptions about the nature of narrative. That is, masculine (or phallocentric) discourse is seen as a representation of the unified symbolic order that attempts to structure narrative, excluding the alien other that disrupts its unity. Rabine's definition of the term *feminine* provides a concise but excellent discussion of the masculine and feminine aspects of narrative:

> I have used "feminine" in the French poststructuralist sense of an unnameable other excluded from the phallocentric symbolic order. Designating neither an eternal essence in opposition to the masculine, nor the complementary reflection of the masculine within our phallocentric symbolic order, the feminine is that which the symbolic order has had to exclude in order to establish itself as a unified structure. (16)

Driving toward unity and coherence, the masculine appears closely akin to that which Bakhtin names the centripetal forces of language. Likewise, in Bakhtin's system the centrifugal forces of language, working as they do to destabilize meaning, appear similar to what Rabine calls the feminine.

One could even say that, at least within the system set up by Rabine, we could benefit by replacing the term *feminine* with *centrifugal.* For it seems obvious that Rabine herself uses the word *feminine* under some duress: the term is an oppositional one which, if it does not take its meaning from *masculine*, surely carries with it some of the word's cultural and ideological baggage. *Centrifugal* may indeed approach Rabine's intentions more closely; the term is able to express in itself the existence of a multiplicity of unnameable others beyond the feminine that are created by the hegemony of the phallocentric order.

If it is true that "centrifugal language" corresponds roughly to what critics such as Rabine have called the "feminine" element of narrative, it is nevertheless imperative that we proceed cautiously at this point in order to avoid conflating the two theoretical systems and thus doing injustice to both of them. To eliminate the term *feminine* from feminist theory would be tantamount to whitewashing the political implications of feminism; it would amount to an attempt to divorce feminist theory from feminist praxis. Certainly Bakhtinian theory shares with feminist theory, as I have indicated, a concern for the excluded others created by the hegemony of dominant languages. Moreover, the Bakhtinian concept of reaccentuation, which postulates that under changed conditions new meanings may surface in the artistic text,[4] resembles revisionary feminist criticism in that it provides a means for revealing those voices once ignored and excluded by centripetal (masculine) discourse. Yet Bakhtinian theory and feminist theory are not always compatible; the concept of dialogue carries with it very different meanings in each theoretical system. *Dialogue*, of course, is a central term in Bakhtinian theory: Bakhtin insists that dialogue is present in every meaningful utterance, that even the weakest of voices can be heard if it is searched for and listened to carefully enough. Feminists more often see dialogue as a form of oppression, a war in which the party with the weakest and least unified voice always loses. According to Susan Griffith:

> There is another aspect of ideological structure. Dialogue—which is finally perhaps the form of all thought—must become a war. One must lose and the other win. There must be a clear victor. One must be shown to be wrong. And therefore, each kind of thought is pitted against the other. The listener must choose between one and the other, either a truth or a falsity.[5]

Despite its brevity, this statement epitomizes one crucial difference between feminist theory and Bakhtinian theory. Griffith begins, as does Bakhtin, by insisting that dialogue is essential to thought: both Griffith and Bakhtin view dialogue as implicit in language, as well as in the thought processes that give rise to language. Bakhtin, however, sees dialogue as basically nonviolent; he does not emphasize the potentially competitive nature of dialogue. In contrast, Griffith sees dialogue as always combative; each side of the dialogue, she might say, attempts to coerce or cajole the other into accepting its own dominance.

Thus, although Bakhtin might have described dialogue as a war without victory, a kind of nonresolved or open-ended ideological skirmish, feminists have difficulty accepting such a view. For them the stakes are indeed much higher; a victory in which the victor fails to gain anything tangible, except perhaps the right to exercise her voice from time to time, is an empty victory indeed. Powerful as it is when used as a tool of textual analysis, Bakhtinian theory leaves little room for actual practice; it is concerned only with detecting the weaker voices in a text, and not with creating and implementing plans for strengthening such voices.[6]

Bakhtinian theory presents another, far more serious problem for critics who attempt to use it in conjunction with feminist literary theory. In "Discourse in the Novel" Bakhtin repeatedly declares that many languages coexist within a single culture:

> All languages of heteroglossia, whatever the principle underlying them and making each unique, are specific points of view on the world, forms for

> conceptualizing the world in words, specific world views, each characterized by its own objects, meanings and values. (292)

Moreover, the novelistic text attempts to represent this linguistic pluralism: "The novel is the expression of a Galilean perception of language, one that denies the absolutism of a single and unitary language" (367). In Bakhtin's system, then, culture and discourse are both inherently heteroglot and linguistically diverse.

Nestled in the middle of the essay, however, is a remarkable statement, one that seems to contradict everything Bakhtin has said:

> What is realized in the novel is the process of coming to know one's own language as it is perceived in someone else's language, coming to know one's own belief system in someone else's belief system. There takes place within the novel an ideological translation of another's language, and an overcoming of its otherness, an otherness that is only contingent, external, illusory. (365)

All languages, according to this passage, are finally identical; because otherness is merely an illusion, presumably at some level heteroglossia ceases to exist, and there is no difference between the languages of individuals. Working upon this assumption, one might easily arrive at the conclusion that the centrifugal forces of language are merely an illusory opposition to the centripetal forces, that language is, at its deepest level, a unified and seamless whole, despite its superficial appearance of diversity.[7]

Such a passage presents serious problems for feminist theory, which celebrates difference and heterogeneity—which is even, to a certain extent, predicated on the concept of heterogeneity. The only way in which to deal with this passage is to assume that Bakhtin is simply unable to push his theory to its proper limits; Bakhtin, we could say, actually falls victim to the circular logic that all too often governs phallocentric texts. He begins by postulating heterogeneity as a force that operates against an imposed homogeneity, but he ends by absorbing heterogeneity into homogeneity, by denying the existence of true difference.[8] It is perhaps difficult to presume that the passage cited is a momentary aberration, a kind of phallocentric slip into which Bakhtin absentmindedly falls, and from which he quickly recovers. Such a presumption, however, seems necessary in order to achieve a working partnership between Bakhtinian theory and feminist literary theory.

If Bakhtin has lost some of his theoretical integrity by iterating such statements as the one quoted, he is sure to gain it back when we consider his work in identifying and describing the chronotope. In fact, a variation on the concept of the chronotope provides the most powerful device with which to stage a reaccentuation of texts such as *Jane Eyre*. In the essay "Forms of Time and of the Chronotope in the Novel" Bakhtin explains that the chronotope is the time/space continuum that gives shape to a novel, directing and in some ways even generating its existence. The chronotope functions, we might say, as a form of setting for the novel. But more than merely a device to locate the plot within a specific time and place, the chronotope actively works to shape and create the plot itself, becoming, in the end, a formal, as well as a thematic, feature of the plot.

According to Bakhtin, any given novel (except, perhaps, a truly monologic one) has not one but several different chronotopes operating within it. I would add that it is in the intersection of chronotopes, in the contradiction and opposition that arises between competing chronotopes, and in the relationships that emerge between various chronotopes, that the workings of different ideologies are revealed in the novel. For each chronotope represents a different ideological view, a competing outlook on the events that take place within the novel. As the novel shifts from one chronotope to another, the gaps and silences that are a necessary part of the representation of an ideology will become increasingly noticeable to the perceptive reader.

Although Bakhtin identifies and describes several types of chronotopes throughout his essay, feminist literary theory must forge a new tool with which to examine texts like *Jane Eyre*, in which female madness figures prominently: the chronotope of the asylum, which exists ostensibly to display female insanity in the novel.[9] Within the chronotope of the asylum, the madwoman emerges and assumes a prominence in the text. A specialized form of narrative annex,[10] the chronotope of the asylum works on two levels: it advances the plot, often displaying the madwoman as a seemingly insurmountable obstacle that threatens the satisfactory outcome of the narrative; at the same time, however, it provides an alternate narrative work space in which the text can represent and explore the deviant world of unrestrained female madness. In addition, the chronotope of the asylum works toward subverting and distorting the primary narrative: in it we find that the normative values of the novel, and with them the drive toward realism, are utterly distorted by the subversive ideology expressed through the representation of female madness. Here, for example, time becomes irrelevant, distorted, and confused; space refuses its normal values, contracting and expanding at will; and the narrative proper is suspended as the chronotope of the asylum interrupts it, becoming for a time, at least, a novel in itself. Inversion figures prominently in the chronotope of the asylum, for insanity represents the most striking form of inversion possible: as the fundamental opposite of sanity, it is most commonly portrayed as the inversion of those values postulated as common to all readers. Thus the chronotope of the asylum works to invert the reader's concepts of gender, of space, even of time. But most important for our purposes here, within the chronotope of the asylum centrifugal language gains the upper hand over centripetal language. Laughs, screams, even silence are valorized in this narrative space, rather than utterances. In short, in the chronotope of the asylum lies the key to an intense linguistic freedom that exists just beyond sanity.

In the chronotope of the asylum, then, female madness—and its concomitant subversion—is represented and refracted in the text. When the madwoman makes her appearance in the chronotope of the asylum, she calls into question issues of normality and abnormality, compliance and deviance, just as she subverts the expectations that the reader has formed in response to the novel's directions. The chronotope of the asylum, camouflaged and obscured, thus becomes an arena in which subversion—and in particular a feminine form of subversion—can be articulated, in which alternate narrative possibilities can be imagined.

Using the tools provided by Bakhtin, we can proceed with our analysis of the novel that Gayatri Spivak has called a "cult text of feminism." For although Bakhtinian theory is not completely compatible with feminism, it nevertheless offers a great deal to the feminist critic who is willing to appropriate its analytical tools. The concept of centrifugal language, for example, is of paramount importance to feminist literary criticism; it brings us a new understanding of the "unnameable" other that has been excluded by phallocentric texts and marginalized by the centripetal language of masculine discourse. Likewise, the chronotope of the asylum allows for the identification of a narrative annex that works to subvert the dominant masculine narrative. Thus, acknowledging the points of conflict between Bakhtinian and feminist theories, but nevertheless equipped with the concepts of centrifugal and centripetal language, authoritative discourse and internally persuasive discourse, and perhaps most importantly, the chronotope of the asylum, we can now examine *Jane Eyre* in an attempt to identify the feminine other at the levels of both plot and utterance.

II

It is no exaggeration to say that *Jane Eyre* is intimately concerned with language and its representation. Throughout the novel, pervading every aspect of it, we find an implicit recognition of language as a device that can define the self, both independently and in opposition to others. Critics are not blind to this emphasis on language and the utterance in *Jane*

Eyre; indeed, it is not difficult to find feminist readings of the novel that point out that Jane and Rochester's courtship proceeds almost entirely through conversation.[11] Given this emphasis, Bakhtinian theory is indispensable here precisely because it forces us to pay close attention to the importance of the word and the voice in this novel. *Jane Eyre* is, in short, a dialogic novel, and thus rests upon a valorization of, as well as an investment in, language and its powers.

Chief among the powers of language is the creation of a self through the narration of one's life history. As all autobiographers (even fictional ones) do, Jane Eyre uses language to create an image of herself, thereby creating an identity. Nevertheless, in the world represented in *Jane Eyre*, language is not a wholly positive force. Although the search for and acquisition of an independent language is Jane's goal throughout the novel, she must also be wary of the pitfalls of language. In other words, language frees Jane from dependency and empowers her; however, it also poses a serious threat to her. Rebellion in this novel is almost always signified by explosive language, by incendiary, subversive, and often involuntary speech.[12] Every one of Jane's spoken outbursts, each of her explosive and rebellious utterances, is characterized by a loss of linguistic and emotional control that is somehow reminiscent of, and compared to, insanity.[13]

Jane's ability to wield several different voices, to adapt to different situations yet maintain her linguistic independence (which we might also call her insistence upon heteroglossia), ensures her survival and, not coincidentally, her success as a narrator, but this stubborn refusal to be silenced, to forgo the pleasure of the utterance, threatens her with a loss of control that is the narrative equivalent of insanity. Thus Jane faces not one but two threats in her search for linguistic independence. On the one hand is the threat of centripetal language: Jane must struggle to free herself from the restrictions of internally persuasive and authoritative language. On the other hand is an equally dangerous threat: linguistic chaos, which is to say insanity. In this novel the ultimate expression of centrifugal language, of language that refuses to be structured and stabilized, is the language of Bertha Mason Rochester, the madwoman whose utterances, laughs, and screams are incomprehensible. As Jane searches for a variety of voices with which to oppose the domination of centripetal language, she must resist the temptation to reject language altogether and fall, like Bertha, into the abyss of linguistic chaos. In other words, Jane must find a middle way, a compromise between the two extremes in the range of communicative possibilities open to her: she must avoid not only the stultified and confining discourse of authority but also the all-too-liberating discourse of madness.

It should come as no surprise that we find this discourse of madness represented most fully in the chronotope of the asylum, that time/space continuum crafted specifically for the representation of female madness. Significantly, the chronotope of the asylum in *Jane Eyre* is not easily identifiable, for it is refracted and defused throughout the narrative. Whenever Bertha appears, snarling or laughing but never communicating through language, always beyond comprehension, she appears within the chronotope of the asylum; she herself is an inversion of woman, a bestial creature with manlike strength and murderous inclinations. The room on the third story of Thornfield in which Bertha is incarcerated is, of course, a powerful representation of the chronotope of the asylum. Here both time and language cease to exist in recognizable forms: in a world in which the passage of time and the acquisition of knowledge and experience are crucial, in which the possession and deployment of language is ultimately a matter of individual survival, Bertha occupies a narrative space that acknowledges the existence of neither time nor language. So powerful a representation is this, in fact, that the chronotope of the asylum invades the outer room in which Mason lies after Bertha's attack, with Jane as his nurse as she cares for him throughout the timeless and silent early-morning hours. We could even say, following Rochester's example (125), that the chronotope of the asylum invades and infects the entire space of Thornfield, tainting the garden in which Rochester courts Jane, the sitting room in which their early conversations take place, and, of course, the corridor on the third floor in which Jane walks to soothe her restless nature before Rochester arrives at Thornfield.

Echoes of the chronotope of the asylum occur throughout the novel, such as in Jane's desperate journey to Marsh End and, much earlier, in her incarceration in the red room. Even Jane's linguistic capabilities fail her when she is placed within this chronotope: in the red room, locked up and terrified by a supernatural light, the young Jane is unable to articulate any words and simply screams in abject terror. As Janet Freeman points out, "That inarticulate sound comes out of her from so far below the level of words that it cannot be narrated, even in retrospect." Freeman adds that "the truth implicit in the child's wordless scream did not serve to free her from bondage: only words, in the world of this novel, have that kind of power."[14] This is the lesson Jane must learn, the lesson that Bertha serves to illustrate and the reason behind the intrusiveness of the chronotope of the asylum in *Jane Eyre:* one must struggle with language but never abandon it, for beyond language lie insanity and chaos. Thus the chronotope of the asylum in *Jane Eyre*, although defused and refracted throughout the novel, and although its effect is never seen in entirety (as if it is too threatening, too tantalizingly seductive to represent fully), contains the warning that the entire novel works to convey to its reader: do not abdicate your control of language, pleasant though this might be, for then language will control you, thereby leading you into madness itself.

Jane's story can be described succinctly as a woman's search for linguistic diversity. Unable or unwilling to accept the centripetal language the Reeds attempt to force upon her, Jane leaves Gateshead, intent upon equipping herself with the ability to wield the forces of centrifugal language. The Reeds insist that Jane conform to their expectations, that she speak in a single, unitary voice—in short, that she use centripetal language, speaking only in the voice of submission and gratitude. But Jane resists, attempting to manipulate the centrifugal forces of language, to speak through as many different voices as she can successfully articulate. For example, in the red room, when she is incarcerated in retribution for articulating a voice of violent rebellion, Jane uses another, very different voice: the voice of contrition. "Oh aunt, have pity!" Jane cries. "Forgive me! I cannot endure it—let me be punished some other way!" Mrs. Reed hastily interrupts Jane's speech with the word "Silence!" (14), and we must wonder at this point whether it is incarceration in the red room or the inability to articulate a voice, any voice, that brings on Jane's fit.

Thus, what makes Charlotte Brontë's novel particularly suited for a Bakhtinian/feminist reading is that representations of language are used in *Jane Eyre* to suggest Jane's search for subjectivity. In her passage from youth to maturity, Jane must fight first to obtain and then to maintain possession of linguistic heterogeneity. Faced with a world that attempts to enforce a unitary, authoritarian language upon her, Jane repeatedly resists this ventriloquism and struggles to maintain heteroglossia; she insists on her right to articulate a multitude of voices. Rejecting the rigid rules of discourse at Gateshead, Jane enters Lowood, where she finds, surprisingly enough, some degree of linguistic diversity and independence, despite having been originally sent to the school in order to effect her complete silencing. At Lowood, Jane finds that, within bounds, she can enjoy a certain amount of linguistic freedom for the first time in her life. For, if conditions at the school are in some ways deplorable, it is a place in which, from time to time at least, voices abound. This circumstance becomes apparent from Jane's description of her first day at school:

> A quarter of an hour passed before lessons again began, during which the schoolroom was in a glorious tumult; for that space of time, it seemed to be permitted to talk loud and more freely, and they [the students] used their privilege. (39)

By the time Jane settles into life at Lowood, she comes to look forward to the late afternoon play hour, for at this time "the ruddy gleaming, the licensed uproar, the confusion of many voices, gave [her] a welcome sense of liberty" (47). It comes as no surprise that Jane, rebelliously insistent on heteroglossia, should take pleasure in the "glorious tumult" and the "licensed uproar" that signify linguistic diversity and the liberty it represents.

Although her years at Lowood cannot entirely satisfy Jane's desire to add to her arsenal of voices and languages, they are certainly an improvement on the stultifying atmosphere of Gateshead. Indeed, at Lowood, Jane's desire to achieve linguistic heterogeneity is even sanctioned (to a certain degree) by her study of French.[15] Thus Jane's tenure at Lowood represents a hiatus in her struggle; once she leaves the school, however, she must again fight against the languages of authority. After she leaves Lowood Jane begins her struggle in earnest; removed from a safe haven, one in which a modicum of linguistic diversity is meted out, Jane must pit the strength of her desire for heteroglossia against the centripetal and authoritarian languages of Edward Rochester and St. John Rivers.

Jane takes the position of governess at Thornfield in order to experience new voices and languages. (Indeed, it is significant that Jane's ability to speak and understand French is one of the primary responsibilities in her new job.) Thornfield appears to offer inviting possibilities. Rochester seems at first to be lined up on the side of the centrifugal forces of language, for he flouts social conventions and speaks out directly and often tactlessly; in fact, his eccentricity (ec-centricity), we might argue, attracts Jane in the first place. It soon becomes obvious that Rochester belongs to the centripetal forces of language, however; despite initial appearances, he generally speaks the language of phallocentrism and patriarchy. A victim of patriarchy himself (his disastrous marriage was a result of his obedience to the system of primogeniture), Rochester has learned from his oppressors, becoming adept at articulating the masterful language of male (and class) dominance. This is most evident during the period of his engagement to Jane, when he speaks primarily the language of male dominance in a stultified authoritative voice. But we also see it in Rochester and Jane's earliest conversations, in his aggressive, imperious manner of questioning Jane about her "accomplishments."

The forces of centripetal (phallocentric) language are best symbolized, even personified, by the character of St. John Rivers, who as he himself explains to Jane, has translated his worldly ambition into a sanctified authority and thus speaks the language of the "fathers."[16] It is surely not coincidence that St. John's very name is associated with the Word of God, which, perceived as unitary, absolute, and authoritarian, is perhaps the ultimate example of centripetal language. Not surprisingly, St. John purports to represent what Bakhtin calls the "authoritative word":

> The authoritative word demands that we acknowledge it, that we make it our own . . . we encounter it with its authority already fused to it. The authoritative word is located in a distanced zone, organically connected with a past that is felt to be hierarchically higher. It is, so to speak, *the word of the fathers*. ("Discourse," 342; emphasis added)

Bakhtin's description of the authoritative word seems to suggest that it is inherently phallocentric. At any rate, it is impossible to distinguish St. John's obvious masculine power from his reliance upon the authoritative word. He presents a serious challenge to Jane's search for independence precisely because he uses the authoritative word in an attempt to enslave her, to bend her to his will. Calling upon the power and the authority of orthodox religious feeling, St. John almost convinces Jane to abdicate her own desires and accompany him on his suicidal mission to India.

If, as I have suggested, *Jane Eyre* is the story of a woman's search for subjectivity through language, then it is clear that St. John performs a crucial role in the novel. Throughout the novel, Jane's objective, I have said, is to obtain some kind of linguistic independence. In Bakhtinian terms, Jane must distinguish her voice from those surrounding her:

> The importance of struggling with another's discourse, its influence in the history of an individual's coming to ideological consciousness, is enormous. One's own discourse and one's own voice, although born of another or dynamically stimulated by another, will sooner or later begin to liberate themselves from the authority of the other's discourse. This process is made more complex by the fact that a variety of alien voices enter into the struggle for influence within an individual's consciousness. ("Discourse," 348)

Jane struggles first with the discourse of the Reeds, then with the discourse of Rochester, and finally with the discourse of St. John Rivers. This last poses the most serious challenge to her linguistic independence, for St. John practices a kind of authoritarian ventriloquism, appropriating the authoritarian word in order to make Jane follow his own desires.[17]

In chapter 35, when St. John makes his last proposal, Jane comes close to capitulating to him. At this crucial point, her voice is, as Bakhtin might say, "dynamically stimulated" by another: Rochester's. In the scene in which Jane comes closest to agreeing to a marriage without love or desire she is prevented from doing so—incredibly and mysteriously—by Rochester's disembodied voice. This scene has met with disapproval by critics for its melodrama, but, looked at in conjunction with Bakhtin's essay, it proves remarkably pertinent. That Jane is able to emerge from St. John's influence through the intercession of an alien voice lends credence to Bakhtin's description of the struggle involved in coming to ideological consciousness. In fact, we need not attempt to explain this supernatural event; the important question is not what this alien voice is, but rather how it functions in the text and why it appears at this particular point in the narrative. Rochester's disembodied voice is that of an alien other that enters into the struggle for influence within Jane's consciousness, leading her to assert her independence. It is alien in that this voice, the voice of desire, proceeds from beyond the social and religious languages—the languages of propriety and duty—in which Jane and St. John have been speaking. With the sound of this voice, then, Jane is able to dispel and nullify the discourse of St. John: "I broke with St. John, who had followed, and would have detained me. It was *my* time to assume ascendency. *My* powers were in play, and in force" (370, emphasis in the original). Aided by an alien voice, Jane liberates herself from the discourse of St. John, raising her own voice against his and successfully articulating her own independent discourse. Having once distinguished her voice from St. John's, Jane is free to follow her own desires; having tested her strength against a powerful opponent, Jane is ready to face the seductively masterful voice of Rochester.

When Jane reaches Ferndean, however, she finds the threat posed by Rochester already dismantled; Rochester's voice is no longer masterful, no longer so compelling as it once was. He no longer deals exclusively in centripetal language. Rochester has, in other words, been transformed to make him worthy of Jane Eyre. I do not propose that Brontë effectively castrates him in order to make this so; that seems to me an oversimplification and misreading of the process as it occurs in the novel. Rather, his injuries are a direct result of his presumptions—he is subjected to an Old Testament, eye-for-an-eye type of law. In the curious terms determined by Brontë's contradictory blend of feminism and patriarchal, talionic justice, the right hand that reaches out to grasp and control its possession must be eliminated completely. Likewise, the possessing gaze of the male subject must be dismantled before he can join with the female subject in an equal partnership. After his transformation, Rochester can no longer treat Jane as an object; now he must listen to her voice. Of course it is profoundly disturbing that Jane can be given a strong voice only at the expense of such violent mutilation; however, the violence of Brontë's solution should not necessarily be condemned as fanciful or malevolent. Instead, we should note with concern that the novel can reach its end only by postulating such a radical solution. That Brontë, a woman gifted with a surprising sense of vision and a superlative imagination, could see no other way to solve the problem of male domination is itself a frightening testimony to the power of masculine authority.

Throughout the novel, then, Jane Eyre must devise a way to raise her voice against the voices lined up on the side of centripetal language—Mrs. Reed, Rochester, St. John Rivers—without falling prey to the temptation to submit completely to the forces of centrifugal language, a submission that would put her beyond the realm of meaningful communication. Thus Sandra Gilbert and Susan Gubar are partially right about the relationship between Jane and Bertha Mason Rochester;[18] it is indeed a monitory one, but no more so than the relationship between St. John and Jane, or between Mrs. Reed and Jane. Just as Jane must avoid the linguistic rigidity of the likes of St. John and Mrs. Reed, so must she avoid the total linguistic chaos represented by Bertha. In short, *Jane Eyre* is the story of Jane's attempt to find a medium way, to devise a compromise between the strict control of centripetal language and the intense linguistic freedom that lies beyond sanity; it is, finally, the story of Jane's search for heterogeneity and heteroglossia. That she finds some degree of both is evident in the structure of the novel. Indeed, this structure can be summed up by stating that Jane constantly initiates narrative action through her frequent movements from one plane to another, through her insistence on conversing in not one but several different narrative languages: the language of gothic, of autobiography, of writing-to-the-moment, of feminism. By the end of the novel, we realize that Jane has indeed achieved heteroglossia, for she can manipulate and control not one narrative voice, but a host of them. Thus the text of *Jane Eyre* is itself a testament to Jane's ability to control language and, consequently, to banish the threat of madness.

III

Although the chronotope of the asylum in *Jane Eyre* is defused and refracted, it nevertheless remains the key to understanding this novel. For, if *Jane Eyre* is a novel that is intimately concerned with language and the representation of language, if it uses the protagonist's relationship to language as a means to represent her search for subjectivity, then it stands to reason that those portions of the novel in which language ceases to perform its normal function—communication—are central to the ideological work undertaken by the novel. By representing the madwoman as a pitiful being beyond communication and thus divorced from community, the novel warns Jane—and her readers—of the dangers involved in seeking heteroglossia.

We can throw some light on this process by mapping out the ways in which competing languages are represented in *Jane Eyre*. To do so it is necessary first to postulate this novel as a spectrum of languages and discourses, in which the left side is dominated by centripetal language and the right by centrifugal language. On the far left end of the spectrum, we place authoritative discourse; on the far right, lies the discourse of madness, which is, in the terms presented by the novel, no language at all. Paradoxically, neither of these discourses can be represented within the novel; they can merely be referred to. Authoritative language, as Bakhtin describes it, is a prior language, monolithic and seamless; it is not fraught with diversity and thus, Bakhtin says, "the authoritative text always remains, in the novel, a dead quotation" ("Discourse," 344). Because it does not interact with any of the other languages represented in the novel, it is, as Bakhtin puts it, merely transmitted and not represented. Likewise, the discourse of madness possesses, as I shall argue shortly, no identifiable language; because it is incomprehensible it is represented as a static discourse, without any discernible traces of internal conflict or meaning. In this spectrum of discourses, just as in the spectrum of light that exists in nature, the extremes remain invisible to the naked eye.

Represented Discourse

Authoritative discourse	Internally persuasive discourse	Idiolect	Discourse of madness (autolect)
Centripetal			**Centrifugal**

Between these extremes we find, toward the left end of the spectrum, internally persuasive language, a discourse that is "half-ours and half-someone else's," according to Bakhtin ("Discourse," 345). Though still invested with authority, this discourse is dialogic; it can be wrestled with, questioned, and interpreted.[19] Before she can dismiss the threat posed by St. John Rivers, Jane must first correctly identify the language in which he speaks; it is not authoritarian language, as he would have her believe, but rather internally persuasive language, which, though still powerful, she can contest. Once she does this, she is free to move still further toward centrifugal language as she develops her own heteroglot discourse, a discourse that we shall call, for convenience, her idiolect.

Jane must keep her idiolect from degenerating into an "autolect," a discourse of madness that is self-enclosed and apparently self-sufficient. It is a discourse, moreover, created through an absence of meaningful language. And, indeed, this is the question raised by *Jane Eyre*: how can a lack of language, or a nonlanguage, be represented within a text made up entirely of language? This is the paradox that rests at the heart of *Jane Eyre*: the insane and all that it stands for can be represented only through its absence, through a silence in the text. That which is truly Other can only be hinted at and referred to, never represented directly. Despite the many references to madness and insane behavior in *Jane Eyre*, insanity always remains beyond the threshold of the world Brontë represents.[20] Brontë can create a space for the Other within her narrative, but it remains an empty space, a mere reference to Otherness, not a description or an endorsement of it.

This lack of direct representation cannot completely dampen the effect of the chronotope of the asylum in *Jane Eyre*. Even the mere reference to a nonlanguage allows Brontë the opportunity to display the limits of language itself. What Brontë represents through Bertha and through Jane's proximity to Bertha is a rejection of language, of all language; what is startling is Brontë's ability to include such a rejection in an art form made up entirely of language. Patricia Yeager argues that "making gaps in one's language and filling in these spaces with other words, with abnormal speech . . . is a productive praxis for the woman writer; it opens within her text a register of extralinguistic metaphors that nonetheless speak."[21] Certainly on one level this is precisely what Brontë does in *Jane Eyre*. On a different level, we see something far more subversive, far more threatening, not only to the dominant social order that Brontë reflects in her novel, but to the textual order upon which she relies to create her novel: Brontë actually creates gaps in her representations and refuses to fill them in with words from any language. That she is able to leave these gaps, these empty spaces, in her text, surrounded and contained by the text but at the same time challenging its authority, is a tribute not only to her artistry, but to her feminism as well.

Significantly, at the same moment Brontë shows us the limits of language she also shows us the limits of dialogic theory. In her ability to represent a lack of language in a text made up entirely of language we find Bakhtinian theory, striking and useful as it is, inadequate. Bakhtin's theories of stylistic language in the novel are powerful indeed; however, they end just at the point where the most radical feminist statements—paradoxically couched in nonlanguage and represented through a rejection of language itself—begin. Thus I do not propose the application of Bakhtin's theories as a panacea to the problems presented by every challenging feminist text, although it is clear by now, I hope, that Bakhtinian theory can enrich a feminist reading of *Jane Eyre*. The concepts of heteroglossia, of the ever-present war between the centripetal and centrifugal forces of language, of the chronotope of the asylum, could become powerful tools in the hands of feminist critics as they work to create what Bakhtin would call a reaccentuated text, revealing feminist values operating in what initially appear to be wholly phallocentric texts. As I have tried to show in my reading of *Jane Eyre*—a reading that depended as much on dialogic theory as on feminist theory—a good deal is to be gained through an interchange between dialogical and feminist theories, particularly when critics consent to be heteroglot themselves in order to effect it.

Notes

I would like to thank Lewis Long and Susan Sage Heinzelman, both of whom read an early draft of this essay, for their valuable criticism and suggestions.

1. Teresa de Lauretis, *Alice Doesn't: Feminisim, Semiotics, Cinema* (Bloomington: Indiana University Press, 1984), 29–30.

2. Leslie W. Rabine, *Reading the Romantic Heroine: Text, History, Ideology* (Ann Arbor: University of Michigan Press), 7,12.

3. M. M. Bakhtin, "Discourse in the Novel," in *The Dialogic Imagination: Four Essays by M. M. Bakhtin*, ed. Michael Holquist, trans. Caryl Emerson and Michael Holquist (Austin: University of Texas Press, 1981), 262. Subsequent quotations from this work will be cited in the text by title and page number.

4. On Bakhtin's concept of reaccentuation, see ibid., 417-22.

5. Susan Griffith, "The Way of All Ideology," *Signs* 7 (1982): 651.

6. This may be why, despite the growth of intellectual conservatism in recent years, Bakhtin has gained such popularity within U.S. academies. Bakhtinian theory celebrates diversity and multiculturalism, but ultimately it remains a purely theoretical, self-contained ideological system. In other words, Bakhtin provides a descriptive theoretical system; feminist theory, in contrast, cannot help but be normative and prescriptive. Unlike feminist theory, then, Bakhtin's work presents little or no threat to the status quo and can be embraced even by those who argue most fervently against Marxism and feminism.

7. It is possible to read this passage in a different light. Bakhtin may actually be arguing that one of the novel's functions or properties is to make the diversity of languages represented within it merely *appear* to be "contingent, external, illusory." Thus we could say that Bakhtin is arguing that the novel has either an ideological responsibility or an inherent drive to make the reader recognize his or her own language in another's language. The passage still presents the same difficulties for the feminist reader, for, whichever view we take of it, at this point in his essay Bakhtin seems to rescind his view of the novel as a form of art that ceaselessly works to represent linguistic diversity and difference.

8. The similarity between this process as it appears in "Discourse in the Novel" and in the romantic narrative as described by Rabine in *Reading the Romantic Heroine* is striking: "The dominant masculine voice of traditional romantic narrative imposes a totalizing structure on romantic narrative and represses an independent feminine other. . . . The hero and/or narrator in . . . these works posits the heroine at first as autonomous other and then in the end absorbs her back into his own identity" (16). If we concentrate on the logical implications of Bakhtin's statement, we find that Bakhtin begins by positing the existence of heteroglossia and centrifugal language but in the end absorbs it back into unitary, centripetal language.

9. Of course, a number of other nineteenth-century British novels besides *Jane Eyre* possess a chronotope of the asylum: Charles Dickens's *Bleak House*, Walter Scott's *The Heart of Midlothian* and *Bride of Lammermoor*, Charlotte Brontë's *Villette*, and Emily Brontë's *Wuthering Heights* could each be examined with a view toward exposing and delineating the chronotopes of the asylum that appear within them.

10. I am referring to Suzanne Keen's term, coined to describe a textual space that differs from, and often contrasts with, the dominant narrative in which it is embedded. "Annexes call attention to their difference from their surroundings. They jolt the reader out of a smooth journey through a fictional world; the map the reader has trusted must be suddenly—perhaps permanently—revised" (108). See Keen's "Narrative Annexes in Charlotte Brontë's *Shirley*," *Journal of Narrative Technique* 20 (2): 107–19.

11. See, for example, Rabine, *Reading the Romantic Heroine*, 117–18, and Janet Freeman, "Speech and Silence in *Jane Eyre*," *Studies in English Literature* 24: 683–700.

12. Hence the maid Abbot's conception of young Jane Eyre as "a sort of infantine Guy Fawkes" (Charlotte Brontë, *Jane Eyre*, ed. Richard J. Dunn [New York: Norton, 1971], 21); apparently Jane Eyre is perceived as a threat to the power structure that rules over Gateshead, and, by implication, England itself. Jane's willingness to use violent speech to vindicate herself is equated with rebellion and treachery. Quotations from *Jane Eyre* will be cited in the text and notes by page number.

13. During one of her confrontations with Mrs. Reed, Jane tells us that "it seemed as if my tongue pronounced words without my will consenting to their utterance: something spoke out of me over which I had no control" (23). Throughout the second of these outbursts, Jane reports that she "thrilled with ungovernable excitement" (31); indeed, even a short time later Jane looks back upon this speech as indicative of "the madness of my conduct" (32). Much later in the novel, Mrs. Reed says of Jane, "I declare she talked to me once like something mad, or like a fiend" (203). Jane uses her angry tirades to speak freely, perhaps too freely; this loss of control is identified, significantly, as madness.

14. Freeman, "Speech and Silence," 688, 689.

15. A good deal of work remains to be done in examining the role of foreign languages and bilingualism in Charlotte Brontë's novels. At this point I will simply point out that, in addition to French, Jane also studies Hindostanee under the tutelage of St. John Rivers. Far from being a liberating linguistic experience for Jane, however, this education seems more deprivation than freedom, for she studies the language under St. John's dictatorial direction, despite her wish to study German with Mary and Diana Rivers. See Patricia Yeager, *Honey-Mad Women: Emacipatory Strategies in Women's Writings*, (New York: Columbia University Press, 1988), chap. 2, "The Bilingual Heroine: From 'Text' to 'Work' ," and Freeman, "Speech and Silence," 692. Significantly, Jane's dismissal of Hindostanee as an "empty" language unworthy of study and application is one way in which we see a colonizing culture at work in *Jane Eyre*. See Gayatri Spivak, "Three Women's Texts and a Critique of Imperialism," *Critical Inquiry* 12 (1): 243ff.

16. According to Sandra M. Gilbert and Susan Gubar, "St. John . . . has an almost blatantly patriarchal name, one which recalls both the masculine abstraction of the gospel according to St. John ('in the beginning was the *Word*') and the disguised misogyny of St. John the Baptist, whose patristic and evangelical contempt for the flesh manifested itself most powerfully in a profound contempt for the *female*" (*The Madwoman in the Attic: The Woman Writer and the Nineteenth-Century Literary Imagination* [New Haven, Conn.: Yale University Press, 1984], 365).

17. I say "ventriloquism" because according to Bakhtin, "authoritative discourse cannot be represented—it is only transmitted" ("Discourse," 344). St. John uses an approximation of the authoritarian word to ensnare Jane, but even an approximation is enough to

threaten her movement toward linguistic independence. I discuss the representation of authoritative discourse in more detail in the final section of this essay.

18. See Gilbert and Gubar, *The Madwoman in the Attic*, 361.

19. Bakhtin describes internally persuasive discourse as follows: "A conversation with an internally persuasive word that one has begun to resist may continue, but it takes on another character: it is questioned, it is put in a new situation in order to expose its weak sides, to get a feel for its boundaries, to experience it physically as an object" ("Discourse," 348).

20. I count fourteen references to madness, delirium, frenzy, and raving, not including references to Bertha and her history, in *Jane Eyre*.

21. Yeager, *Honey-Mad Women*, 45.

On veult responce avoir: Pernette du Guillet's Dialogic Poetics

Karen Simroth James

> Imagine a dialogue of two persons in which the statements of the second speaker are omitted, but in such a way that the general sense is not at all violated. The second speaker is present invisibly, his words are not there, but deep traces left by these words have a determining influence on all the present and visible words of the first speaker. We sense that this is a conversation, although only one person is speaking, and it is a conversation of the most intense kind, for each present, uttered word responds and reacts with its every fiber to the invisible speaker, points to something outside itself, beyond its own limits, to the unspoken words of another person.
>
> Bakhtin, *Problems of Dostoevsky's Poetics*

Although this passage by Bakhtin refers to the phenomenon of "hidden dialogicity" in Dostoevsky's novels, it also serves as a strikingly accurate description of the dialogic essence of Pernette du Guillet's *Rymes*. The seventy-eight poems of the collection, published in 1545 just months after the young poet's death, embody a multifaceted principle of dialogism through which Du Guillet questions the relationship between truth and language and explores the acquisition of subjectivity through speech, through poetic creation, through the exchange of knowledge and of language. Not only do her poems explore the emerging voice(s) of her poetic subjectivity, but they also enact a dialogic exchange with Scève's *Délie* and sustain an intertextual dialogue with other contemporary works. This aspect of Du Guillet's poetry reflects in part the atmosphere of both intellectual and economic exchange that characterized mid-sixteenth-century Lyon. Jacqueline Risset, in the introduction to her study of

Scève's *Délie,* notes that each text of the *Ecole Lyonnaise* is caught up in a network of numerous contemporary texts.[1] This network in fact extends beyond Renaissance Lyon. Engaging an intertextual dialogue with works of the Italian Renaissance and of antiquity—in particular with those of Leone Ebreo, Ficino, Petrarch, and Plato—Du Guillet's poetry provides us with an example of what Thomas Greene has termed "dialectical" imitation in Renaissance literature.[2]

Despite this atmosphere of intellectual exchange in Lyon, any Renaissance woman wishing to speak or write for a public audience risked censure for these acts. In fact, her virtue depended upon her silence. Furthermore, the dominant, patriarchal literary conventions available to the woman who might choose to write, in spite of society's censure, offer no models of women's independent speech. In the Petrarchan tradition, for example, the woman remains the silent object of the male gaze, her very silence simultaneously inspiring the male poet/lover's suffering and his language. The Neoplatonist tradition, although allowing for a certain theoretical reciprocity in love, in practice silenced the woman or relegated her to the role of Echo in the service of the male poet/lover.

Not only were the literary models of women's speech severely limited, but Du Guillet—at the same time she was composing her *Rymes*—also found herself objectified, in a position of silence, in the love poetry of Maurice Scève. The beloved woman at the center of Scève's *Délie* becomes indeed an "objet de la plus haulte vertu" (object of the highest virtue), remaining the silent source of the poet/lover's tormented discourse. In a question very pertinent to this discussion of the Renaissance woman poet, Toril Moi asks, concerning the woman writer under patriarchy: "If the author is defined as male and she finds herself already defined by *him* as his creature, how can she venture to take up the pen at all?" The women writers of the Renaissance chose a variety of strategies to overcome this "anxiety of authorship," described by Moi, and the constraints placed upon them by patriarchal ideology.[3]

Modern feminist criticism examines this "anxiety" in its various forms, and its profound effect on feminine voice and language, particularly as they express resistance to patriarchal hierarchies. This important element of feminist criticism parallels Bakhtin's (nongendered) concern with polyphonic novelistic discourse. Although Bakhtin's theory of dialogism in novelistic discourse does not take into account gender or sexual difference, his dialogic paradigm provides the feminist critic with a model that encompasses multiple and opposing voices without granting authority or dominance to any single voice or discourse and without silencing the marginalized and/or resistant voices. Dale Bauer and Susan McKinstry comment on this aspect of dialogism, defining feminist dialogics as "a way of recognizing competing voices without making any single voice normative."[4] In addition to recognizing the appeal of this model for twentieth-century feminist critics, as well as its importance for the modern novel, I argue here that the dialogic paradigm mirrors the poetic strategy of Pernette du Guillet, a Renaissance woman writing in a prenovelistic, prebourgeois era. In Du Guillet's case, the dialogic quality of her poetry, which I will examine in some detail in the following pages, allows her to circumvent and to challenge the ideal of silence that Renaissance society and literary conventions imposed upon women. Du Guillet develops a dialogic poetics in which the speaking and writing subject refuses to be relegated, or in turn to relegate the other, to the role of silent object, emphasizing the exchange of speech and of knowledge as the necessary condition for the individual's subjectivity.

Deborah Jacobs opposes this sort of critical approach, criticizing the "transhistorical" use of Bakhtinian "models of subversion and resistance." She refers in particular to Bakhtin's notions of carnival and the grotesque body, making the important point that Renaissance culture did not separate the grotesque body from the "aristocratic," authoritative body. The problem, as Jacobs observes, lies in the way in which modern critics use the Bakhtinian theories of the carnivalesque and the grotesque, and the bourgeois " 'sovereign' individual consciousness of subjectivity."[5] Jacobs is right to warn against the "novelization" of prebourgeois, prenovelistic literature, but the complex relationship—or dialogue—between the carnivalesque body and the classical, authoritative body in the Renaissance warrants further study and in fact supports a dialogic reading of certain texts of this earlier era. Dialogism implies polyvocality rather than opposition and refuses to allow the authoritative, dominant voice to silence any resistant voice, no matter how grotesque or marginalized.

According to Jacobs, any feminist dialogic reading must be strictly historicized, taking into account the time and culture in which the text was written. Specifically, Jacobs argues that gender is not a useful category in the analysis of works from early modern Europe. In the case of Pernette du Guillet, however, the historical and cultural context of Renaissance Lyon clearly emphasizes dialogue and the exchange of ideas through poetry, juxtaposed with strict social codes that silenced women. The Renaissance concept of gender may differ from our modern version, but Du Guillet's *Rymes* provides an example of a prebourgeois literary text that dramatizes and foregrounds an ongoing dialogue in which the speaker/character's gender is an essential element. Further analyses of the *Rymes* will show to what extent dialogue and dialogic relationships are fundamental to the creation of a female poetic subject.

Before examining this dialogic poetics in greater detail, we must stop for a moment and ask what exactly dialogue is—and more precisely, what is a dialogic text? Furthermore, we must eventually question the limits of dialogism within the lyric genre. In her article on dialogue in sixteenth-century France, Eva Kushner makes the important point that "the disposition of a text in dialogue form does not suffice to confer upon it a dialogic structure or to assure the presence and reality of the other in it."[6] It is essentially this presence and reality of the other in the work, rather than the actual physical format of the text, that guarantees its dialogicity.

If the disposition of the text on the page, then, does not guarantee the dialogic nature of the work, we can hypothesize, conversely, that a work that does not overtly present itself as a dialogue, or overtly convey its polyphonic nature, may in fact possess dialogic qualities. To test this hypothesis we can examine several of Du Guillet's poems in the light of Bakhtin's remarks on dialogism.[7] It must be noted that Bakhtin himself believed lyric poetry to be essentially monologic in nature. According to Bakhtin, only the novel can embody multivoicedness, the heteroglossia informing all dialogic possibilities; the lyric genre precludes such possibilities:

> The language of the poet is *his* language, he is utterly immersed in it, inseparable from it, he makes use of each form, each word, each expression according to its unmediated power to assign meaning (as it were, "without quotation marks"), that is, as a pure and direct expression of his own intention.[8]

Bakhtin's remarks on poetry reflect widely accepted notions as to the unity of the lyric voice. Many critics and readers continue to be influenced by the assumption that the lyric poet's "voice" expresses direct and intense personal emotion in soliloquy form. Wayne Booth, in his introduction to Bakhtin's work on Dostoevsky and dialogue, echoes this belief in the inherently unified lyric voice:

> Lyric poems, for example, marvelous as they can be, tend toward becoming monologues—the poet inventing a single voice, one that belies the actual polyphony of his inner chorus.[9]

The lyric, according to Bakhtin, Booth, and others, revolves around monologue and excludes dialogicity. A first reading of Pernette du Guillet's *Rymes*, however, undermines this theory that restricts lyric poetry to one monologic voice directly expressing the poet's sentiments. As Thomas Greene has pointed out, Bakhtin may have too narrowly defined his category of the dialogic mode by restricting it to novelistic discourse. Poetry too "is open to the challenge of divergent or opposing utterances."[10]

Not surprisingly, Greene's description of the dialogic potential of poetic discourse calls to mind the network of texts in which Du Guillet's *Rymes* participates:

> Every poem contained in a collection maintains a dialogic relation with the other poems surrounding it, and also with the antecedent poems of its tradition. (101)

The *Rymes* clearly possess this essentially dialogic quality that juxtaposes divergent, and at times opposing, voices. Although the speaker/poetic narrator can often be associated with the persona of the poet herself, "Scève's beloved," this voice repeatedly emphasizes its changeable nature and draws attention to the interior dialogue that marks her thoughts and therefore her speech. This speaker repeatedly calls attention, for example, to the conflict within herself between the voices of virtuous, spiritual love and of physical desire. She insists, as in chanson 6 and elegy 1, on the continuous struggle to leave "amour" and "folle affection" (love/physical passion) behind in favor of "amytié" (friendship/Platonic love), but as the one leads to the other, the two types of love are in reality inseparable, and therefore constantly in conflict.

Although critics have long characterized the speaking voice throughout the *Rymes* as that of the humble pupil and beloved of Scève, seeking to praise his eloquence and embracing Neoplatonic ideals wholeheartedly, such an account vastly oversimplifies the case.[11] Throughout the collection, the poetic voice adopts alternately a Neoplatonic stance, a Petrarchan tone, and a playful "style marotique," among other stylistic variations. Furthermore, the "je" (I) in many instances does not represent the persona of the admiring apprentice poet—Scève's beloved—at all. Epigrams 55-59, for example, entitled "Mommerie de cinque postes d'Amour," are narrated by five lovers serving as Cupid's messengers. Likewise, in elegy 4 the speaker is the male lover who recounts his suffering and despair due to his lady's silence. In elegy 5, an unidentified speaker (whose gender is never indicated) gives advice to the suffering poet/lover, the same one who expresses his complaints in elegy 4.[12]

Even this shifting poetic "I," however, does not suffice to explain the dialogic essence of this poetry. More important is the context in which each of these poetic voices speaks. Do they express different emotions on the part of the poet in a monologic form, or does each speaking voice take into account the views and the discourse of an interlocutor? In fact, the interlocutor is nearly always explicitly present in the poems in the form of a "tu" or "vous" (you) that often represents the male poet/beloved, but at times indicates a contemporary observer (a witness of sorts), the ladies of Lyon, Cupid, or the reader. Many of the poems in the collection evoke the presence of the male poet/beloved but the role attributed to him varies in each case. The speaking "I" may address him directly ("tu" or "vous") or may refer to him in the third person, sometimes in an appeal to a third party who serves as a witness or a judge. Although Du Guillet inscribes Scève's name in anagrammatic form in several of her epigrams, openly acknowledging her dialogue with the other poet, we must also recognize that each poem in the *Rymes* creates (or re-creates) a new fiction of both speaker and interlocutor, each time with important variations and differences.

Occasionally the poetic voice shifts to a "nous" (we) that encompasses the lover and the beloved, or that serves to identify the speaker with other interlocutors. Such is the case in chanson 5, which opens with an apostrophic address to all ladies experiencing love's perfidy. The speaker here aligns herself with the "dames" (ladies) against "ilz," the men who love them inconsistently and imperfectly:

Dames, s'il est permis
Que l'amour appetisse
Entre deux cueurs promis,
Faisons pareil office:
Lors la legereté
Prendra sa fermeté.
S'ilz nous disent volages
Pour nous en divertir:
Asseurons noz courages
De ne nous repentir,
Puis que leur amytié
Est moins, que de moytié.
(ll 1-12)

Ladies, if love's allowed
To wander and take wing
Away from what lovers vowed,
Let us try the same thing.
Then fickle hearts
Will learn faith's arts.
If they say we wander too free,
To convince us to return,
Let's keep on, courageously,

Their pleading let us spurn,
For their oaths of devotion
Belie true emotion.
(ll. 1-12)[13]

The speaker in this chanson switches briefly to the first person, "je" (I), in the fourth stanza, referring to her own first experiences with the dangers of love, and expressing the realization that knowledge of these dangers beforehand could have allowed her to avoid this pain. She reverts then to the plural "nous" (we) in the remaining stanzas, which remind the ladies (and herself) that "amour" will eventually avenge the neglect they have suffered:

Mais puis qu'occasion
Nous a esté donnée,
Que nostre passion
Soit à eulx adonnée:
Amour nous vengera,
Quand foy les rengera.
(ll. 31-36)

But given our chance
To lead the dance,
Let us return
If true hearts can learn.
Love will relieve us,
Once lovers believe us.
(ll. 31-36 [228])

This assertive and confident voice certainly bears little resemblance to the persona of the humble, admiring apprentice poet often cited as the central (or only) voice of the poet in the collection. In fact, many of the poems I discuss in the remainder of this essay provide further examples of this diversity of voices—and of contexts in which they speak—in the *Rymes*.

In addition to these various scenarios involving dialogues of two or more persons, Du Guillet uses a number of linguistic flags or markers to draw our attention to the fact that what is at issue here is the exchange of words and ideas. For example, verbs that signal an act of speech (spoken or written) abound in the *Rymes*. Forms of the verbs "dire" (to say or tell), "demander" (to ask), and "supplier" (to implore), and expressions such as "motz" (words), "propos" (remarks), "argumentz" (arguments), "discours" (speech), "querelle" (quarrel), and "entretient" (conversation) occur frequently in these poems, much more so than in the works of Du Guillet's contemporaries. The verb "dire" appears at least once in twenty-three of the seventy-eight poems in the *Rymes*, nearly twice as frequently as in the *Délie*.[14] Moreover, these expressions that signal a speech act are paired with the various interlocutors as well as with the speaking "I." (I say something, and you respond; you say/ask something and I answer; we quarrel; he converses with someone else, and I overhear the conversation, and so on.) The verb "dire" is conjugated with "je" (I), as well as with "tu" and "vous" (you), "ils" and "elles" (they), and "nous" (we) throughout these poems. In this manner, expressions implying a discursive act repeatedly highlight the range of possibilities for a dialogic exchange of language and ideas.

Clearly, Du Guillet rejects the dichotomy that juxtaposes a speaking subject with a silent object, a dichotomy upheld by dominant Renaissance literary discourses and often associated with lyric poetry to this day. Du Guillet's second elegy dramatizes this decision not to relegate the other (poet/beloved) to the role of silent object. This does not mean, however, that the female voice will remain silent. The conclusion of this elegy establishes the speaker's refusal to require the beloved's silence and servility as a condition of her own poetic activity. After painting a forceful image of her wish for power over the male poet/lover—to the extent that the goddess Diana would envy her (ll. 35-36)—this voice concludes:

> Mais, pour me veoir contente à mon desir,
> Vouldrois je bien faire un tel deplaisir
> A Apollo, et aussi à ses Muses,
> De les laisser privées, et confuses
> D'un, qui les peult toutes servir à gré,
> Et faire honneur à leur hault choeur sacré?
> Ostez, ostez, mes souhaitz, si hault poinct
> D'avecques vous: il ne m'appartient point.
> Laissez le aller les neuf Muses servir,
> Sans se vouloir dessoubz moy asservir,
> Soubz moy, qui suis sans grace, et sans merite.
> Laissez le aller, qu'Apollo je ne irrite,
> Le remplissant de Deité profonde,
> Pour contre moy susciter tout le Monde,

Lequel un jour par ses escriptz s'attend
D'estre avec moy et heureux, et content.
(ll. 39-54)

But finally, to satisfy my desire,
would I really want to cause displeasure
to Apollo and also to his Muses,
by depriving them and leaving them bereft
of a man who can serve them exactly to their taste
and bring glory to their lofty, holy chorus?
Away, my hopes!—away with such
a high ambition; it does not belong to me.
Let him go, to serve the nine Muses,
I must not insist on enslaving him to me,
to me, who lacks both grace and merit.
Let him go; let me not anger Apollo,
filling him with powerful divinity
so that he stirs up the whole world against me,
which, one day, expects through my love's writing
to be, along with me, blessed and content.
(ll. 39-54 [230])

The humility topos in line 49 cannot erase the potent image that precedes this conclusion. The poet may be concerned about public censure of a woman who dares to envision such power for herself, hence the claim to humility in line 49 and the recognition of the importance of public opinion in line 52. Despite these claims, however, the vision of power remains. It has only been tempered by the speaker's realization that her poetic powers do not require the beloved's silence. By resisting the temptation to exert her power over the lover, by refusing to silence him, she allows the world's enrichment by her lover's poetry. This conclusion does not imply her own silence, despite her claims of humility, for she continues to write poetry and to focus on her speech and on her writing within these poems. This situation is quite the reverse of what we find in the *Délie*—and in the typical Petrarchan plight—where the silence of the lady and the servitude of lover *inspire* poetic creation. Here, servitude and silence *inhibit* this creation. Rather than relegate the other to silence, she opts instead for dialogue, invoking the possibility of union in poetic "escriptz," both his and hers, for they both serve the same muses. Just as she rejects the role of object herself, the speaking poetic voice refuses to adopt the male literary convention that demands the silence of the other, the beloved. The result is subtle, even paradoxical: her apparent "submission" allows her to create a difference and a distance from the male poet and the discourses he embodies. In turn, this distance allows her to establish a dialogue with the patriarchal literary and philosophical discourses of the Renaissance. Twentieth-century feminist theory is still grappling with the question of whether women need to create their own discourse, completely outside of patriarchal traditions, or whether they must rewrite phallocentric discourses to suit their needs. The debate rages on, so it comes as no surprise that a position such as that reflected in Du Guillet's elegy should elicit opposing interpretations from modern readers of this poetry.[15]

Du Guillet adopts neither what twentieth-century readers might call a feminist essentialist point of view nor a feminist position inspired by the humanist (and patriarchal) ideal of an equal but seamlessly unified self. She chooses instead to highlight the many discourses that construct the individual, and through which the shifting poetic subject emerges. This aspect of the *Rymes* underlines the importance of the dialogic paradigm in Renaissance literature, despite Deborah Jacobs's objections to such a "transhistorical" critical approach. If we speak of a poetic subject/self in this poetry, we must recognize that this is a contradictory and constantly decentered self, conveyed by a variety of voices that focus simultaneously on the exchange of ideas and language, and on the essentially duplicitous nature of language, as we shall see later in this discussion.

Bakhtin observes that "to affirm someone else's 'I' not as an object but as another subject" is the essence of the dialogic principle. The affirmation—in elegy 2—of the other's "I" as subject is characteristic of Du Guillet's dialogic poetics. According to Bakhtin, "only in communion, in the interaction of one person with another, can the 'man in man' be revealed, for others as well as for oneself" (*Problems of Dostoevsky's Poetics*, 252). Bakhtin's remarks recall Benveniste's account of the link between subjectivity and language:

> Consciousness of self is only possible if it is experienced by contrast. *I* use *I* only when I am speaking to someone who will be a *you* in my address. It is this condition of dialogue that is constitutive of *person*, for it implies that reciprocally *I* becomes *you* in the address of the one who in his turn designates himself as *I*. . . . It is in a dialectic reality that will incorporate the two terms and define them by mutual relationship that the linguistic basis of subjectivity is discovered.[16]

Du Guillet's poetry embodies this notion of a dialogic subjectivity described by both Bakhtin and Benveniste. The linking of subjectivity with the dialogic in the *Rymes* reflects and is rooted in the acceptance of the relative nature of truth, as opposed to monologism, which claims to possess the preconceived/predetermined truth. Bakhtin's discussion of philosophical monologism represents the scenario that Du Guillet repeatedly rejects in the *Rymes*:

> Someone who knows and possesses the truth instructs someone who is ignorant of it and in error; that is, it is the interaction of a teacher and a pupil, which, it follows, can only be a pedagogical dialogue. (*Problems*, 81)

In epigram 28, the voice of the woman/poet overtly refuses this pedagogical model, reminding her beloved: "Qu'en me traictant rudement, comme maistre, / Jamais sur moy ne gaignerez le prys (ll. 3-4)" (That by treating me harshly, as a master/teacher, you will never win me over).

Rejecting this didactic monologism in favor of a dialogic truth, with all its inherent ambiguities, Du Guillet repeatedly foregrounds her concern for the manner in which all signs, and words in particular, are interpreted in the dialogic pursuit of the truth. Epigram 7 revolves around the very notion of the multiple interpretations possible in the dialogic quest for answers. The cryptic "R" written in the margin of a ten-line poem puzzles the speaker:

> R, au dizain toute seule soubmise
> M'a, à bon droict, en grand doubtance mise
> De mal, ou bien, que par R on peult prendre.
> Car, pour errer, R se peult comprendre.
> Signifiant que le loz, qu'on me preste
> Soit une erreur, ou que R est riens, ou reste:
> Mais si par R on veult responce avoir,
> Je dy, combien que n'aye le sçavoir,
> Ne les vertus que ton R m'advoue,
> Qu'errer je fais tout homme, qui me loue.
>
> R, alone added to the *dizain*,
> Has with reason caused me great uncertainty,
> As to the bad or the good that this R implies.
> Because R can be understood as "to err,"
> Signifying that the praise given to me
> Is an error, or that R is nothing [*riens*] or remainder:
> But if this R indicates a response is desired,
> I say, although I possess neither the knowledge

> Nor the virtues that your R attributes to me,
> That I cause every man to err who praises me.

She examines the possible meanings that can be attached to this sign that has been added to the text, stressing the process of interpretation with the expressions "comprendre" (to understand), "signifiant" (signifying), and "responce" (answer/response). Because ambiguity prevails in this case, she proposes a resolution based on only one of the possibilities proposed, and the resolution is presented as a hypothesis ("but if"). This conditional structure is linked to the notion of a dialogic truth, for in the search for truth, opposing points of view and different conditions will affect the answers obtained. The conditional or hypothetical structure in this poem accompanies a claim for humility that recalls the use of this topos in elegy 2, but here too the power that she attributes to herself (and to her poetry) in the last line of the epigram belies the tentative tone that prepares the conclusion. In the end, her boast also includes a subtle reminder that she herself has provoked a problem of interpretation, given the double meaning of the verb "errer," to err and to wander, as in the erratic steps of the suffering lover.

The other's words, and the problem of how to evaluate their meaning, recur in epigram 31, which begins with the blunt accusation, "Je ne croy point ce que vous deites" (I do not at all believe what you said). The entire epigram revolves around the problem of speech and belief, with the speaker first telling her admirer that she does not believe what he says, because his actions contradict his words, because he exhibits more desire for "celle" (that woman), than for herself (line 3). In the second quatrain, she shifts from accusation to question, asking her lover which he himself would believe, truthful actions or false words, wondering whether he will be able to interpret her actions (and her silence) correctly and to recognize the deceitful nature of her rival's language:

> Mais quelle plus estimeriez:
> Ou celle qui, d'un cueur tremblant,
> N'ose dire ce que vouldriez,
> Ou qui le dict d'un faulx semblant?
> (ll. 5-8)

> But who will you esteem more highly:
> She who, with a trembling heart,
> Dares not say what you would like to hear,

Or she who says it under false pretense?
(ll. 5-8)

The words of the interlocutor (of the lover, but also of the rival), although not directly recorded here, certainly influence the accusation made and the question asked. The verb "dire" (to say/tell) after all appears three times in the poem; everyone speaks in this scenario—the jealous woman, the lover, and the rival. This phenomenon recalls Bakhtin's description of hidden dialogicity in the passage cited at the beginning of this chapter. Although the speaker's point of view dominates the poem, the speaker does not and cannot impose a resolution to this dilemma of interpretation because the truth, after all, will only be attained through the continuation of the dialogue.

Jealous accusations recur in several of the *Rymes*, notably in epigram 36, which again raises the question of actions that belie words:

Si descharger je veulx ma fantasie
Du mal que j'ay, et qui me presse fort,
On me dira que c'est la jalousie
(Je le sçay bien) qui faict sur moy effort.
Mais qui pourroit estre en propos si fort,
Et d'argumentz si vivement pourvueu,
Que ce que j'ay de mes propres yeulx veu
Soit une folle imagination
Il feit accroire à mon sens despourveue?
Il me feroit grand' consolation!

If I want to rid my imagination
Of the pain with which I suffer excessively,
They will tell me it is jealousy
(I know it well) which has this power over me.
But who could be so skilled with words,
And so well-equipped with arguments,
That he could make me believe I have lost my reason
And that what I saw with my own eyes
Is but a wild fancy?
He would give me great consolation!

Markers—linguistic "flags"—indicating an exchange of speech draw our attention to the framework of dialogue in which the speaker expresses the link between her jealousy and the difficulty involved in interpreting both words and actions. She knows that her jealous reaction may simply be a product of her imagination and realizes that others will tell her so. Lines 1-4 juxtapose the speaking "je" (I) to an impersonal "on" (they, one), but this third party assumes a speaking role ("On me *dira*"). The speaking "I" then asks a question about the powers of persuasion this third person (or persons) may possess. Though someone (perhaps the lover himself) may try to tell her that jealousy causes her imagination to run wild, the speaker here wonders who could possibly command the language ("propos" and "argumentz") that could convince her that she is mistaken in her interpretation of what she saw with her own eyes. In this case, the dialogic path to truth involves the juxtaposition of actions and words, of reason and imagination, and the dialogue between the skeptical, jealous speaker and the lover or his defenders.

In fact, the question asked here is a hypothetical one, expressed in the conditional mode. Only one voice actually speaks in this epigram, and this speaker doubts whether arguments exist that could console her and convince her that she is mistaken in her fears. Despite the hypothetical, imaginary status of the interlocutors, however, the entire epigram creates and revolves around dialogue, stressing speech and the *potential* exchange of words and interpretations. The inner dialogue related by the speaker evokes a potential debate in terms that conjure up the presence of the imaginary or absent interlocutor(s) and that leave the conclusion of this scenario uncertain. The jealous woman does not impose a solution; her dilemma persists even at the close of the poem. Still jealous, she has not resolved her doubts in one way or the other, and she remains open to the possibility of different interpretations and points of view.

Epigram 40 takes up these themes of jealousy and the evaluation of words and actions in a humorous vein, founded on a play of words:

Mon jour estoit assis tout aupres d'une,
L'entretenant à l'aise, et à repos,
D'affection non autre, que commune,
Mais comme on vient d'un à autre propos.
Voicy Amour sur eulx gay, et dispos,
Portant un arc, et traictz à la Gregeoise,
Lequel lascha deux mots à la Bourgeoise,
Et au partir luy dit: callimera!
Lors souspeçon en mon cueur myt grand noyse,

Doubtant qu'il dist d'elle: qu'il l'aymera!

My day was seated very near a lady,
Conversing with her, at ease and with delight,
But with affection none other than of the common sort,
Flitting from one topic to another.
Then Cupid, gay and nimble, happened upon them,
Carrying a bow and flaming Greek arrows.
He shot two words at the Bourgeoise,
And upon leaving said to her: "hello!" [*callimera*]
Then suspicion raised a great clamor in my heart,
fearing that he said: "He will love her." [*qu'il l'aymera*]

In the first quatrain the speaker (again the jealous woman) construes in an unfavorable light the sight of her beloved, her "jour," seated near and engaged in conversation with another woman. Their conversation may concern an affection "of the common sort" (l. 3), but even so, their exchange leads to a dangerous problem of interpretation. As Cupid, armed with bow and arrow, approaches the seated couple, he fires two of his weapons at them: "Lequel lascha deux mots à la Bourgeoise" (l. 7). The weapons turn out to be words, not arrows. If the danger inherent in language is not yet clear to the reader, the speaker/narrator explains further. Observing the scene, the narrator tells how she overheard "Amour" pronounce the Greek word "callimera" (hello) to her rival, "la Bourgeoise."[17] The problem arises from the narrator's doubts as to how to construe this parting word that she has overheard. Did Cupid simply bid the other woman a good day, or did he perhaps mean "qu'il l'aymera" (he will love her, or may he love her), easily confused with the nearly identical "callimera," but representing instead a proclamation that the beloved (the "day") would fall in love with the rival? The narrator recognizes that her suspicion fuels her doubt, that her emotions may have affected her ability to interpret correctly the signs before her, making the "truth" more elusive than ever.

In these last three examples (epigrams 31, 36, and 40), the speaker juxtaposes what she sees to what she hears. Language possesses no visionary quality; it does not represent what the eye sees.[18] No ideal, Cratylitic link exists between images and words, and this recognition of the duplicitous nature of language is the primary assumption upon which Du Guillet builds the dialogic model in her poetry. Duplicity of language, divergent voices, and opposing points of view allow for a new poetic subjectivity, one that refuses the traditional dichotomy that opposes the speaking subject to the silent object. Critical of and seeking to deconstruct this dichotomy that represents the very core of Western (patriarchal) thought, Luce Irigaray maintains that women have traditionally been assigned the role of silent object, and specifically that of the mirror that reflects the achievements and speech of a speaking (male) subject. Irigaray wonders what would happen, in this traditional scenario, "if the 'object' started to speak?" Irigaray envisions not a reversal of the subject/object dichotomy, but a dissolution of this logical, hierarchical category, "with no possibility of returning to one single origin."[19] Although Du Guillet's poetry does not dissolve the subject/object dichotomy to the extent that Irigaray describes, the *Rymes* nevertheless repeatedly reject any such static hierarchy, emphasizing instead the exchange of speech and the coexistence of multiple voices and speaking subjects, as well as the relative nature of truth itself.[20]

Epigram 50 dramatizes this absence of a monologic, univocal truth, highlighting the relative nature of truth (and of language) as the only possible resolution to a friendly debate:

> Deux amys, joinctz par estroicte amytié,
> Eurent, sans plus, une dissention:
> L'un soubstenoit (par raison la moytié)
> Que le Thuscan a plus d'affection
> L'autre disoit par resolution
> Que le François parle plus proprement.
> Pour les vouloir mettre d'appointement,
> Je dy: qu'ilz sont tous deux beaux à descrire:
> Mais, pour en faire au vray le jugement,
> Celuy despeinct ce que cestuy veult dire.

> Two friends, joined by close friendship,
> had a disagreement, nothing more:
> One (by reason, half of this friendship) maintained
> That Tuscan [Italian] has more merit,
> The other said with resolution
> That French is more precise and elegant.
> In order to reconcile them,
> I say: that they are both beautiful for describing:
> But to make a real judgment of the case,
> Each one depicts what each speaker wants to say.

The opening lines of the poem emphasize that this "dissention" occured between two very close friends, otherwise joined in "amytié," the term that elsewhere in the collection describes the ideal, spiritual love sought by the persona of the speaking poet. These first two lines serve as a reminder that discussion and disagreement are possible, perhaps normal, even between two individuals joined in the sort of friendship or love that traditionally implies a perfect accord between the two souls as they become one.

The disagreement between these two friends involves the use of language, a topic of debate that appears frequently in the *Rymes*, notably in the last four poems discussed. The solution proposed by the speaker in epigram 50 resembles the conclusions of the previous examples; there is no unequivocal answer, the truth depends on one's own perspective. The speaker (and judge, in this case) admits the beauty of both languages, but refuses to give preference to either. The only resolution to this disagreement between "amys" is a reminder of the relative merits of each language and the conditional nature of truth.

The specific topic of epigram 50—the question of the relative merits of the French and Italian languages ("le François" and "le Thuscan")—represents a concern shared by other poets of the French Renaissance and undoubtedly of particular interest to those in Lyon, as a result of the extensive Italian influence there. In his allegorized version of this debate earlier in the century, Jean Lemaire de Belges situates the Temple of Venus, focal point of the noblesse and glory of the French language, in the city of Lyon. Like Pernette du Guillet's later epigram, Jean Lemaire's *Concorde des deux langages* seeks to reconcile the partisans of each language and to eliminate the notion of an opposition between them. Whereas Du Guillet's poem provides no further resolution to the debate than a recognition of the validity of each language and their necessary coexistence, Jean Lemaire's text envisions an ultimate reconciliation in the Temple of Minerva:

> Là se treuvent conjoinctz, vivans en paix sans noise,
> Le langaige toscan et la langue françoise.
>
> (ll. 73-74)
>
> There are found united, living in peace without discord,
> The Tuscan language and the French tongue.[21]

More than coexistence, this conclusion involves a union of a mystical nature, both future and imaginary, on the summit of the Temple of Minerva, which remains inaccessible to the living. It is only "après le decours de ma vie, et non devant" (after the passing of my life, and not before) (Lemaire, 45), that the poet narrator hopes to meet up with the two guides who will show him the site (and sight) of the mystical union of the two languages, an image he has thus far only glimpsed in a magic, artificial mirror:

> Lors il feroit tant que j'auroie deux guides . . . lesquelz me feront veoir à plain la tresvertueuse et tresnecessaire concorde des deux langaiges, ou temple de la deesse dessus speciffiée, dont en ung miroir artificiel, fait par art magicque, il me monstra les vifves ymaiges embrassans l'une l'autre en la presence de la deesse. (Lemaire, 46)

> Then he would make it so that I would have two guides . . . who will make me see clearly the very virtuous and necessary concord of the two languages, in the temple of the above-mentioned goddess, of which in an artificial mirrror, made by magic art, he showed me the vivid figures embracing each other in the presence of the goddess.

Unlike Jean Lemaire de Belge's vision of a future embrace in which all differences are resolved (and dissolved), Du Guillet's poem discards any notion of a mystical union in favor of continuing dialogue.

Spiritual Union or Dialogic Distance?

Although the texts of the *Rymes* continually remind us of the impossibility of this sort of ultimate, mystical union (of languages or of lovers), Du Guillet nevertheless provides a Neoplatonic framework for her poetry that allows the notion of an ideal, spiritual union to hover in the background, nearly always implicit as a goal (or standard), however unattainable. Certain poems, such as those that describe the spiritual birth of the poet, give more prominence to this desire for Platonic union. Elegy 1 describes this "parfaicte amytié." In the eyes of the speaker, "amour" is but a dream, or lie, while "amytié" (friendship or Platonic love), given to her by the gods and founded on "si sain jugement" (such sound judgment), makes her lover as content as she.

The ideal that seems to have been realized in this elegy, however, recedes to some distance in many other poems, as we have seen in the numerous epigrams that revolve around jealous accusations and playful reproaches directed at less than ideal lovers. In these examples, any implied desire for spiritual union with the other does not extend to or provide a resolution to the debates or disagreements. The poet imposes no ultimate solution that would reconcile the dialogic differences of opinion and perspective at work in her poems, realizing that in order to express a goal of unity, she requires a voice separate and different from the other's. Even when the poetic voice adopts its humblest tone, it continues to insist on the differences that separate the woman/poet from the "source" of her love and knowledge.

The necessity of difference to express the self recalls the passages from Benveniste and Bakhtin cited earlier in this discussion that link subjectivity with dialogue. Toril Moi expands upon this model of a dialogic subjectivity, rejecting the possibility that any union between subject and object could sustain the two separate self-identities and voices:

> Logically speaking, there are only two possible forms of such communion: either the object engulfs the subject, in which case there is nobody around to do the communing: or the subject engulfs the object, thereby radically destroying it as other. There is of course a sense in which the Chodorovian account of "male" science presents us with a third solution: the image of a transcendental, *lost* unity (the original, symbiotic relationship between mother and child) to be *re-established* through "female" empathy. As paradoxical and prone to fissures as any other "unity" of different self-identities, such a strategy can be no more than a dissolution of a real problematics.[22]

Although Bakhtin's work does not address questions of gender, his realization that the union of subject and object would imply the silence of at least one of the two individual voices is an underlying principle of the dialogic model. As Caryl Emerson explains in her preface to Bakhtin's work on Dostoevsky, "Life in language is in fact dependent upon the preservation of a gap"(*Problems*, xxxii). The two speakers must never completely understand each other:

> They must remain only partially satisfied with each other's replies, because the continuation of dialogue is in large part dependent on neither party knowing exactly what the other means. (*Problems*, xxxii)

In a similar vein, Anne Herrmann distinguishes the dialogic from the dialectic based on the resolution or synthesis that is absent from the former:

> Unlike the dialectic, which seeks to transcend oppositions by means of a synthetic third term, the dialogic resists the reconciliation of opposites by insisting on the reciprocity of two or more antagonistic voices.[23]

Even Du Guillet's use of the plural pronoun "nous" (we), while suggesting the union of speaker and interlocutor, does not actually allow any true union of the two voices. Rather than to preserve the "gap" necessary for dialogue, however, the "we" subjects the interlocutor to domination by the speaking "I." Benveniste explains this phenomenon in linguistic terms:

> "We" is not a multiplication of identical objects but a *junction* between "I" and the "non-I." . . . . in "we" it is always "I" which predominates since there cannot be "we" except by starting with "I"[24]

Du Guillet uses this plural pronoun sparingly in her poetry, prefering scenarios in which the speaking "I" addresses an interlocutor, either present on the scene or imagined ("you" or "he," for example). In chanson 5, the "we" refers to the speaker and the ladies who are neglected by their lovers, and in this way the "I" simultaneously addresses the ladies while setting up an opposition with "them," the remiss lovers. There is perhaps a solidarity among the ladies here, but the "we" does not imply any sort of union of subject or object, of lover and beloved. Elsewhere, when this plural pronoun does refer to the speaker and her beloved, the "we" alternates with the singular pronouns "I" and "you," never giving the impression that the two individuals speak with one voice.

Given this paradoxical presence in the *Rymes* of an ideal unity that is constantly undermined by debate and differences of opinion and perspective, the poet's preference for a dialogic mode of self-expression proves all the more appropriate. In dialogism there is no ultimate resolution of doubt, no union or fusion of subject and object, but the model allows the exchange of language and of ideas in the pursuit of a unity of a higher (and in all likelihood unattainable) order. This juxtaposition of a dialogic poetics of difference with an ideal of union and unity creates some difficulty in the identification of the *Rymes* as a truly dialogic work in the same category as, for example, Dostoevsky's novels.

Questions of genre aside, can we speak of polyphony (in the modern sense of the interaction of submerged consciousnesses) in the case of a Renaissance poet? We have already seen that historical context and literary tradition in this case served to foster the poet's dialogic poetics. Certainly, this is not a monologic work, for the examples discussed in this chapter show a variety of voices and perspectives that are never unified in a single voice or truth. Although this plurality of voices may not match the modern phenomenon of the "splintered" consciousness, the Renaissance, as Kushner has shown, fostered an atmosphere in which the image of the other in the text begins to waver, to assume a variety of positions and points of view.[25] Kushner concedes that the "I" remains relatively stable in Renaissance dialogue, but we should not neglect the important variations that characterize this first-person pronoun—and the figure of the self—in the *Rymes*. Furthermore, as to the presence of a unifying factor in Renaissance dialogue (such as the Neoplatonic goal of spiritual union that plays an important, if ambiguous, role in Du Guillet's poems), Bakhtin himself recognized the possibility of a unity that would require a plurality of consciousness:

> It is quite possible to imagine and postulate a unified truth that requires a plurality of consciousness, one that is, so to speak, by its very nature *full of event potential* and is born at a point of contact amoung various consciousnesses. (*Problems*, 81)

This is not a static unity that silences one of the voices participating in the dialogue. Instead, this unity exists at the moment of exchange, in the act of dialogue.

Beyond this question of a unified truth, Bakhtin also took into account the practical limits of polyphony faced by the writer. Although he insisted that dialogue was not plot-dependent, Bakhtin points out that even Dostoevsky was influenced by his readers' expectations, by their need for some sort of thematic closure and formal unity (*Problems*, 252). Booth comments on this paradoxical status of dialogue in literature, describing the two opposing tendencies in human existence and language:

> There is a "centrifugal" force dispersing us outward into an even greater variety of "voices," outward into a seeming chaos that presumably only a God could encompass. And there are various "centripetal" forces preserving us from overwhelming fluidity and variety. The drive to create art works that have some kind of coherence—that is, formal unity—is obviously a "centripetal" force. (*Problems*, xxi-xxii)

Booth then goes on to postulate that lyric poets follow this centripetal drive too far and thus tend to impose a monologic unity on their work. Du Guillet's *Rymes* give us an example of lyric poetry that maintains a balance between the "centrifugal" and "centripetal" forces (in language and in the pursuit of truth). In fact, her poetry focuses on the attempt to balance these two forces in life and in art.

Beyond the notion of polyphony inherent in the dialogic text, Bakhtin delineates different versions or manifestations of dialogism. Perhaps we may not be able to relate all of these to Renaissance texts, but we have seen, for example, that Bakhtin's concept of "hidden dialogicity" quite aptly describes the way in which the speaking voices in the *Rymes* respond to their absent interlocutors.[26] On the level of the individual poem, because the interlocutor remains silent for the moment, the dialogue in which the speaking voice participates is more likely to be a "hidden" one. The statements of the other speaker are omitted, but his (or her) words profoundly influence the discourse of the poetic voice. Despite traditional notions of a solitary lyric voice (that of the "poet"), the different voices that emerge throughout the collection of Du Guillet's poetry, responding at times to one another, show clearly to what extent "hidden" dialogicity can become overt.

The combination of the dialogic model and an ideal of unity represents the central paradox of Du Guillet's poetry. The goal of spiritual union with the beloved is continually questioned and undermined by voices that call attention to their diversity, to their difference from the various interlocutors, and to the relative nature of truth. As the preceeding discussion has shown, the *Rymes* provide numerous examples of this characteristic absence of a monologic, univocal truth. By highlighting the dialogic nature of truth and focusing on the very problem of interpreting signs, and language in particular, Du Guillet moves beyond what might otherwise have been considered mere uncertainty or insecurity on the part of an apprentice poet. Instead she clearly bases her poetics on a dialogic model in which doubt plays a powerful role in the acquisition of knowledge and of subjectivity.

Any reading that searches only for an overriding unity of vision or self within the *Rymes* proves, then, to be falsely reductive and ignores the extent to which the poet exposes the duplicitous nature of human discourse and questions the patriarchal, humanist notion of an underlying, essential meaning (a transcendental signifier) in language. Kristeva identifies such a position on the part of a writer as embodying, if not a social revolution, certainly a poetic one.[27] In the case of Du Guillet's *Rymes*, the revolution is grounded in and inextricably linked to gender; this dialogic poetics allows Du Guillet to reject the silence (the Renaissance ideal of woman as silent object of male desire and discourse) imposed upon women by her society, by literary tradition, and by Scève, within the *Délie*. The twentieth-century reader may not at first find that Du Guillet's work conveys a strong feminist position; after careful reading, however, we must recognize the subtle but revolutionary manner in which the *Rymes* question, reject, and transform the patriarchal literary codes and laws of language that dominated the Renaissance, and that remain powerful even today.

Notes

1. Jacqueline Risset, *L'anagramme du désir*, 20. The group of poets writing in Lyon at this time, contemporaries of Du Guillet and Scève, are often referred to as the Ecole Lyonnaise, although the term *school* fails to convey the spirit of exploration, collaboration, and exchange that characterized these writers and their works. For further discussion of this point, see Risset, chap. 1, and Ann Rosalind Jones, *The Currency of Eros*, chap. 3, 79-82.

2. Thomas Greene, *The Light in Troy*, 45-46.

3. For further discussion, analysis, and documentation of these strategies, see Jones, *The Currency of Eros*, chap. 1, and "Surprising Fame"; Colette Winn, "La femme écrivain au XVIe siècle"; Katharina Wilson, ed., introduction to *Women Writers of the Renaissance and Reformation*; and Tilde Sankovitch, *French Women Writers and the Book*. See also Peter Stallybrass "Patriarchal Territories," and Constance Jordan, *Renaissance Feminisim*, for their analyses of the social and literary status of women in the Renaissance.

4. Dale M. Bauer and Susan Jaret McKinstry, eds., *Feminisim, Bakhtin, and the Dialogic*, 6.

5. Deborah Jacobs, "Critical Imperialism and Renaissance Drama," 74, 77.

6. Eva Kushner, "Le Dialogue en France au XVIe Siecle," 143; my translation.

7. I refer primarily to Bakhtin's theories of dialogism as they are developed in *Problems of Dostoevsky's Poetics* and the essay "Discourse in the Novel" in *The Dialogic Imagination*, 259-432. See also *Rabelais and His World*.

8. Bakhtin, *The Dialogic Imagination*, 285; emphasis in the original.

9. Wayne C. Booth, "Introduction," xxii. Quotations from this work will be cited by title and page number in the text.

10. Thomas Greene, *The Vulnerable Text*, 102.

11. Robert Griffin takes such an approach to Du Guillet's *Rymes*, concluding that "the degree of Neo-platonism in her poetry is far greater than is generally imagined" ("Pernette du Guillet's Response to Scève," 110). While the Neoplatonic current is important in the collection, an overemphasis on this aspect of the *Rymes* obscures the complexity of the poet's voice. Fortunately, however, recent essays on the *Rymes* have shed new critical light on this poetry, examining from a variety of angles the manner in which Du Guillet creates a poetic identity—and a voice (or voices) to express this identity—within a society and a literary tradition dominated by patriarchal discourse and power. Lance K. Donaldson-Evans ("The Taming of the Muse") briefly examines the feminine voice in Du Guillet's *Rymes* and provides an interesting overview of the status of women poets in Medieval and Renaissance France. In her discussion of several of Du Guillet's more enigmatic epigrams, Gisèle Mathieu-Castellani highlights the poet's status as subject, concluding that a "weak voice" seeks a way to affirm its own autonomy, refusing to act only as an echo (La Parole Chétive," 60). Colette Winn underlines the paradoxical nature of this voice, which is simultaneously rebellious and submissive ("Le chant de la nouvelle née," 213). Both Winn and Jones call attention to the strategies devised by women writers of the Renaissance as they sought voices of their own within patriarchal discourses. Lawrence Kritzman uses psychoanalytic theory to identify and examine the rhetorical strategies by means of which Du Guillet "transcends the dominance-submission paradigm of petrarchism and instead theorizes in figurative language a utopian discourse of equals derived from the neo-platonic tradition" (*The Rhetoric of Sexuality and the Literature of the French Renaissance*, 5).

12. Entitled "Desespoir traduict de la prose du parangon italien" (Despair translated from the prose of the Italian model), elegy 4 imitates an unidentified Italian source, which could serve to justify the masculine "I." François Ier imitated the same source in his "Parangon translaté d'ytalien en françoys par le Roy." Verdun L. Saulnier's "Etude sur Pernette du Guillet et ses *Rymes*" includes the text of the king's prose translation of the Italian model (42-44). Victor E. Graham speculates, in his notes on elegy 4, that Du Guillet probably would not have read the royal manuscript, but that the king might have seen one of the two editions of the *Rymes* published in his lifetime. As Graham points out in his 1968 edition of *Rymes*, it is more likely that the two French writers would have each imitated the Italian source independently (103).

13. Here I have quoted Ann Rosalind Jones's excellent English translation of Du Guillet's chanson 5, published in Wilson's *Women Writers* (228). In the remainder of my essay,

I also quote Jones's translation of elegy 2 (Wilson, *Women Writers*, 229-30). The page reference to the Wilson anthology appears in brackets following each of the Jones translations. Where no page reference appears, the translation is mine.

14. Jerry Nash's *Concordance de la "Délie"* makes such a statistical comparison possible. Keith Cameron has recently published a concordance to Du Guillet's *Rymes*, but this volume was not available to me in the preparation of my study. Fortunately, the size of the collection (seventy-eight poems) permits a simple count of the number of times that certain words—forms of the verb "dire" (to say/tell), for example—appear in the poems.

15. Although she notes the reversal of the typical Petrarchan model in elegy 2, Gillian Jondorf ("Petrarchan Variations in Pernette du Guillet and Louise Labé") concludes that Du Guillet's use of Petrarchan convention is strained and reveals a woman uneasy writing in a male poetic tradition. I argue the opposite in my article on this poem. Joann DellaNeva interprets the conclusion of this elegy as the "ultimate failure of the female poet" to find a voice of her own ("Mutare/Mutatus," 51-52). According to DellaNeva, the female lover/poet comes to realize, in this elegy, that "her rightful place is that of the silent object, not speaking maker, of poetic discourse, by virtue of her sex alone" (55). As I maintain here and in my article on this topic, however, the woman poet's decision not to silence the beloved (male poet) does not mean that she accepts silence for herself. Donaldson-Evans in "Taming of the Muse" comments on the nature of the poet's decision in the elegy: "Beneath this self-deprecation, Du Guillet is also, paradoxically, proclaiming her power, both as woman and poetess, for it is not simply because she cannot subjugate Scève that she renounces doing so, but because she will not out of respect for his poetic gifts." (94). Kritzman too recognizes the power that the speaker possesses at the conclusion of the elegy—"the power to endow Apollo with deity while at the same time permitting Scève to find the path to spiritual perfection as poet rather than as chaste lover" (*Rhetoric of Sexuality*, 27).

16. Emile Benveniste, *Problems in General Linguistics*, 224-25.

17. In his critical edition of the *Rymes*, Graham confirms that this is very likely a reference to Clémence de Bourges, to whom Louise Labé dedicated her collection of poetry, first published in 1555 in Lyon. Scève later composed an epitaph to this same Clémence de Bourges (66).

18. Joel Fineman in *Shakespeare's Perjured Eye*, examines the relationship between vision and language in the Renaissance love sonnet from Petrarch to Shakespeare, and finds that—before Shakespeare—tradition called for the poetic "I" to become a "speaking eye" (14). According to Fineman, Shakespeare rewrites and revises the "visual poetics of the poetry of praise," characterizing language "as something corruptingly linguistic rather than something ideally specular, as something duplicitously verbal as opposed to something singly visual" (15). Well before Shakespeare, however, Pernette du Guillet explored these same issues in her poetry, and the poetic subjectivity that emerges from her *Rymes* sets up an opposition between language and vision, as does Shakespeare's "perjured eye" (16).

19. Luce Irigaray, *Speculum of the Other Woman*, 135, 142. Gail Schwab criticizes essentialist readings of Irigaray and proposes instead the reading of Irigaray's work through a dialogic model. Schwab concludes that "no other feminist writer is so profoundly dialogic" ("Irigarayan Dialogism," 59).

20. Although we must remain cautious in the use of twentieth-century critical theory to examine texts of a much earlier era, in this case the historical context and literary traditions of the Renassance support this line of investigation. The Renaissance woman was silenced and objectified by the patriarchal society in which she lived, as well as by the dominant (patriarchal) literary discourses within which she wrote. Although emphasizing this need to account for the historical and cultural context in our critical reading of a literary text, Wayne Booth also observes that the cultural context of the Renaissance has not really

changed that much when it comes to questions of gender and voice: "The specific ideology on which Rabelais' laughter often depends is in 1982 still a dominant ideology of our culture; women are fair game, they are sillier than men, as nine out of ten television comedies proclaim" ("Freedom of Interpretation," 73).

21. The translations of Jean Lemaire de Belges's *La concorde des deux langages* are mine. Quotations from this work will be cited in the text by author and page number.

22. Moi, "Patriarchal Thought," 192. Moi argues for a psychoanalytic model of knowledge and subjectivity that "questions and displaces traditional notions of subject-object relationships" (198).

23. Anne Herrmann, *The Dialogic and Difference*, 15.

24. Benveniste, *Problems in General Linguistics*, 202.

25. Kushner, "Le Dialogue en France," 144-46.

26. Dialogue also characterizes Du Guillet's poetry on an intertextual level. Among the many types or variations of dialogue identified by Bakhtin, his concept of "double-voiced discourse" aptly describes the phenomenon of the intertextual dialogue with Scève's *Délie* inscribed in the *Rymes*. This type of discourse, according to Bakhtin, is simultaneously directed "both toward the referential object of speech, as in ordinary discourse, and toward another's discourse, toward someone else's speech" (*Problems*, 185). The texts in the *Rymes* that respond, refer to, or "rewrite" various dizains from the *Délie* exhibit this double-voicedness. For Julia Kristeva's discussion of this phonomenon, linked with her theories of intertextuality, see "Word, Dialogue, and Novel" (36-37, 41-42). Chansons 7 presents a similar dilemma of interpretation in a dialogic mode. Speaker refutes accusations or insinuations pronounced against her virtue, contrasting duplicitous language with statements she interprets as truthful. See Robert Cottrell's discussion of Chansons 7 in his essay "Pernette du Guillet and the Logic of Aggressivity," 381.

27. I refer here to Kristeva's *Révolution du langage poétique*. In her essay on Bakhtin, Kristeva calls attention to the manner in which dialogic (and carnivalistic) discourse represents a revolutionary break from the laws of language ("Words, Dialogue, and Novel," 36).

Bibliography

Bakhtin, M. M. *The Dialogic Imagination: Four Essays by M. M. Bakhtin*, ed. Michael Holquist, trans. Caryl Emerson and Michael Holquist. Austin: University of Texas Press, 1981.

———. *Problems of Dostoevsky's Poetics*, ed. and trans. Caryl Emerson. Minneapolis: University of Minnesota Press, 1984.

———. *Rabelais and His World*. Trans. Helene Iswolsky. Cambridge, Mass: M.I. T. Press, 1968.

Bauer, Dale M. *Feminist Dialogics: A Theory of Failed Community*. Albany: State University of New York Press, 1988.

Bauer, Dale M., and Susan Jaret McKinstry, eds. *Feminism, Bakhtin, and the Dialogic*. Albany: State University of New York Press, 1991.

Benveniste, Emile. *Problems in General Linguistics*. Trans. Mary Elizabeth Meek. Coral Gables, Fla.: University of Miami Press, 1971.

Booth, Wayne C. "Freedom of Interpretation: Bakhtin and the Challenge of Feminist Criticism." *Critical Inquiry* 9 (September 1982): 45-76.

———. "Introduction." In *Problems of Dostoevsky's Poetics*, by Bakhtin.

Cameron, Keith. *A Concordance to Pernette du Guillet*, Rymes. University of Exeter Press, 1988.

Cottrell, Robert. "Pernette du Guillet and the Logic of Aggressivity." In *Writing the Renaissance*, ed. Raymond C. La Charité. Lexington: French Forum, 1992. 93-113.

DellaNeva, Joann. "Mutare/Mutatus: Pernette du Guillet's Actaeon Myth and the Silencing of the Poetic Voice." In *Women in French Literature*, ed. Michel Guggenheim. Saratoga, Calif.: Anma Libri, 1988. 47-55.

Donaldson-Evans, Lance K. "The Taming of the Muse: The Female Poetic Voice in Pernette du Guillet's *Rymes*." In *Pre-Pléiade Poetry*. Ed. Jerry C. Nash. Lexington: French Forum, 1985.

Du Guillet, Pernette. *Rymes*, ed. Victor E. Graham. Geneva: Droz, 1968.

Fineman, Joel. *Shakespeare's Perjured Eye: The Invention of Poetic Subjectivity in the Sonnets*. Berkeley: University of California Press, 1986.

Greene, Thomas. *The Light in Troy: Imitation and Discovery in Renaissance Poetry*. New Haven: Yale University Press, 1982.

______. *The Vulnerable Text: Essays on Renaissance Literature*. New York: Columbia University Press, 1986.

Griffin, Robert. "Pernette du Guillet's Response to Scève: A Case for Abstract Love." *Esprit Créateur* 5(1965): 110-16.

Herrmann, Anne. *The Dialogic and Difference: "An/other woman" in Virginia Woolf and Christa Wolf*. New York: Columbia University Press, 1989.

Irigaray, Luce. *Speculum of the Other Woman*, trans. Gillian C. Gill. Ithaca, N.Y.: Cornell University Press, 1985.

Jacobs, Deborah. "Critical Imperialism and Renaissance Drama: The Case of *The Roaring Girl*." In *Feminism, Bakhtin, and the Dialogic*, ed. Bauer and McKinstry, 73-84.

James, Karen. "Pernette du Guillet: Spiritual Union and Poetic Distance." *French Literature Series* 16(1990): 27-37.

Jondorf, Gillian. "Petrarchan Variations in Pernette du Guillet and Louise Labé." *Modern Language Review* 71(1976): 766-778.

Jones, Ann Rosalind. "Assimilation with a Difference: Renaissance Women Poets and Literary Influence." *Yale French Studies* 62(1981): 135-53.

______. *The Currency of Eros: Women's Love Lyric in Europe, 1540-1620*. Bloomington: Indiana University Press, 1990.

______. "The Lyonnais Neoplatonist: Pernette du Guillet." In *Women Writers of the Renaissance and Reformation*, ed. Wilson, 219-31.

______. "Surprising Fame: Renaissance Gender Ideologies and Women's Lyric." In *Poetics of Gender*, ed. Nancy Miller. New York: Columbia University Press, 1986. 74-95.

Jordan, Constance. *Renaissance Feminism: Literary Texts and Political Models*. Ithaca, N.Y.: Cornell University Press, 1990.

Kristeva, Julia. *La révolution du langage poétique*. Paris: Seuil, 1974.

______. "Word, Dialogue, and Novel." In *The Kristeva Reader*, ed. Toril Moi. New York: Columbia University Press, 1986. 34-61.

Kritzman, Lawrence D. *The Rhetoric of Sexuality and the Literature of the French Renaissance*. Cambridge: Cambridge University Press, 1991.

Kushner, Eva. "Le Dialogue en France au XVIe siècle: quelques critères génologiques." *Canadian Review of Comparative Literature* 5(1978): 141-53.

Lemaire de Belges, Jean. *La concorde des deux langages*, ed. Jean Frappier. Paris: Droz, 1947.

Mathieu-Castellani, Gisèle. "La Parole chétive: Les *Rymes* de Pernette du Guillet." *Littérature* 73 (February 1989): 47-60.

______. "Parole d'Echo: Pernette au miroir des *Rymes*." *Esprit Créateur* 30 (Winter 1990): 61-71.

Moi, Toril. "Patriarchal Thought and the Drive for Knowledge." In *Between Feminism and Psychoanalysis*, ed. Teresa Brennan. London: Routledge, 1989. 189-205.

———. *Sexual/Textual Politics: Feminist Literary Theory*. London: Methuen, 1985.

Nash, Jerry C., ed. *Maurice Scève: Concordance de la* Délie. 2 vols. Chapel Hill: University of North Carolina Studies in the Romance Languages and Literatures, 1976.

Risset, Jacqueline. *L'anagramme du désir: essai sur la* Délie *de Maurice Scève*. Rome: Mario Bulzoni, 1971.

Sankovitch, Tilde. *French Women Writers and the Book: Myths of Access and Desire*. Syracuse: Syracuse University Press, 1988.

Saulnier, Verdun L. "Etude sur Pernette du Guillet et ses *Rymes*." *Bibliothèque d'Humanisme et Renaissance* 4(1944): 7-119.

Scève, Maurice. *The* Délie *of Maurice Scève*, ed. I. D. McFarlane. Cambridge: Cambridge University Press, 1966.

Schwab, Gail. "Irigarayan Dialogism: Play and Powerplay." In *Feminism, Bakhtin, and the Dialogic*, ed. Bauer and McKinstry, 57-72.

Stallybrass, Peter. "Patriarchal Territories: The Body Enclosed." In *Rewriting the Renaissance: The Discourses of Sexual Difference in Early Modern Europe*, ed. Margaret W. Ferguson, Maureen Quilligan, and Nancy J. Vickers. Chicago: University of Chicago Press, 1986. 123-42.

Wilson, Katharina, ed. *Women Writers of the Renaissance and Reformation*. Athens: University of Georgia Press, 1987.

Winn, Colette. "Le chant de la nouvelle née: Les *Rymes* de Pernette du Guillet." *Poétique* 78 (April 1989): 207-17.

———. "La femme écrivain au XVIe siècle: écriture et transgression." *Poétique* 84 (November 1990): 435-52.

Contributors

Siobhan Craig is a Ph.D. candidate in comparative literature at the University of Massachusetts in Amherst. Her research interests include feminist and postmodern theory and film, and her dissertation explores constructions of subjectivity and history in selected postwar Italian and German films and literary texts.

Elizabeth Butler Cullingford is associate professor of English at the University of Texas at Austin. She is the author of numerous articles on W. B. Yeats and has published two books, *Yeats, Ireland and Fascism* and *Gender and History in Yeats's Love Poetry.*

Lisa Gasbarrone is associate professor of French at Franklin and Marshall College, where she has also chaired the women's studies program. A *dix-huitièmiste* by training, her current work, on Tocqueville and Québécois writer F.-X. Garneau, addresses travel writing, history, colonialism, and cultural identity.

Denise Heikinen is a Ph.D. candidate in rhetoric and technical communication at Michigan Technological University.

Karen Hohne is an independent scholar and artist. She received a Ph.D. in Russian language and literature from Indiana University, and has previously taught English composition and Russian literature at Moorhead State University, and humanities and literary theory at the University of Minnesota. Her research has primarily concerned popular literature.

Karen Simroth James is assistant professor of foreign languages at Roanoke College. Her current research interests include French women poets of the Renaissance, theories of lyric voice, and the contributions of Bakhtinian dialogism and feminist literary theory to the study of Renaissance poetry.

Patrick D. Murphy is associate professor of English and director of the Graduate Program in Literature and Criticism at Indiana University of Pennsylvania. He is the author of *Understanding Gary Snyder*, and recently he completed a collection of essays on ecofeminist dialogics and literary criticism. His work with dialogics and environmental criticism has appeared in such journals as *Hypatia* and *American Studies*.

Virginia L. Purvis-Smith is the associate pastor of Cary Presbyterian Church, Cary, North Carolina, and the research associate at the Resource Center for Women and Ministry in the South. Her doctoral work at the University of Michigan focused on gender and rhetoric, especially concerning women and their experiences of preaching.

Julie A. Schaffer has written several articles examining how eighteenth- and nineteenth-century women writers used the marriage plot to challenge repressive views of women and subvert ideologies working against women. Her work has appeared in *Misogyny in Literature: An Essay Collection*, edited by Kathy Ackley.

Suzanne Rosenthal Shumway received a Ph.D. in English from the University of Texas at Austin. She teaches at the University of St. Thomas and at the School of Continuing Studies at Rice University. She is currently working on studies of female madness in the English novel.

Eleanor Ty is assistant professor of English at Wilfrid Laurier University in Waterloo, Ontario, Canada. She has edited Mary Hays's *Victim of Prejudice* and has published on women novelists of the late eighteenth- and early nineteenth-centuries including Mary Wollstonecraft, Elizabeth Hamilton, and Mary Shelley. Her book, *Unsex'd Revolutionaries: Five Women Novelists of the 1790s*, is forthcoming.

Helen Wussow is assistant professor of English at Memphis State University. She has authored several articles on Virginia Woolf and is currently transcribing the manuscripts of *Mrs. Dalloway,* as well as editing a collection of essays about Woolf.

Index

Compiled by Robin Jackson and Helen Wussow